Humana Festival 2002
The Complete Plays

Humana Inc. is one of the nation's largest
managed health care companies
with approximately six million members in its health care plans.

The Humana Foundation was established in 1981
to support the educational, social, medical and cultural development
of communities in ways that reflect
Humana's commitment to social responsibility
and an improved quality of life.

SMITH AND KRAUS PUBLISHERS
Contemporary Playwrights / Collections

Act One Festival '95
Act One Festival '95

EST Marathon '94: The One-Act Plays
EST Marathon '95: The One-Act Plays
EST Marathon '96: The One-Act Plays
EST Marathon '97: The One-Act Plays
EST Marathon '98: The One-Act Plays

Humana Festival: 20 One-Acts Plays 1976–1996
Humana Festival '93: The Complete Plays
Humana Festival '94: The Complete Plays
Humana Festival '95: The Complete Plays
Humana Festival '96: The Complete Plays
Humana Festival '97: The Complete Plays
Humana Festival '98: The Complete Plays
Humana Festival '99: The Complete Plays
Humana Festival 2000: The Complete Plays
Humana Festival 2001: The Complete Plays

New Dramatists 2000: Best Plays from the Graduating Class
New Dramatists 2001: Best Plays from the Graduating Class

New Playwrights: The Best Plays of 1998
New Playwrights: The Best Plays of 1999
New Playwrights: The Best Plays of 2000
New Playwrights: The Best Plays of 2001

Women Playwrights: The Best Plays of 1992
Women Playwrights: The Best Plays of 1993
Women Playwrights: The Best Plays of 1994
Women Playwrights: The Best Plays of 1995
Women Playwrights: The Best Plays of 1996
Women Playwrights: The Best Plays of 1997
Women Playwrights: The Best Plays of 1998
Women Playwrights: The Best Plays of 1999
Women Playwrights: The Best Plays of 2000
Women Playwrights: The Best Plays of 2001

If you require pre-publication information about upcoming Smith and Kraus books, you may receive our semi-annual catalogue free of charge, by sending your name and address to *Smith and Kraus Catalogue, PO Box 127, Lyme NH 03768. Or call us at (603) 643-6431, fax (603) 643-1831. www.SmithKraus.com.*

Humana Festival 2002
The Complete Plays

Edited by
Tanya Palmer and Amy Wegener

Contemporary Playwrights Series

SK
A Smith and Kraus Book

A Smith and Kraus Book
Published by Smith and Kraus, Inc.
177 Lyme Road, Hanover, New Hampshire 03755
www.SmithKraus.com

Manufactured in the United States of America
First Edition: October 2002
10 9 8 7 6 5 4 3 2 1

Cover and Text Design by Julia Hill Gignoux
Layout by Jennifer McMaster
Cover artwork © Chris Gall

Library of Congress Cataloguing-in-Publication Data
Contemporary Playwrights Series
ISSN 1067-9510
ISBN 1-57525-317-8

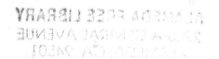

Contents

Acknowledgments

The editors wish to thank the following persons for their invaluable assistance in compiling this volume:

Nicole Burgund
Claire Cox
Susannah Engstrom
Brenda Harger
Don Marinelli
Marc Masterson
Jennifer McMaster
Steve Moulds
Elizabeth Nolte
Carrie Nutt
Alexandra Peterson
Jeff Rodgers
James Seacat
Kyle Shepherd
Alexander Speer
Nancy Vitale
Jason Yann

Beth Blickers
Judy Boals
John Buzzetti
Sam Cohn
Libby Edwards
James Flynn
Nicole Graham
Ronald Gwiazda
Peter Hagan
Mary Harden
Morgan Jenness
Joyce Ketay
Carl Mulert
Wendy Streeter
Mark Christian Subias
Megan Wanlass Szalla

Foreword

Ultimately it is about people, isn't it? The way we think, feel, act and make decisions about our lives. In a world driven by money and technology, a good play encourages us to share our common humanity with each other without barriers. It involves a kind of sacrifice—a collective storytelling where dozens of people put their heads together to tell a story to thousands of others. When we laugh, cry, or gasp in amazement together, we do something important—especially when artist and audience are in the same room.

The Humana Festival of New American Plays is a celebration of new work with a long history of honoring and embracing the playwright's vision—because we believe that part of our responsibility in premiering new work is to allow the writer to see the play that he or she imagined. To this end, we strive to create an environment in which playwrights are involved in major creative decisions—by inviting writers into the room for the rehearsal process, and by ensuring them complete control of their texts. We believe that this simple practice is what makes our festival unique, and that it's this support that brings exciting playwrights to Actors Theatre each year.

While every play will not appeal to all tastes, what is wonderful about the Humana Festival is the sense of discovery and adventure that this approach to producing new work yields. We take seven full-length plays (and a number of shorter pieces) through full production each year, and we believe that we have a responsibility to both our local and national audiences to include a cross-section of the most vital work being written in the American theatre today. By presenting this diverse range of styles and worlds to our audiences—whose participation is essential to the evolution of these new plays—we can capture the aspects of life as we know it, and send these new works into a world that sometimes needs to be reminded of the importance of the rich collective human imagination found in the theatre.

Marc Masterson
Artistic Director
Actors Theatre of Louisville

Editors' Note

At the time of this writing, several months have passed since the wild and wonderful event that was the 2002 Humana Festival of New American Plays wound to a close. But the texts at the center of this remarkable celebration of American playwriting continue to live and breathe, finding new homes at other theatres, and transforming before their creators' watchful eyes. What you will find in this book—a document of the variety, imagination, and brilliance that made up this year's festival—is that which lies at the heart of the whole endeavor: the writers' words on the printed page. What you won't see in this volume are the years of thought, the months of conversation, the weeks of fevered activity, debate, technical brilliance, ardent prayers, exaltation and plain hard work that went into bringing these plays to life in three dimensions.

A play is a slippery, suggestive creature, employing language and a keen theatrical sensibility to evoke a whole visual and aural experience—a world of possibility made out of words. The words you'll encounter in these pages represent both an endpoint and a new beginning in the lives of these plays: they are records of where the playwrights arrived following their rehearsal process here, as well as rich invitations to imagine how these worlds might be reincarnated in the future. In each of these texts, the playwright has fashioned a complete universe out of his or her own unique vocabulary, a detailed blueprint for an experience that can be accessed in the mind's eye, but is ultimately meant to confront us in real time and space.

Rather than feeling left out of the three-dimensional experience, though, we hope you will see this collection as an invitation. Maybe you weren't—as we were—running from rehearsal room to rehearsal room, witnessing a scene transform completely from one day to the next, witnessing the struggle toward understanding or, conversely, the joy of discovery when the secret of a moment was unlocked for all to see. But these words are ready to come alive again at your touch. "Therein lies the pact twixt artist and viewer," Tina Howe's Rembrandt tells us in her warm and witty play, *Rembrandt's Gift*. "'Tis the former who sets the scene, but the latter who must complete it." The words on these pages may be fixed, precise, and chosen with great care, but if you look a little more closely, you may notice that the paint is still wet. That's because the playwright's art is to invite many minds into the endeavor of seeing and hearing (and yes, even smelling) a dramatic universe—and that imaginative gesture begins with readers like you.

Tanya Palmer and Amy Wegener

Humana Festival 2002
The Complete Plays

Score

Conceived and directed by Anne Bogart
Adapted by Jocelyn Clarke
Created by SITI Company

BIOGRAPHY

Anne Bogart is the artistic director of SITI Company. Recent productions with SITI include *Hay Fever* by Noël Coward (Actors Theatre of Louisville), *Lilith* (New York City Opera), *bobrauschenbergamerica* (Actors Theatre/25th Humana Festival), *Room* (Wexner Center and City Theatre), *War of the Worlds* (Actors Theatre/24th Humana Festival, Edinburgh International Festival and BAM's Next Wave Festival), *Bob* (Wexner Center for the Arts/SITI), *Culture of Desire* (a co-production of SITI, City Theatre, and Portland Stage Company), *Private Lives* by Noël Coward and *Miss Julie* by August Strindberg (Actors Theatre of Louisville/SITI), and *Alice's Adventures* (Wexner, City Theatre City Stages, SITI), as well as *Small Lives/Big Dreams*, *Going, Going, Gone*, and *The Medium* (SITI). She is the recipient of two Obie Awards, a Bessie Award, and a Guggenheim Fellowship. Ms. Bogart is currently an associate professor at Columbia University.

Jocelyn Clarke is commissioning manager of the National Theatre, Ireland (Abbey Theatre). He was lead theatre critic with *The Sunday Tribune* for nine years, and was a contributor to *Irish Theatre Magazine*, *The Irish Times* and *American Theatre*. He has lectured in theatre criticism and dramaturgy at the Samuel Beckett Centre, University College Dublin, and Dartington College in the UK. He has written three adaptations for SITI Company—*Bob*, adapted from interviews with theatre director Robert Wilson; *Alice's Adventures*, from Lewis Carroll's *Alice's Adventures Underground*; and *Room*, from the writings of Virginia Woolf. For the Blue Raincoat Theatre Company in Sligo, Ireland, he has written two adaptations of Carroll's *Alice's Adventures in Wonderland* and *Through the Looking Glass*.

SITI Company, celebrating its tenth anniversary, is an ensemble-based theatre company based in New York City. The company's mission is to create new works for the theatre, to perform and tour these productions nationally and internationally, to provide ongoing training for young theatre professionals, and to foster opportunities for cultural exchange with theatre professionals and audiences from all over the world.

HUMANA FESTIVAL PRODUCTION

Score premiered at the Humana Festival of New American Plays in March 2002. It was directed by Anne Bogart with the following cast:

Tom Nelis

and the following production staff:

Scenic Designer .... Neil Patel
Costume Designer .... James Schuette
Lighting Designer .... Christopher Akerlind
Sound Designer............................ Darron L. West
Properties Designer .... Mark Walston
Stage Manager .... Elizabeth Moreau
Assistant Stage Manager .... Debra A. Freeman
Music Consultants................ Jeff Halpern and George Steel
Dramaturg .... Steve Moulds

Tom Nelis
in *Score*

26th Annual Humana Festival of New American Plays
Actors Theatre of Louisville, 2002
photo by Larry Hunt

Words and Action

by Anne Bogart and Jocelyn Clarke

Anne Bogart and Jocelyn Clarke conducted the following interview via e-mail on the fly over three weeks between different rehearsals, workshops and readings in Salt Lake City, Dublin, Copenhagen, and New York.

ANNE: What did you look for when starting to piece together *Score*?

JOCELYN: I looked for a voice. I read as many of Leonard Bernstein's writings as I could find—I spent a day crawling around Strand Books in New York City looking for books by and about Bernstein. Reading his writings, I was struck by Bernstein's erudition and passion. They display a rigorous and promiscuous intelligence—he gleefully added ideas from science, psychology, sociology, history and art to his own idiosyncratic musicology—and radiate a fervent and intense excitement about his subject, the creation and performance of music. Moreover, Bernstein's desire to communicate his ideas and experience of music to a diverse audience—young and old, professional and amateur, academic and unschooled—infuses his writings with an urgency and necessity that was inherently performative.

The voice I began hearing in Bernstein's writings was at once playful and serious, demanding and generous, arrogant and self-conscious, passionate and frivolous, earnest and ironic, democratic and snobbish, childish and wise, radical and traditional... Bernstein's character, in terms of the character I perceived in his writings, was so contradictory and complex that the biggest problem I faced in creating the text for *Score* was not what to put in but what to leave out. Reading two biographies helped clarify for me an image I had for *Score*'s Lenny, an image which could contain and sustain the various contradictions inherent in Bernstein's writings—particularly between learning and intuition, creation and interpretation, flesh and soul: Lenny as a fierce *rebbe* fighting with God as much as with himself.

• • •

"In some very important part of me, I will always be that exiled, frightened little boy of ten, singing the Megillah, and praying for a chance to make music in my lifetime."

—Leonard Bernstein, *Findings*

• • •

JOCELYN: Why did you want to make theatre pieces (*Bob, Room, Score*) about creativity?

ANNE: The issue of human creativity is of great personal interest to me, and I believe that I share this fascination and its accompanying curiosity with many others. But because the subject is so complex, I chose to approach the same issue from different angles and through contrasting lenses. Each of the three artists—Wilson, Woolf and Bernstein—experiences creativity and expresses their own truths in vastly different ways. I wanted to get inside their bodies, their minds, and their sensibilities in the hopes that some of it would rub off on me and on my collaborators, and ultimately, could be shared with diverse audiences.

• • •

ANNE: What do you find fruitful and unique in the collaboration with Anne?

JOCELYN: What I enjoy most in our collaborations are the discoveries. All of our projects together have required that I learn something new—researching *Score*, for example, I had to read up on music composition and theory. Our collaborations have started with an idea or an impulse, and the process of articulating and expressing that impulse or idea is what excites me about our collaborations. *Bob* began as a conversation on a beach in Dublin about a director called Bob who gives a talk about his work… and something happens. What happens? We didn't know, but figuring it out was the beginning. How we get there, why we are going there and what we find along the way not only make our collaborations fun to do but also offer an exciting challenge: the idea or impulse must be communicated to the other collaborators in the process—the designers and actors—as well as an audience. Working with you is like hanging out but with something to do. And you have the goofiest sense of humor.

• • •

JOCELYN: Why do you make theatre?

ANNE: A great deal of the world seems unjust, vicious and, at times, unbearable to me. I see pain, destructive behavior, entropy and suffering. I dislike the damaging behavior and blindness of the political sphere. I watch wars declared, social injustices that inhabit the streets of my hometown, and a planet in unnecessary meltdown. I have to DO something. My chosen field of action is the theatre.

As a director in the theatre I am in charge of the atmosphere inside a particular ROOM at a particular time. I can determine the politics and the values and can insist on justness, mutual respect and listening. I can create a non-hierarchical environment in which creation is a collective act within a sphere that I determine via imagination and a connection to a history of ideas, aesthetics, literature and human striving. In short I can create a place of rapture to share with fellow human beings. The influence of this space of rapture radiates out to colleagues, to audiences and even to people flung far in the world who only hear about what we are doing and inspires hope in them.

• • •

ANNE: How does *Score* fit into the contemporary developments in the theatre?

JOCELYN: If theatre is at core a meeting place, not only of people and ideas, but also of technologies and art forms, then *Score*, as well as *Bob* and *Room*, embraces and explores that idea directly: a man, or a woman, talking to a group of people is the initial act of theatre of all three pieces. All three are giving lectures about art and creativity—theatre in *Bob*, literature in *Room* and music in *Score*—in which they talk about what they do and how and why they do it. They have arrived into the space in a state of crisis, which they begin to articulate, at first unexpectedly and unknowingly, but then wilfully, courageously, dangerously. They are not trying to solve their crisis—after all, it defines who they are as artists—but rather to articulate and communicate it to the people in the theatre.

The characters of *Bob*, *Room* and *Score* are not characters in the conventional sense—they remain unchanged at the end of each, but our perceptions of them change. There is no plot in the conventional sense, and what narrative there is is not an exploration of character, but rather an explosion of character: ideas, gestures, phrases and images tumble chaotically from their mouths and bodies in their attempt to communicate what is happening to them now, in this space, in front of an audience.

The distinction between character and actor is deliberately blurred in the course of each piece—what happens to the characters in the lecture is what happens to the actors in the performance: both are trapped on stage by the audience's gaze, each trying to negotiate their way off. Ellen Lauren and Tom Nelis, the performers of *Room* and *Score*, once asked Will Bond what was his secret as an actor when he performed *Bob*, particularly its very awkward ten-minute introduction, and he said, "It's about getting through it… until you stop," which is what each of the characters in *Bob*, *Room* and *Score* is doing in their attempts to communicate with the audience.

Bob, *Room* and *Score* were conceived and developed out of our mutual interest in audiences—particularly the audience's role and relationship to what happens on stage. While presenting the audience with the lecture, each piece also casts the audience, assigning it a particular role, identity and function—as a roomful of theatre students, female students, and music lovers respectively. Then each deliberately subverts its casting because an audience can never be a single gaze, a single identity, a single intelligence but rather is composed of myriad individual gazes, identities and intelligences. Bob continually checks in with the audience, reminding them that this is a performance and that it will be over soon. Virginia speaks to an exclusively female audience, asserting its unique identity, only to interrogate and subvert it—and ultimately re-cast it as a collection of individuals. Lenny talks to the audience as a group with a specialist knowledge and interest, while using his show and tell about music as a metaphor for everything non-musical—"music is a metaphor for men and women, women and women, men and men." All three pieces deliberately locate the audience at the core of the theatre experience, not as passive spectators but as active individual participants, and ultimately witnesses.

•　　•　　•

Jocelyn asks Anne four questions for her long flight home from Copenhagen to New York.

JOCELYN: What is theatre in the 21st century?

ANNE: Theatre is presence and energy coursing through bodies, and it is a meeting place of many languages. Because we now live in a society dominated by mediated experiences, that is, technologically arbitrated communication controlled and owned by huge conglomerates, the theatre has become an exotic plant—and like an exotic plant, it issues novel fragrances, shapes and pleasures that ignite dark places in the soul where our daily existence meets eternal issues of perception and how we live.

A Sanskrit saying suggests that all good theatre experiences accomplish three feats simultaneously: 1. Amuse the drunk. 2. Answer the question, "how to live." 3. Answer the question, "How does the universe work?" I feel that this ancient notion is still a contemporary issue.

Each theatre experience is an expression of a philosophy of living. Working in the theatre and being part of its evolution demands that we study history, forge philosophies, see the present without the baggage of inherited assumptions, and develop the capacity to receive the world in an open and sensitive way. It is only with receptivity and articulation that what we produce and share with audiences can pierce through time and find eternity behind it.

JOCELYN: How can theatre make a difference—or still be meaningful—now? (I am thinking post-9/11, post-Afghanistan, intra-Corporate America, intra-Bush, pre-possible Iraq attack.)

ANNE: To answer your question, I'm going to make a list.

1. Of the top ten corporations in the world, seven of them control the media. The theatre is a forum that does not need to be owned by large corporations. In this context, one can speak freely and personally about the times in which we live.

2. The theatre is a place of great intensity, where we meet one another in a charged field, where we can decide to set the stakes high and select tasks that ask us to function from deep and demanding parts of ourselves. Rather than the wash of manipulated experience found in the commercial world, the theatre can be a place of high moment-to-moment differentiation.

3. The theatre is a forum, and it is a place where we can ask questions.

4. The theatre is unique in that it intersects with and utilizes many art forms—painting, design, music, sculpture, architecture—and calls upon us to keep up with the innovations in all of those fields. We are painting the future in the present moment. We are creating the future in our description of it in the present moment.

5. The theatre is, at its heart, democratic; fed by countless amateur companies, stand-up comics, parlor singers and street performers. Its roots are ancient and necessary. It keeps us in touch with one another on a deeply visceral level.

JOCELYN: How important is memory?

ANNE: Consciousness is the place where attention and memory meet. Without memory, there can be no consciousness. The theatre must be a place of intense consciousness and awareness.

JOCELYN: What inspires you?

ANNE: Right now, paintings and painters inspire me. The process that painters undergo is one of intense receptiveness to the world. This inspires me deeply, and I want it to alter my work and life. I've discovered Edgar

Degas all over again and wonder now why I had not previously been able to really see the full extent of his brilliance. I've just become aware of the work of the Danish painter Vilhelm Hammerschoi, and I've fallen deeply in love.

I am inspired by the architects Daniel Liebeskind and Zaha Hadid.

I am inspired by all the living composers who are struggling to transcend the hegemony of minimalism, twelve-tone-ism, and romanticism in order to forge a new experience in music.

I am inspired by the nutty world of opera because of its impossibility.

Bridges forged between people inspire me. I'm inspired when real exchanges happen. I'm inspired by perseverance and love. I'm in awe of people who manage to create heightened aesthetic experiences for others.

I am inspired by living writers who can think with passion, such as Charles Mee, Margaret Atwood, John Berger, Michael Cunningham, Jeanette Winterson, Susan Sontag and so on.

• • •

ANNE: What do you hope for?

JOCELYN: I hope for challenge and resistance. That theatre artists continue to make theatre that will provoke audiences about their lives and the world they live in. That theatre continues to be a meeting place for asking questions, exchanging ideas and experiences, embracing new technologies and art forms—to be a necessity rather than a luxury. Of course, by theatre artists I mean all of us, actors, directors, designers, dramaturges, and producers, technicians, everybody who works in the theatre, and by theatre I mean any space where audiences come to participate—their very presence is an act of engagement.

In a time when there is a simultaneous disintegration of foundational beliefs and values, as much religious as political and economic, and a reassertion of fundamentalist dogma and certainties, again religious and political, then theatre must continue to be a place of resistance. It must continue to offer a space in which to debate philosophies and beliefs, and to interrogate values and certainties—in the bawdiest comedy, the bloodiest tragedy, the soppiest musical or the most stirring drama—because increasingly the space to discuss and to question, never mind to dissent, is shrinking and disappearing. To misquote *Star Trek*, resistance is fertile— it is in resistance that great art and ideas are born.

•   •   •

JOCELYN: What do you hope for?

ANNE: Personally I hope for grace. I imagine a lightness that rises above the natural entropy of dying. I want to leave a sliver of hope for coming generations. I want to be useful in the world. I hope that we can learn to live in the midst of paradox and ambiguity and not make blind or easy choices. I hope that we can learn to love that state of not-knowing and at the same time make bold and visible choices. I hope that we can find new shapes that can communicate and express the present ambiguities of our lives. When George W. Bush announces that he plans to invade Iraq, I want to find expressions for the ensuing state of horror, helplessness and absurdity that will wake us all up to the situation in which we live.

Excerpts from the Text

Some of this material has been sampled from published sources as noted.

What is this?

Who is this?

Good evening.

You've come so far to see me.

On the one hand, I am very pleased to see you all.

On the other hand, I cannot help asking the question, "Why me?"

I realize that I am speaking to a highly diverse and composite group, all, I am sure, devoted music-lovers.

You know, just being in this room is an inspiration.

You're an oasis in the desert!

I am just guessing at this.

I assume further that you are all highly educated and sophisticated in your particular disciplines—which may be the whole trouble. Socrates would say to you: Experts, learn from one another; this is the moment to begin your education.

We've just begun.

May I take the liberty of skipping the customary formal salutations and address myself directly to you?

My name is Leonard Bernstein.

Let me start with a confession.

I'm pretty tired—but... of course, I'm excited.

I'm going to give it everything I have.

What am I supposed to do for you?

What can I say? Do I have to make a speech?

I've been seized with all kinds of tremors contemplating this lecture because I've read over the brochure describing the nature of this series and it said something about creativity and psychiatry, and the creative personality, and all kinds of mysterious and wonderful phrases like those. I then asked myself, of course, by what right on God's earth did I dare to speak on this subject? After all, I don't spend twenty-four hours a day as a composer. Therefore I'm not properly a full-time creator; therefore I'm not properly qualified to discuss this. [1]

Then, I thought, well, maybe I'm better qualified to discuss it just because of that. And because half the time I cease to be a creator and switch off that magic little off-and-on switch and become a performer again, perhaps I thereby earn a certain kind of objectivity that I otherwise might not have. At this very moment I have just ended a performing period and started a creative one again, and so the switch went on again last week; but for the last few months I've been conducting. Now the conducting's over and will be over for seven months while I write another show, a rather serious and tragic musical comedy for Broadway—figure that one out. [1]

When you're conducting, you itch to compose, and when you're composing, you itch to conduct.[2]

I feel I have to give myself a chance to find out about the importance of composing.

And so, since I find myself just at the beginning of this period, and having left this long performing period, I think I'm probably just on the threshold of objectivity about the creative process or some aspect of the creative process. [1]

Therefore, I thought maybe I have the right to say something about it. On the other hand, I'm not by nature a lecturer; when I teach I ask a lot of questions of my students and I like very much to learn from them. The thing that attracts me about addressing groups like this are the questions. [1]

Would you like me just as well if I were a composer and not a conductor?

In a way my job is an educational mission.

A work of art does not answer questions: it provokes them; and its essential meaning is in the tension between their contradictory answers. For each question there are two answers, roughly corresponding to Yes and No, and attended by innumerable variations. [3]

All our lives are spent in the attempt to resolve conflicts; and we know that resolutions are impossible except by hindsight. We can make temporary decisions (and do, a thousand times a day); but it is only after death that it can be finally perceived whether we ever succeeded in resolving our conflicts. [3]

As long as we live we continue the attempt to resolve them. That attempt is the very action of living. [3]

So okay, you say, thanks a lot.

(If this is news to you, I hope it's good news.)

I could, of course, end my remarks right here, and everybody would be happy as a clam.

But there are still those questions,

Those unanswered questions.

What is music?

Why is music?

What does music mean?

The way it makes you feel when you hear it?

Perhaps a good way to begin would be to recall a question I am very often asked about a practical aspect of the creative process which is, perhaps, a superficial question, but which brings up a lot of others. The question is, "Do you compose at the piano, or at a desk, or where?" [1]

Well.

Hmm.

Well, the answer to that is that I sometimes do compose at the piano, and sometimes at a desk, and sometimes in airports, and sometimes walking along the street; but mostly I compose in bed, lying down, or on a sofa, lying down. I should think that most composing by almost any composer happens lying down. Many a time my wife has walked into my studio and found me lying down and has said, "Oh, I thought you were working, excuse me!" And I was working, but you'd never have known it. [1]

Now, this is a kind of trance state, I suppose, which doesn't exactly sound like a very ideal condition for working, but rather a condition for contemplating, but there is a very strong relation between creative work and contemplation. It's very hard to describe it. People have tried to describe it for centuries. [1]

Okay. Let's invent a fantasy together, right now—and I mean a fantastic fantasy.

As you lie on a bed or on the floor or wherever, and the conscious mind becomes hazier and hazier, the level of consciousness begins to lower, so that you find yourself somewhere at the borderland of this twilight area, which is the area, let's say, wherein fantasies occur at night when you're falling asleep. Everybody has that experience whether he is creative or not. [1]

Wouldn't it be marvelous if everyone could consciously, then, preserve just enough awareness, observation, and objectivity to be able to watch himself fantasizing? If, in other words, you can allow yourself this freedom of fantasy, then I think you've hit it. That's kind of the moment you want. [1]

And if the fantasy happens to be a creative one, if it happens to be taking place in terms of notes, or, if you're a writer or painter, in terms of words or design—in other words, if it is a creative vision you are having and you are still awake enough to remember it and appreciate it and know how to go about making it permanent (that is, when you arrive back in consciousness to formulate the vision into something communicable to other people)—then I suppose you've hit the ideal state. [1]

• • •

What is this? Who is this?

That's a perfect portrait of me.

That's me.

How did we get here?

Perhaps the most theatrical thing in the world is a room full of hushed people, and the more people… are silent, the more dramatic it is. [4]

I think we have a show. What do you think?

Be-ba-bom-ba

I believe in man's unconscious, the deep spring from which comes his power to communicate and to love. Art is nothing to me if it does not make contact between the creator and the perceiver on an unconscious level. Let us say that love is the way we have of communicating personally in the deepest way. What art can do is extend this communication, magnify it, and carry it to vastly greater numbers of people. [5]

I believe in art, of the warmth and love it carries within it, even if it be the lightest entertainment, or the bitterest satire, or the most shattering tragedy. For if art is cold it cannot communicate anything to anybody. [5]

I believe in people. I feel, love, need, and respect people above all else.

If I can write one real, moving American opera that any American can understand, I shall be a happy man.

People say I don't belong in the concert hall. What's wrong with theater in the concert hall and concert hall in the theater? [6]

Do you mind if I smoke? I really should give it up but I like it too much.

Stillness is our most intense mode of action. It is in our moments of deep quiet that is born every idea, emotion, and drive which we eventually honor with the name of action. Our most emotionally active life is lived in our dreams, and our cells renew themselves most industriously in sleep. We reach highest in meditation, and farthest in prayer. In stillness every human being is great; he is free from the experience of hostility; he is a poet, and most like an angel. [5]

Be-ba-bom-ba

I remember now the music I played at my first public performance at Temple Mishkan Tefila in Roxbury. I can remember my own excitement because I—I remember now—played a composition of my own.

My first composition.

It was a series of variations on a tune my father was very fond of singing in the shower.

I will always be a chip off the old *Tanach*.

But one thing I still know: beauty is truth, and truth beauty.

You've had a bellyful of rhetoric, I know that. So have I. But here I am.

I am an artist. I run off at the mouth.

I would like to leave you with what I consider a real shocker along these lines.

The only theme that interests me at this point is the great question of our time—are we headed for destruction, or is there hope? [7]

What have we artists to do with it? The answer is Everything. Our truth, if it is heartfelt, and the beauty we produce out of it, may perhaps be the only real guidelines left, the only clear beacons, the only source for renewal of vitality in the various cultures of our world. Where economists squabble, we can be clear. Where politicians play diplomatic games, we can move hearts and minds. Where the greedy grab, we can give. Our pens, voices, paintbrushes, *pas de deux*; our words; our C-sharps and B-flats can shoot up far higher than any oil well, can break down self-interest, can reinforce us against moral deterioration. Perhaps, after all, it is only the artist who can reconcile the mystic with the rational, and who can continue to reveal the presence of God in the minds of men. [5]

It's the artists of the world, the feelers and the thinkers, who will ultimately save us; who can articulate, educate, defy, insist, sing and shout the big dreams. Only the artists can turn them into reality.

All right, how do you do it? Like this: Find out what you can do well, uniquely well—You. Unique. And then do it for all you're worth. [5]

Relax. Invent. Perform. Have fun. [8]

Fun is the "x" of the equation that tries to solve the riddle of why art exists at all. [8]

It all happens while you are not looking. If you're looking, nothing will happen.

Life is juicy.

This is my last bit of sermonizing, for which I humbly beg pardon.

And at the very least you must admit that nothing I have fantasized, lunatic-artist though I may be, is actually inconceivable. After all, we did imagine it together, from beginning to end.

And this artist challenges you to pursue the fantasy, all your fantasies, while there is still time.

Now, that's a tall order, but a magnificent goal.

I want things to last...

Je veux vivre.

Just being in this room is an inspiration.

When we touch one another through music, we are touching the heart, the mind, and the spirit, all at once.

Cherish your love of music.

It is a glorious feeling.

Oh, it's getting late.

Good night.

Thank you.

[1] Bernstein, Leonard. *The Infinite Variety of Music.*
[2] Quoted in *Time,* December 21, 1953.
[3] Quoted in *The New York Times,* October 24, 1965.
[4] Quoted in *Opera News,* September 1972.
[5] Bernstein, Leonard. *Findings.*
[6] Quoted in *The Boston Sunday Globe,* February 2, 1964.
[7] Quoted in *The Baltimore Morning Sun,* January 5, 1967.
[8] Quoted in *Dance Magazine,* June 1946.

a.m. Sunday
by Jerome Hairston

for James Hairston
with love and admiration

BIOGRAPHY

Originally from Yorktown, Virginia, Jerome Hairston received his B.A. from James Madison University and is a graduate of Columbia University's M.F.A. playwriting program. His plays include: *L'Eboueur Sleeps Tonight, Forty Minute Finish,* and *Method Skin.* His work has been developed and presented at theaters such as Playwrights Horizons, The Atlantic Theatre Company, Hartford Stage, and New York Stage and Film, as well as The Sundance Theater Lab and The Eugene O'Neill Theater Center's National Playwrights Conference. He was featured twice in the Young Playwrights Festival in New York (1993, 1994) and was also the recipient of the 1998 Kennedy Center/American College Theater Festival's National Student Playwriting Award. He has received commissions from The Kennedy Center, The Public Theater/NYSF, and the Manhattan Theatre Club, where he was a 2001 playwriting fellow.

HUMANA FESTIVAL PRODUCTION

a.m. Sunday premiered at the Humana Festival of New American Plays in March 2002. It was directed by Timothy Douglas with the following cast:

Denny	H.J. Adams
R.P.	Ray Anthony Thomas
Helen	Barbara Gulan
Jay	Jason Cornwell
Lorie	Tarah Flanagan

and the following production staff:

Assistant to the Director	Rajendra Ramoon Maharaj
Scenic Designer	Paul Owen
Costume Designer	Christal Weatherly
Lighting Designer	Tony Penna
Sound Designer	Vincent Olivieri
Properties Designer	Doc Manning
Stage Manager	Cat Domiano
Production Assistant	Sarah Hodges
Dramaturg	Amy Wegener
Assistant Dramaturg	Nancy Vitale
Casting	Orpheus Group Casting

CHARACTERS

R.P.: Black, mid-thirties. Helen's husband.
HELEN: White, mid-thirties. R.P.'s wife.
JAY: Age fifteen,
AND DENNY: Age eleven. Helen and R.P.'s children.
LORIE: White, fifteen. A girl from school.

SETTING

The home of R.P. and Helen.
A bus stop.
The woods.

TIME

a.m. Sunday to Thursday morning.
Early November.

Tarah Flanagan and Jason Cornwell
in *a.m. Sunday*

26th Annual Humana Festival of New American Plays
Actors Theatre of Louisville, 2002
photo by Fred Furrow III

a.m. Sunday

Sunday, late a.m.

Helen at the stove. Denny is by the patio window. R.P. looks out from behind him.

DENNY: Ebony's running.

R.P.: When's the last time you two been out there?

DENNY: Yesterday. Remember we tried that trick.

R.P.: I mean out there for real. Look at that. It's a dog shit ocean. All that soggin' shit. Rain just knockin' it all to hell. Everywhere. Grass all out of control. The house is surrounded, surrounded by all this... Shameful. Shameful is what it is. Now I shouldn't have to tell you.

DENNY: You shouldn't.

R.P.: You or your brother.

DENNY: I'll tell Jay. Me and him. We'll do it.

(Pause.)

R.P.: What's wrong with this dog?

DENNY: She heard the train.

R.P.: She's all messed up in the head.

DENNY: She's excited.

R.P.: We got took.

DENNY: Whenever she hears the train. She tries to chase it, but the fence. She goes back and forth like that.

R.P.: Honey, I said we got took.

HELEN: *(From the stove.)* Did she hear the train? I think she hears the train.

R.P.: Ain't no train out there. It's come and gone already.

DENNY: But she still hears, you know. Even though it's going instead of coming. It's like the coming and going is the same thing. Like it don't matter. It don't matter to her.

R.P.: We got took, I'm tellin' you.

HELEN: *(Approaching the window.)* No, she's smart.

R.P.: Not too smart. Look at her. She's retarded.

HELEN: I've seen her, seen her do things. She's a smart dog. Like yesterday when the boys…

R.P.: She ain't even full bred, look at her. Cocker Spaniels don't even have noses like that.

DENNY: What do you think she is?

R.P.: She ain't no Cocker, I can tell you that much. We got took.

HELEN: Well, she's pretty. She's a pretty dog, and that's something.

R.P.: *(To Denny.)* What's the matter with you?

DENNY: Huh?

R.P.: Why you doin' that?

DENNY: What?

R.P.: What you grabbin' yourself for?

DENNY: I'm just sittin' here.

R.P.: Denny, get off the floor.

DENNY: I was just feelin' the vent.

R.P.: Dirty down there.

DENNY: I was just feelin' the air. I can go get warm some other way if you want.

R.P.: Just stay off the floor.

> *(Denny exits.)*

R.P.: Did you see him? You saw him, didn't you?

HELEN: What?

R.P.: Grabbin' himself.

HELEN: So?

R.P.: Hear that? The bathroom. He's pissin'. He needed to piss.

HELEN: Well, there you go.

R.P.: Why didn't he just get up? Get up and piss?

HELEN: He did.

R.P.: No, he was sitting there. Watchin' the dog instead of gettin' up and pissin'.

HELEN: You want applesauce?

R.P.: Two days ago, you know what I saw him doin'? Ducked on his knees lookin' through the crack of the bathroom.

HELEN: If you want applesauce, tell me. So, I can time it.

R.P.: You know who was in there?

HELEN: Time it with the toast.

R.P.: It was you. You was in there.

HELEN: I didn't mind.

R.P.: You ain't mind, 'cause you ain't seen him.

HELEN: So, no on the applesauce.

R.P.: No, no. Go ahead and cook that up.

HELEN: And the bacon?

R.P.: We ain't got no Sizzlean?

HELEN: Just regular bacon.

R.P.: How about hot dogs? We got any hot dogs? You can split 'em. Split 'em like you did.

HELEN: Like I did?

R.P.: That one time.

HELEN: What time?

R.P.: That one time. You don't remember?

HELEN: No.

R.P.: Back when we was broke.

HELEN: Well, I remember that.

R.P.: We ain't have nothin' worth cookin', so, you improvised.

HELEN: Did I?

R.P.: Yeah. I remember. Breakfast. Out of nothin'. Out of the nothin' I made back then. I remember, 'cause, it was a surprise. You surprised me. Conjurin' somethin' like that. I remember feelin', felt like I did somethin' right. Havin' you around. Yeah, I remember. You improvisin'. Improvisin' breakfast. *(Pause.)* It was a Sunday then, too. *(Silence.)*

R.P.: The other one up?

HELEN: He will be.

R.P.: He sleep?

HELEN: He is if he's not up.

R.P.: *(Listening.)* He's showerin'. Denny done finished his pissin', now he's in the shower. I hear the water runnin'. He soak in there too long, eat up all that hotness, his brother gonna beat his ass.

HELEN: His brother should get up.

R.P.: What you think he does in there?

HELEN: Gets clean.

R.P.: Clean only takes so much.

HELEN: What do you do in the shower?

R.P.: I do my business. I get out.

HELEN: You gonna get the other one up?

R.P.: The rain ain't stoppin' no time soon.

HELEN: He still got to eat.

R.P.: He can eat it cold. Jay got a choice. Ain't much can be done on the lawn, so, he can choose whatever. *(Pause.)* We need to shave that dog. Did you call that lady?

HELEN: Didn't know I was supposed to.

R.P.: She gets that coat of shit on her. Every time she gets wet. The bitch needs a shavin'.

HELEN: Fine.

R.P.: I want it tight this time. Where the skin's showin'. We got took last time.

HELEN: She cut it like a Cocker.

R.P.: But she ain't no Cocker. She's some sort of mutt. If she ain't one, she can't look like one. So, I want the hair cut, off her body. So, she don't drag that shit in here.

HELEN: You want it bald? Bald with no style?

R.P.: I want it cut.

HELEN: Well, they're gonna style it regardless.

R.P.: Regardless of what? Of me sayin' I want the shit shaved?

HELEN: All I'm saying is that they're gonna style it. It's the nature of the work. They see hair, they're gonna see what can be. Besides, it's cold out there. And it gets colder.

R.P.: It's a practical thing. They shave that shit off, we ain't worryin' about no dirt. No ticks to be hiding. 'Cause they hide in that mess, you know that. *(Enter Denny. A towel clings tight to his wet body.)*

R.P.: They hide inside.

DENNY: Can we bring her in?

R.P.: What the hell you doing?

DENNY: She's cold. I know. 'Cause I'm cold now.

R.P.: Get back in the shower.

DENNY: When you're wet, the air makes you cold.

R.P.: Take your naked ass on, now, I'm serious.

DENNY: See here. Even though the heater's on, the warm air's making me cold.

HELEN: Honey, back to the shower.

DENNY: I'm just gonna let her in first.

R.P.: Get away from the window.

HELEN: She's dirty now. Maybe later.

DENNY: I'll hold her. She won't touch the ground.

R.P.: Come here.

DENNY: But I...

R.P.: ...I said...

DENNY: ...I'm doing the right...

R.P.: Now you get in there, and you don't come out till you're clean and with some God Damn clothes.

DENNY: Neighbors will think we're mean. They can't think that.

R.P.: Look. The water. All this, everywhere. Don't make me pick your scrawny ass up.

DENNY: It's important, Dad. Don't you think it's important? She's ours.

HELEN: Honey, he's concerned. Denny's just concerned.

DENNY: She's ours.

HELEN: *(To R.P.)* He's worried. *(To Denny.)* Denny, finish your shower, Sweety. I'll look to her. *(To R.P.)* He's worried, is all. *(To Denny.)* Denny?

R.P.: I'm countin' seconds now, boy. Hear me? Seconds.

HELEN: Denny?

DENNY: I'll shower. Okay, Dad. Dad okay, look. I just...
 (Denny moves to the window, opens the towel, and presses his body against the glass. It leaves a print.)

DENNY: So, she'll know. Know someone's here. That we didn't forget. She'll see the glass, my shape. Think someone's lookin' over her. *(Pause.)* See?
 (Silence.)
 I'll go finish now.
 (Denny returns to his shower.)
 (Silence.)

HELEN: Should it be me?

R.P.: What?

HELEN: Taking the dog. To the lady, I mean.

R.P.: No mistakes this time. I'll take the dog in. End of the week.

HELEN: Today's Sunday.

R.P.: Yeah?

HELEN: It *is* the end of the week. Tomorrow is when it starts.

R.P.: So, the end after tomorrow, then.

HELEN: I can do it, R.P. I can find the time.

R.P.: *(To the glass.)* Are you seein' this? Nose all up against the glass. Sniffin'.

HELEN: It's just a matter of when you want.

R.P.: Sniffin' that boy's shape like there's somebody there.

HELEN: But you have to tell me, 'cause.

R.P.: We got took.

HELEN: 'Cause I'm leavin'.

R.P.: What did you say?

HELEN: I said I'm leavin'.

R.P.: What do you mean by that?

HELEN: It means what I say. Thursday. Afternoon.

R.P.: What's Thursday afternoon?

HELEN: *(Pause.)* It's her birthday. The whole day it is.

R.P.: What are you talking about?

HELEN: The twelfth. That's this week. Thursday. I was gonna take the day.

R.P.: It's no one's birthday, Helen.

HELEN: Just the day.

R.P.: Ain't mine. Ain't Denny's. Ain't Jay's.

HELEN: It's her birthday. I should at least try.

R.P.: Try what?
> *(Nothing.)*
> You plan on taking them? The two of them.
> *(Nothing.)*
> Are you?

HELEN: Just pictures. Pictures of them. Of us. I got stacks. A box. I'm gonna wrap it.
> *(Denny enters. He's dressed and sits at the table, looking at a piece of paper. Helen and R.P. continue as if he's not there.)*

HELEN: It's just me, R.P. All alone. Just me.

R.P.: You don't need to be takin' you either.

HELEN: We'll see. We'll just have to see.
> *(Enter Jay. He hovers over Denny.)*

R.P.: *(Pause.)* Nothing changes, Helen. A long time you've known that. Nothing changes.

HELEN: I don't know, R.P. I'm alone in bed. Twelve, one-thirty at night. In bed. Alone. And I find myself thinking. *(Pause.)* The one thing she's given me and still... I've forgotten. I've forgotten my mother's face.

R.P.: We need to get the other one up.

HELEN: I think I miss her.

R.P.: Just felt the hour.

HELEN: I was alone.

R.P.: It's past late.

HELEN: And I missed her.

R.P.: Way past.
> *(Silence.)*

HELEN: So you want me to...

R.P.: Yeah. *(Pause.)* Get him up.
(*Helen and R.P. remain.*)

Monday, 3:30 p.m.

Denny and Jay at the table.

JAY: Here. Johnny does what?

DENNY: Goes to the store.

JAY: What happens?

DENNY: He buys oranges.

JAY: What next?

DENNY: He goes home.

JAY: Okay, yeah. He goes home, but home to what?
(*Fade Helen and R.P.*)

DENNY: Huh?

JAY: To do what? What does he do?

DENNY: He splits them.

JAY: Splits them how?

DENNY: In the middle, I guess.

JAY: The number, Denny. How many pieces?

DENNY: See, it's numbers. They always get me.

JAY: C'mon now. Just look. You got one thing, it splits in half, what do you got?

DENNY: You still got one thing. It's just split.

JAY: No. You got two separate things. It's something new. You got two things. And what does Johnny do?

DENNY: He splits.

JAY: That's right. He does that to each one. And how many of each?

DENNY: Eight.

JAY: Now, Johnny's mom, dad, brother, sister. What's that?

DENNY: The family. That's why he bought them.

JAY: But how many are they? Mom, dad, brother, sister? What is that?

DENNY: Four.

JAY: You forgot Johnny.

DENNY: But he splits.

JAY: But still, you got to count him. How many?

DENNY: Five.

JAY: And how many pieces has he split?

(He circles his answer from before.)

JAY: Now, count how many each can have so that they'll all have the same thing.

DENNY: I did that before.

JAY: And what happened?

DENNY: There was one left.

JAY: That's the remainder.

DENNY: That's wrong.

JAY: What is?

DENNY: The remainder. It doesn't fit.

JAY: It's not supposed to.

DENNY: I'm telling you, I'll go in there tomorrow and she'll tell me. In front of everybody. It's wrong. It has to fit.

JAY: Not always.

DENNY: It does, Jay. I know you're older and you know things. But you're not the teacher. It may be right now, but tomorrow. The remainder. They'll laugh.

JAY: Just star the ones you don't understand. We'll work them out later.

DENNY: I have to do this now. I'm only right when you're here, but once you go... And I take it slow, Jay. I do. I go bit by bit, real careful, but I know in the end. The numbers. The numbers won't be what I need them to.
(The phone rings. The two stop dead and listen. It rings four times. They do nothing. It stops.)

JAY: An hour, something like that. An hour from now, I'll help you. That's plenty of time.

DENNY: But that's when we walk.

JAY: We'll do this instead.

DENNY: Our dog needs to walk, Jay. We said we would.

JAY: This is schoolwork. You got to get it done, right?

DENNY: But we said. *We* take care of her. We have to walk.

JAY: We'll do it after.

DENNY: Is she smart?

JAY: What?

DENNY: Her, in there. In your room, the pretty girl in your room, can she help me?

JAY: I'll help you.

DENNY: She looks like she could be smart. She walks smart. She has a smart walk.

JAY: I can't do this now.

DENNY: I'm not talking about you. If she says it's right. Maybe it is. Me, you, and her look at the same numbers. See the same things.

JAY: There's nothing wrong here. What we've done. What we've been doing. The numbers come out the same each time. Each time, Denny. So, what are you doing?

DENNY: I'm doing homework.

JAY: What are you doing, Denny?

DENNY: When you leave things happen.

JAY: What things?

DENNY: I must turn stupid or something. Nothing makes sense. They should, but they don't.

JAY: I'm not staying. That's it. I'll be here. Right in there. But I'm not staying.

DENNY: I'm going to be wrong, Jay.

JAY: Understand for me, huh?

DENNY: I feel bad. I feel so bad.

JAY: You work. I'll walk her later. Alright?

DENNY: Will she? You know, your friend, go with you?

JAY: She's going home soon.

DENNY: Oh. I thought she might...

JAY: She's going home.

(Lights up on Lorie. She has on big earphones. One ear listens, the other free.)

JAY: *(Indicates his room.)* Now, how many times?

DENNY: Four. Real slow.

JAY: Denny.

DENNY: Sorry. I keep thinking the code: four.

JAY: You want me to make it four?

DENNY: No, I can know. If someone comes home, three real slow. Like: Bang. Bang. Bang. You make it four instead of three, I'll remember three and forget one, and you'll be waiting.

JAY: Try to remember, Denny? Try?

DENNY: I don't mean to bother you.

JAY: Star the ones you don't understand. Then later.

DENNY: Tell her, would you? That I don't mean to.

(Jay walks to Lorie.)

DENNY: It's just these numbers. They get the best of me. They do. They get me.

Same day. Jay's bedroom.

JAY: They're $6.99.

LORIE: Hmmm?

JAY: $6.99. If you want your own. $6.99. On sale.

LORIE: I figured I'd listen first. Get a sense. If I liked it as a whole. I mean, there's the one song, on the radio, but, you know, that's one song.

(Denny fades.)

JAY: Sorry about the speakers. My little brother. He wrecks things.

LORIE: No, I like this. Close to your ear. You hear more. All the little things.

JAY: Well, the next one, actually the next one after the next. You'll hear. There's this time where he kinda sings to himself.

LORIE: To himself.

JAY: It's a trick, when it's recorded. It's the lyrics regular in one ear, and in the other, he sings it a different way. The same song different. He repeats, no, he replies? No, he… echoes himself. Like a second him pushing the song along. But you got to have both sides on to hear it.

LORIE: But if I do that, I can't hear you.

JAY: It's just a few minutes.

LORIE: What will you do?

JAY: When?

LORIE: You'll just be sitting there.

JAY: I'll watch.

LORIE: What fun is that?

JAY: I want to see if you hear the same things I did. Or do.

(Lorie listens a moment. She takes off the earphones.)

JAY: What?

LORIE: Ear's all sweaty.

JAY: I'd stop it, but Milton has me recording…

LORIE: A few minutes, I'll put them back on. I won't miss it, promise.

(Silence.)

Your brother. He's…

JAY: Outside. In the living room.

LORIE: And your door?

JAY: It locks.

(Pause.)

LORIE: Look at your hair.

JAY: What's wrong with it?

LORIE: You have a big line.

JAY: What? Are you saying the phone head? I got the phone head, don't I?

LORIE: Looks funny.

JAY: I'd re-comb it. But then I'd have to wet it down. And re-comb.

LORIE: Is it soft?

> (Lorie approaches Jay. She feels through his hair.)
>
> I guess not really. Looks softer than it is.

JAY: I'd re-comb it, but...

LORIE: I don't mind.

> (Lorie continues a soft exploration into Jay's hair. Jay moves away.)

JAY: Guess you don't have that problem, do you?

LORIE: What's that?

JAY: The re-comb factor.

LORIE: My hair? No, it pretty much just lays there. It's boring. Thin and boring. Get it from my dad. My mom and dad actually. Guess I was doomed from the start.

> (Pause. Lorie explores the room, discovers a photo.)

LORIE: Is your dad funny?

JAY: What?

LORIE: Your dad. Is he funny?

JAY: Funny how?

LORIE: Seeing here, your face in his. Figured, you know, your talents. If that's where you got them from?

JAY: Talents?

LORIE: Yeah.

JAY: I'm not talented.

LORIE: How can you say that?

JAY: I can say it over and over. 'Cause it's true.

LORIE: Jimmy was crying. He was. Crying. When you did those impersonations.

JAY: Oh, those.

LORIE: The way you can just push your face into something like that. It's amazing.

JAY: Ain't that hard. Just think you're someone else. Convince your face it's the truth.

LORIE: Jimmy's head was 'bout to split laughing so hard. We were just talking about it.

JAY: You were talking?

LORIE: Uh huh.

JAY: Talking about me?

LORIE: Yeah.

JAY: And laughing?

LORIE: Well, about your talents.

JAY: With who?

LORIE: Well, everybody.

JAY: Where?

LORIE: Just the other night. At the alley, remember?

JAY: I don't think I do.

LORIE: You don't?

JAY: No. Maybe 'cause, I don't think I was there.

LORIE: Really? I could've swore. Well, something must've got, jumbled, I'm
    sure you were invited.

JAY: Surely.

LORIE: Still, even if you weren't there. You were still a hit, you know.

JAY: No, I'm kinda having trouble.

LORIE: With?

JAY: It's just these talents you say I have. Not sure they're all you crack them
    up to be.

LORIE: Am I cracking them up to be something?

JAY: Maybe we should put it to a test.

LORIE: Test?

JAY: See how my talents hold up.

LORIE: I don't understand.

JAY: What I'll do is, be somebody. You take a look. See if you could tell me
    who it is. What do you say?

LORIE: I say it's not necessary.

    (Jay turns around.)

JAY: *(Pause.)* Ready?

LORIE: This is silly, really.

JAY: Alright. Here it is.

LORIE: Jay…

    (Jay turns around. His face hasn't changed.)

JAY: Well?

LORIE: *(Pause.)* I don't see it.

JAY: Give me a second. *(Pause.)* How about now?

    (His face remains. Silence.)

LORIE: I guess you were right. I'm looking at you, but I'm not seeing a thing.

JAY: They must've been laughing at something.

LORIE: Must be me then. Must just be something with me.

    (Silence.)

JAY: What did you wear?

LORIE: Wear?

JAY: At the alley.

LORIE: I don't know. Just some sort of whatever, I guess.

JAY: Was it green?

LORIE: I don't wear much green.

JAY: Sometimes you do.

LORIE: When?

JAY: You have the one thing, it swoops.

LORIE: What thing is this?

JAY: The green thing, it kind of swoops down. It'd be too cold to wear now, 'cause, well, it exposes.

LORIE: Exposes what?

JAY: Your back. You wear it in the summer. I saw it that one time at the pool.

LORIE: I don't remember.

JAY: No, I guess you wouldn't.

LORIE: What does that mean?

JAY: Your back was turned.

LORIE: Oh. Sorry.

JAY: No, I didn't mind.

LORIE: How exciting is someone's back?

JAY: You'd be surprised.

LORIE: Would I?

JAY: Depending on the way you move. Your muscles. They change.

LORIE: I don't have muscles.

JAY: Everyone has muscles.

LORIE: I mean I don't have real ones. I'm not some bodybuilder or something.

JAY: Well, whatever they are. They move. Like when you. Your hair. When you take it back.

LORIE: You mean behind?

JAY: When you up and tie it. Your skin moves, and the hairs on your back…

LORIE: I'm hairy back there?

JAY: The tan, I'm saying. The sun accents the little you got back there. And these two freckles…

LORIE: I don't have freckles.

JAY: You have two.

LORIE: Where?

JAY: Towards the middle. To the side.

LORIE: Which side?

JAY: The left.

LORIE: Are they close together?

JAY: Somewhat.

LORIE: Somewhat how?

JAY: See my finger? From the tip to the knuckle. That's how far.

LORIE: *(Turning her back to Jay.)* Show me.

JAY: Show you?

LORIE: Point.

JAY: Well, I don't know if I can exactly.

LORIE: Why not?

JAY: I could tell you in general. But I couldn't give you… specifics.

LORIE: 'Cause you can't see. 'Cause of my shirt, you're saying?

JAY: Not that I have to see. I just don't want to steer you wrong. In the facts of, of what you have.

LORIE: *(Pause.)* Well, you can lift it up, I guess. To where they are and all. But only to the freckles, though. Just to where you need.

(Jay carefully pulls up the back of Lorie's shirt.)

LORIE: You see them?

JAY: Yeah. You want me to, you know, tip to knuckle? So you'll know.

LORIE: Umm. Okay. Yeah, sure.

(Jay points then gently presses the rest of his finger down.)

LORIE: Does it measure the distance?

JAY: It measures.

LORIE: How about that.

JAY: I could be lying, you know. You can't see, so I could be.

LORIE: You could be.

JAY: Am I making you cold?

LORIE: Why are you asking?

JAY: It's fifty-four outside. Just wanted to make sure it didn't make its way inside.

LORIE: Inside your hand?

JAY: Yeah.

LORIE: I can't tell anymore.

JAY: What if I placed it somewhere else? Should I do that?

LORIE: *(Pause.)* Yes.

JAY: There?

LORIE: I feel you, but. It doesn't make me cold.

JAY: There?

> *(Pause.)*

LORIE: Your brother?

JAY: The living room.

LORIE: The door?

JAY: It locks.

> *(Pause.)*

LORIE: I'm sorry about your speakers.

JAY: Why are you sorry?

LORIE: I just wish we had some sound. Sound to blanket the room, you know. It's so quiet.

> *(They listen.)*

JAY: It's the next.

LORIE: What?

JAY: The song I was talking. It's next.

LORIE: *(Pause.)* Aren't we going to?

JAY: I want to watch you. Please.

> *(Lorie places the headphones back on. She waits for the song.)*

LORIE: *(Loudly, over the music.)* It's starting now.

JAY: I hear you.

LORIE: WHAT?

JAY: Shhh. I hear you.

> *(Lorie listens. Jay watches. A few moments. Lorie takes the phones off.)*

JAY: The song over?

LORIE: No.

JAY: Why did you stop?

LORIE: Did I listen alright? The little I did?

JAY: I think you heard enough.

LORIE: How do you know?

JAY: 'Cause you stopped right after.

LORIE: After what?

JAY: After he stopped singing to himself. Not much to hear after that.

> *(Silence.)*

JAY: You know, I really want to walk you home today.

LORIE: I know. I know but...

JAY: Yeah.

>   (*They look at each other a moment. Lorie then takes off her shirt. Jay sees her. Lorie sees him seeing. She covers herself.*)

LORIE: It's so quiet.

JAY: It's alright.

>   (*Jay approaches her. He opens her up. He touches her breast.*)

LORIE: It's so quiet.

JAY: Shhhh.

LORIE: It's so quiet.

>   (*Monday fades as lights rise on...*)

Tuesday, Late Night

>   *Helen and R.P. in the bedroom.*

HELEN: Do you think they heard?

R.P.: Depends.

HELEN: On what?

R.P.: If they was listenin'.

HELEN: That answers that then.

R.P.: Do it?

HELEN: It's a small house. Sound doesn't have too many places to hide.

R.P.: They shouldn't go lookin'.

HELEN: You don't look for sound. If it's there you hear.

R.P.: They should be sleep. Two-thirty. They should be in deep.

HELEN: Maybe they couldn't help it.

R.P.: Help what?

HELEN: I know that I... I may of let loose more than I should've.

R.P.: You let loose?

HELEN: Well, I giggled.

R.P.: You what?

HELEN: I giggled. You didn't notice?

R.P.: I noticed somethin'.

HELEN: What did you think it was?

R.P.: Just didn't figure it was a giggle.

HELEN: What else would I be doing in a moment like that?

R.P.: It wasn't your laugh, that's all.

HELEN: A small laugh, isn't that what a giggle is?

R.P.: If it was your laugh, I would've recognized. After all these years I think I would've.

HELEN: So, if it was a laugh, you'd take notice.

R.P.: Ain't that what I said.

HELEN: Like the last time you heard me. Laugh that is.

R.P.: Right.

HELEN: When was that? The last time that I. Laughed. Do you remember? 'Cause I.

(Pause.)

R.P.: Whatever it was. I don't think they heard. I wouldn't worry.

HELEN: I didn't say I was.

R.P.: Not now you didn't.

HELEN: You mean earlier. Before. Earlier.

R.P.: I'm gonna go ahead and go. Take a look 'round.

HELEN: It was nothing.

R.P.: Seemed like something awhile ago.

HELEN: I was nervous, that's all it was.

R.P.: Nervous about what?

HELEN: What I meant was...

R.P.: It won't take long.

HELEN: You shuffle around out there, you'll wake them for real.

R.P.: It's two-thirty, Helen.

HELEN: It's something outside.

R.P.: I'll take a look.

HELEN: Just something outside, trying to make its way in.

R.P.: So, I'll check.

HELEN: Like a cat or something. Something harmless, I'm sure. She stopped, so. I'm gonna assume it's gone.

R.P.: The cat?

HELEN: The cat or whatever it was.

R.P.: Just to make sure. To set you at ease.

HELEN: I am at ease.

R.P.: We stopped.

HELEN: That was then.

R.P.: We stopped so you could...

HELEN: My imagination. I'm fine now.

R.P.: You're fine.

HELEN: I am.

R.P.: Just don't want to be waiting. To see. To hear her. 'Cause if there's something out there, she'll start again.

HELEN: Isn't that a reason why we got a dog in the first place? To warn us. Announce invaders, thieves, strangers out to take...

R.P.: She'll bark up the neighborhood. Then what?

HELEN: The neighborhood would wake up.

R.P.: And those two in there?

HELEN: If they weren't awake already.

R.P.: It's two-thirty.

HELEN: It might've been us. That's got them up. That they heard...

R.P.: Like they would even know...

HELEN: They might've...

R.P.: Even know what they was listenin' to.

HELEN: Don't be so sure.

R.P.: What?

HELEN: I'm just saying. Don't be so sure. What they know. Don't know.

R.P.: We were quiet. Careful. I remember.

HELEN: I giggled.

R.P.: So, what's that mean? What they gonna get from that?

HELEN: Maybe he knows. What a giggle like that is supposed to mean.

R.P.: They ain't hear nothin'.

HELEN: I didn't say they. I said he.

R.P.: What's he know?

HELEN: He's fifteen.

R.P.: We was careful.

HELEN: He's fifteen and I wash his sheets.

R.P.: What are you sayin'?

HELEN: That there are things he might know.

R.P.: Let's not talk about this.

HELEN: Why not?

R.P.: What he does with himself is his business.

HELEN: I found a strand of hair. A long strand. That's not his and it's not mine.

R.P.: So, whose is it?

HELEN: His business isn't all his own.

   (Pause.)

R.P.: What color?

HELEN: What's that?

R.P.: The color. Of the hair, the color of it.

HELEN: Like mine. Slightly.

R.P.: In his room?

HELEN: Where else?

R.P.: I thought he had just the one.

HELEN: Who?

R.P.: We saw her. The other week, we were passing in the car. Him and that girl on the corner.

HELEN: That's not the one.

R.P.: You know the one I'm sayin', don't you? Yellow jacket. Dark, dark skin. You know what I'm talkin' about, right?

HELEN: Yes. I remember. It's not her.

R.P.: You sure? 'Cause I could've swore. I saw somethin' there.

HELEN: They were just walking.

R.P.: But there's ways a boy can walk. I mean, he wasn't walkin' like he didn't care. He was takin' his time. You know, slow, like he was keepin' in sync. Gettin' familiar.

HELEN: Familiar.

R.P.: Yeah, you know.

HELEN: Not sure I do.

R.P.: The way you move next to somebody when you're, well, taking them in. Like he was lookin' for somethin'. In her. Lookin' at her, waitin' for a look back. Ain't you see his face? His face all tensed up. Like his life, his whole life. Depended on it. On that one look. That tells him he's... he's where he should be. Tellin' him he's free. Free of any and everything that makes him... unsure. Of himself, the world, his world in particular. A boy gets a lot on his mind when he gets a certain age. Comes a time, seems everything's in question. And he waits, he waits for that moment. That look. That answers all of it. Answers by ain't askin'. By ain't askin' anything at all. *(Pause.)* And I'm sure he got it. She was into him. I can tell. They looked good. They looked good together.

HELEN: You got all this, while we were passing?

R.P.: You only got to see but so much. The rest ain't complicated. *(Pause.)* Just hope he don't mess things up for himself. With this other girl, I mean.

HELEN: Which one?

R.P.: You should know, you're the one who brought it up.

HELEN: Just that "other" can go either way. Just want to be clear who we're talkin' about.

R.P.: *(Pause.)* The one with the hair.

(Silence.)

When exactly does this happen?

HELEN: Does what happen?

R.P.: His sheets.

HELEN: Home's not always home, R.P.

R.P.: What's that?

HELEN: Home's not always… It's not always what you think it is. When you leave…

R.P.: I'm gonna talk to him.

HELEN: When you leave. We're not here. Things happen. They're alone so much. Alone and getting ideas. You can't expect him to help it.

R.P.: Me and him. We'll talk.

HELEN: All I wish is that he would tell us.

R.P.: What's he gonna say? Give us the play-by-play. Dirty details of what he does in there.

HELEN: Maybe bring her over.

R.P.: Sounds like he did enough of that.

HELEN: For us to meet. To see.

R.P.: Maybe she ain't the girl to bring home.

HELEN: What kind of girl is that?

R.P.: It's no barber shop in there. There's ways hair falls. And the way they ended up in his sheets ain't exactly wholesome.

HELEN: To explore. To find out. That's what young people. When you're young…

R.P.: It's a matter of respect.

HELEN: To who?

R.P.: To the house.

HELEN: The home?

R.P.: That's right.

HELEN: Where's he gonna go? Where do you go for such…

R.P.: You don't got a home, then you ain't got the right.

HELEN: Where did we go?

R.P.: Who?

HELEN: Those first times.

R.P.: You talkin' us?

HELEN: It wasn't a home.

R.P.: I don't know. I can't…

HELEN: Why can't you?

R.P.: Time. You know. It was awhile ago.

HELEN: Yeah. It was. Suppose I don't remember either.

R.P.: That the truth?

HELEN: *(Pause.)* No.

    (Silence.)

R.P.: Are you taking the Charger?

HELEN: What?

R.P.: Thursday. If you're still doing this.

HELEN: I am.

R.P.: It rattles. The Charger. The engine, I'm talkin'.

HELEN: I wasn't planning.

R.P.: You'd risk being stuck. Stranded somewhere. And I'm working, it would take a while for me to come...

HELEN: ...Like I said...

R.P.: ...To come save you...

HELEN: ...I wasn't....

R.P.: ...The engine. It won't last the day. 'Cause that's what it would take. The whole day.

HELEN: I know.

R.P.: Back and forth. Majority of the time that's what you'll be doing. On the road goin' and comin'.

HELEN: It's not like I've never been.

R.P.: I ain't say you ain't know the way. I'm sayin', you find that front door not opening. Like the time before. And before that. You find yourself coming straight back. Still, the day will be gone. So if you're going to take the day. Leave the Charger.

HELEN: I understand.

R.P.: It rattles.

    (Pause.)

HELEN: You really don't remember, do you?

R.P.: Remember what?

HELEN: The places we'd find. Back then.

R.P.: Back then?

HELEN: Yes.

R.P.: If I tried maybe.

HELEN: Then why don't you?

R.P.: Think about it.

HELEN: I have. More than I should lately. Thinking backwards. Why am I
doing that, R.P.?

R.P.: Those were places we ain't want to find. We had to. Why is it you're not
remembering that?

HELEN: It was silly.

R.P.: I just don't see the reason.

HELEN: It was a silly thing for me to ask.

R.P.: What's wrong with here. With right here and now. Ain't that somewhere
to find?

HELEN: Here is fine, R.P. It is. It's fine.

(Silence. The dog is heard barking.)

R.P.: Just a matter of time.

HELEN: Hmm?

R.P.: A matter of time.

HELEN: *(Listening.)* It's nothing.

R.P.: I'm gonna go.

HELEN: A night train's coming. That's all.

R.P.: Still, I should.

(R.P. gets out of bed. He heads for the door.)

HELEN: It was seventh time.

(R.P. stops. He turns around.)

The seventh time I ever held your hand. I looked down and stretched out
your fingers. I stared so deep. Every crease. Every line. Spoke to me. I
studied it, your palm. The color, this creamy pale. So different from the
rest of you. It was the only part of you I could see myself in. These strong
hands. And I felt safe. Purer than four years old. I felt like such... I was
such a child. *(Pause.)* Come to bed.

R.P.: I should secure the house.

HELEN: I... want to.

R.P.: Again?

HELEN: Yes. Again.

R.P.: The boys.

HELEN: I'll giggle soft this time.

R.P.: The barking. You'll get nervous, I know you.

HELEN: I won't stop you this time. We won't stop. I'll hear only what needs to
be heard. The rest, I'll block out. I'll control it. What's heard. The sounds
I make, the noises I hear, no matter how strange. I'll make it the quiet it
needs to be.

R.P.: It'll only take a second.

HELEN: Then you'll be back.

R.P.: Where else is there to go?

HELEN: Stay, R.P. Please. Stay.

R.P.: *(Pause.)* You really are being silly, now.

(He leaves. She notices. Helen slides out of bed and puts on her robe. She realizes herself in a "mirror." Soft spotlight as she gazes into herself.)

Lights rise on Jay and Denny's room, same night. Jay is faced forward, also looking at himself in a "mirror." He is fully dressed in carefully chosen clothes. He combs and pats down his wet hair. Denny looks on behind him in his pajamas.

DENNY: Maybe if you concentrate. Think flat things. Like cardboard pancakes, steam-rolled Play-Doh, stuff like that.

JAY: What's that gonna do?

DENNY: Think hard enough, maybe the curls will listen. Lay down like you want them to.

JAY: That's not gonna work.

DENNY: Why not?

JAY: Been tryin' to think you to sleep the last hour, hasn't done me any good.

DENNY: It's 'cause I've been thinkin' harder. I done out-thank you is what it is. How you think that shirt happened?

JAY: I put it on.

DENNY: No. I thought it looked best, then thought that thought to you, which made you think: This is it, this is the one. And it is.

JAY: I liked the blue one better.

DENNY: Don't matter.

JAY: I know what I like, Denny.

DENNY: But it's what I like.

JAY: It's not about what you like.

DENNY: Oh. It's about what she likes, right?

JAY: Who?

DENNY: Nobody.

JAY: Go to bed, Denny.

DENNY: *(Pause.)* You think she's scared?

JAY: Scared of what?

DENNY: Of what Mom and Dad's thinkin'?

JAY: Mom and Dad can't think about what they don't know.

DENNY: But they do.

JAY: Did they say something?

DENNY: They don't have to. They can hear.

JAY: Hear what?

DENNY: Hear Ebony. Hear her cryin'. 'Cause that's what that is. You think it's just a bark, but it ain't. That's cryin'.

JAY: What she got to cry about?

DENNY: She thinks Dad's gonna get rid of her.

JAY: Dogs don't think.

DENNY: No, they cry. They cry 'cause they can't think. But still they can know. Where things are headed.

JAY: Ebony ain't goin' nowhere.

DENNY: That's what I've been hopin'. Doin' my best to hope that into happenin'. You think you can do that? Hope your way into somethin'?

JAY: No.

DENNY: What about your shirt?

JAY: What about it?

DENNY: I hoped you into wearin' that tomorrow.

JAY: No you didn't.

DENNY: I did. You're gonna wake up tomorrow and it'll be the first thing you throw on.

JAY: How do you know?

DENNY: 'Cause it goes. Goes with you, your face, your flat head. It just goes. I may not know my math, but there's some things I can put together. There's just certain ways things should be.

(Denny slides into his slippers.)

JAY: Where you going?

DENNY: Ebony needs me.

JAY: Mom and Dad are awake.

DENNY: How do you know?

JAY: I just do.

DENNY: She needs comfort, Jay. What other reason is there to cry at night?

(Denny exits.)

(Jay looks to himself in the "mirror." Spotlight. He takes a quick look around, making sure he's alone. He places his face close to the "mirror" glass and breathes hot air onto the surface. He fingers the letters L-O-R-I-E. He smiles as the letters fade away. The soft pools on Jay and Helen remain.)

Lights rise on Denny and R.P. The kitchen. R.P. sitting at the table, the phone in front of him. Denny stands nearby, holding something behind his back.

DENNY: Were you talkin' to somebody?

R.P.: It's late.

DENNY: I thought I heard you talking.

R.P.: Who is there to talk to this hour?

DENNY: The ring could wake them.

R.P.: What ring?

DENNY: The ring of the phone. If you dialed. If you were talking to somebody.

R.P.: I wasn't.

DENNY: Oh.

(R.P. takes out a cigarette, lights it.)

R.P.: Why are you up?

DENNY: Couldn't sleep.

R.P.: Why not?

DENNY: 'Cause you were talking.

R.P.: What I just say?

DENNY: Not the *you* you, but the "thought it was" you. I heard a voice. Started getting scared.

R.P.: About what?

DENNY: About people. Dog people.

R.P.: Dog people?

DENNY: Take-the-dog-away people. Is that who you were talking to?

R.P.: I haven't been talkin' to anybody.

DENNY: But would you? Ever talk to them.

R.P.: Dog people aren't up this late.

DENNY: It's just I was listening. To you and Mom.

R.P.: When?

DENNY: About Ebony's coat the other day. You sounded so… disappointed. Like you maybe wanted to, send her away or something.

R.P.: What is that?

DENNY: What's what?

R.P.: Behind your back.

DENNY: I don't know.

R.P.: Put it on the table.

(Denny reluctantly places hair clippers onto the table.)

R.P.: What you plan on doin' with that?

DENNY: Surprise you.

R.P.: How?

DENNY: By making her the way you said you wanted. Where the skin's showin'.

R.P.: That was just talk, Denny.

DENNY: Sounded like you meant it.

R.P.: People don't always mean what they say.

DENNY: Then why say it?

(The phone announces itself. The house hears. R.P. picks it up mid-ring. R.P. begins to hang up, but stops. He places the open receiver on the table. R.P. stares at it a second then turns to Denny.)

R.P.: Where you find those clippers?

(Denny takes the clippers from the table.)

DENNY: I'll put them back.

R.P.: You ain't putting anything back like that. Cord all hangin' loose.

(Denny awkwardly wraps the cord around the clippers.)

R.P.: You want me to show you?

(Denny walks to his father.)

R.P.: Alright, you grab on to the end.

(Denny does.)

R.P.: Now start steppin' back.

DENNY: Till what?

R.P.: Till you can't any more.

(Denny walks backward. The cord is taut.)

R.P.: Now when the pull says. You follow, understand?

(Denny nods.)

(R.P. slowly spins the clippers inward, reeling the cord in tight, slowly drawing Denny closer.)

R.P.: Somebody open that closet not knowing what you left undone, they could get hurt. Now, you don't want to hurt nobody, now do you?

(Denny shakes his head.)

R.P.: So, you got to be aware what you're doin'. 'Cause what you do, don't effect just you. Other people live in this house, too. A whole family lives here. In this house. You see what I'm sayin'?

DENNY: Guess, I wasn't thinkin'.

R.P.: Well, next time you will. Know why?

DENNY: Why?

R.P.: *(Pause.)* 'Cause your father told you.

(Silence.)

(Denny is reeled in close to R.P. Both their hands grip the clippers.)

DENNY: Is it safe now?

(R.P. takes the clippers.)

R.P.: You head on to sleep.

DENNY: I can't.

R.P.: Why?

(Denny indicates the phone. R.P. picks up the open receiver, holding it in his hand.)

R.P.: It's not the dog people.

DENNY: You sure?

R.P.: Just a wrong number. You go on now.

DENNY: Aren't you going to bed?

R.P.: Your mother heard something.

DENNY: Like me?

R.P.: No. Something different than you.

DENNY: Was she right?

R.P.: I checked. There's nothing.

DENNY: Then why are you still here?

R.P.: Why are you?

DENNY: I don't know. Guess I'm still scared.

R.P.: Of what I might do?

(Denny timidly nods his head. R.P. takes a drag. He hangs up the phone. Exhales.)

R.P.: *(Softly.)* So am I.

(R.P. holds his cigarette ash upwards. He watches the thin line of smoke fade into the air. Denny watches his father.)

(Fade R.P. and Denny.)

(The lights change to…)

Wednesday

Jay's room. Helen straightens Jay's sheets. Jay enters.

JAY: Yes.

HELEN: Took you long enough.

JAY: Didn't hear you the first time.

HELEN: Clearly.

JAY: You didn't have to.

HELEN: Then why am I?

JAY: I would've got to it.

HELEN: What you say and what you do, Jay.

JAY: It's four-thirty.

HELEN: No excuse.

JAY: What's the point if it's four-thirty?

HELEN: You gave your word. Your word is all you got. And you gave it.
  (Pause.) Now what's the cause of that?

JAY: What?

HELEN: What's with the bulldog expression?

JAY: Nothing.

HELEN: Something happen at school?
  (Nothing.)
  At school? Something?
  (Helen pulls the sheets over the pillow.)

JAY: Don't.

HELEN: What?

JAY: I don't like it that way. Over the pillows like that.

HELEN: What's the right way then, Sir Jay? Would you kindly fill me in?

JAY: Never mind.

HELEN: No, if you find my work sub-standard. Please tell me. Tell me where I
  went wrong. You must let me in on these things. Your preferences. Above
  the sheets?

JAY: Mom...

HELEN: Above the sheets. I'm asking.

JAY: Mom, what happened to the phone?
  (Nothing.)
  Mom?
  (Nothing.)
  Mom?

HELEN: I don't have to do this for you. Your age, I *shouldn't* have to do this for
  you. The least you can do is show some appreciation for my efforts here.
  You know, a little cooperation, that's all I'm asking for.

JAY: *(Pause.)* Above the sheets, yeah.
  (Helen rearranges the pillows.)

HELEN: Doesn't look right. Cases don't match the sheets. Exposed like that, it
  completely draws attention.

JAY: Not like it's a big deal.

HELEN: It looks better the other way.

JAY: I just sleep in it, Mom.

HELEN: Is that really?

JAY: What?

HELEN: All you do.

JAY: *(Pause.)* Yeah.

HELEN: Jay?

  (Nothing.)

  Jay, you can tell me her name.

  (Nothing.)

  Well, let's say, if. If there is a girl you've been spending time with. If a girl like that indeed exists. I was thinking, maybe. You should invite her.

JAY: Here?

HELEN: Yes. I think you should ask her over.

JAY: For what?

HELEN: Dinner. Sunday. I'll make something. I've dog-eared the cookbooks. You can flip and pick something. Whatever you feel would make the evening… However you want it.

JAY: I don't think I do. Want it.

HELEN: Well, I know if I suddenly found myself, by some miracle, once again a young girl, I believe I'd be… flattered. Be deemed a guest of honor. Walk into a home, see sophistication on my behalf. Silk napkins. Candles and such.

JAY: Sounds like a hassle.

HELEN: Then we'll keep it simple. You can be simple and elegant at the same time. No law against that. I mean, there are worse things. Worse things in this world, you can ask somebody.

JAY: So, you're sayin' it's up to me?

HELEN: I don't know this girl, Jay. I haven't had the chance to look at her, looking at you. And I'd like to. *(Pause.)* I mean it's obvious. Very obvious. That she's, well, very fond of you.

JAY: What do you mean by that?

HELEN: By what?

JAY: Obvious. What's obvious?

HELEN: What you've been doing. It's expected. I expect it. It's just the secrecy. That you're keeping things hidden. Like all this. You feel there's something shameful, or dirty about it.

JAY: I haven't done anything dirty.

HELEN: These are grown-up decisions you're making. Grown-up actions. So, let's talk honest. Straight and honest here.

JAY: We just talk.

HELEN: Talk.

JAY: We listen to music. To each other. Nothing grown up about it. So there's no need. For straight and honest. For any of this.

HELEN: A girl needs to be seen, Jay. Seen in a certain way. There's these changes. These inevitable changes. She needs to know. Where she stands in the world. In the world of you, Jay.

Do you love this girl?

JAY: I don't know.

HELEN: I think maybe you need to. 'Cause there's things you're saying by, well, in this room. You need to show her, that she's... valued. A girl doesn't give herself...

JAY: I told you we just...

HELEN: It's all she has. It's all she's ever going to have. You have to take responsibility for that.

JAY: Responsibility.

HELEN: Secrets are no good, Jay. For you. For her. For anybody. They cause damage. Unseen damage. Understand what I'm saying?

JAY: I guess.

HELEN: Seriously. Do you? Why it's important, that you ask her. What this is all about?

(Lights up on R.P. in the kitchen. He cradles a broken phone. In one hand, he holds a tumbler full of ice. In the other, a bottle of liquor, a roll of duct tape hanging around its neck.)

JAY: Straight and honest? Is that what we're being?

HELEN: I'd like to think so.

JAY: *(Pause.)* You haven't left the house.

HELEN: What?

JAY: Your robe. You've spent the day in your robe.

(Silence.)

I need five dollars.

HELEN: What's that?

JAY: *(Pause.)* I need five dollars.

HELEN: Why?

JAY: I just felt the need to buy something. *(Pause.)* Mom?

HELEN: I don't have it. The little I have. I need.

JAY: For what?

HELEN: You need new sheets. Ones that match your cases. Your father will be home soon. You can ask him.

(Silence.)

You will at least consider asking her over?

JAY: I'll consider it.

HELEN: It's just that this. This is your home. And it could be such, such a lovely time. *(Pause.)* If your father asks. Your sheets. You tell him. *(Pause.)* I had to go.

(Helen exits. R.P. tosses the phone onto the table.)

R.P.: So. You gonna tell me?

JAY: I can't.

R.P.: Can't or won't.

JAY: *(Walking to R.P.)* It's the way I found it.

R.P.: What you hidin'?

JAY: Nothin'.

R.P.: Your brother?

JAY: He's in our room.

R.P.: Bring him in here.

JAY: He's been in there working. He doesn't even know.

R.P.: Know what?

JAY: What happened.

R.P.: And what exactly is that? What's happened here?

JAY: Somehow. It cracked. Everywhere.

(R.P. pours a drink. He takes a sip, then picks up the phone.)

R.P.: Come here.

JAY: Why?

R.P.: I said here.

JAY: I didn't do it.

R.P.: You testin' me?

(Jay complies.)

R.P.: *(To the phone.)* Press your palm down.

JAY: Where is this?

R.P.: Right down on it.

(Jay does.)

JAY: Is it?

R.P.: Empty house. You boys. You boys fuck around. And these things hap-
pen. These things. Havoc.
(Jay's hand slips.)
R.P.: Dammit.
JAY: Sorry.
R.P.: Jay. Down. Tight. Or else it gets open.
JAY: Down, tight. I got it.
R.P.: *(Pause.)* I can hear your mother now.
JAY: She's gone.
R.P.: What?
JAY: She wasn't here. When this happened. No one was here.
R.P.: Don't tell me *no one.*
JAY: No, that's what's crazy. I just came home and there it was. But she wasn't.
Mom wasn't here.
(R.P. rips some tape.)
JAY: Can you fix it?
R.P.: You can't fix this, Jay. Even if I get it to work. Still, it won't be fixed.
JAY: So, you're saying you can't.
R.P.: Look at the thing. *(Jay does.)* But, still hold it.
*(Jay holds the phone together. R.P. steps back and takes a drink. He takes a
look at his son. Jay feels him looking, but keeps his eyes down.)*
R.P.: You afraid? Is that the case?
(Nothing.)
How old are you? Look at me, now.
JAY: Fifteen.
R.P.: You're too old. Too old for me to whup it out of you. Too old for both
of us. So, what you afraid of?
JAY: I don't know.
R.P.: Just a question, Jay. Simple facts. You do this?
JAY: No.
R.P.: Then tell me who did.
JAY: House was empty. Been empty this whole time.
R.P.: You ain't betrayin' anybody by sayin'.
JAY: I know I'm not.
R.P.: *(Pause.)* Where is this place?
JAY: Huh?
R.P.: Where you wanted to go? What you asked earlier.
JAY: Just out.

R.P.: Priorities, Jay. What you want and what's expected. A choice you gonna have to make the rest of your life. Better start now. Now you tell me the truth, you can go.

JAY: Does it matter?

R.P.: Say again?

JAY: The phone wasn't working anyway, right? I mean it would ring. Ring and ring. But when me or Mom pick up, no one's ever there. I mean, who would do that? Can you explain it? I mean, if you can explain it, maybe that'll shed light on the whole thing.

(Silence.)

Did you mean it?

R.P.: What?

JAY: That if I don't tell.

R.P.: Tell the truth is what I said.

JAY: If I don't. Then I can't go?

R.P.: I guess, we got a situation here, don't we? *(Pause.)* Sometimes you got to let it fall, Jay. 'Cause if you don't. Lessons don't get learned. It's all placed crooked, and stays that way. Wrong just feeds wrong. You're the oldest and you need to act as such. *(Pause.)* It takes courage. Courage. To see that. To know who you are. And what you got to do.

(Silence.)

JAY: I lied.

R.P.: About the phone?

JAY: Yeah.

R.P.: I'm listening.

JAY: It's not always silence. When the phone rings, and there's no one there. There was once, this one time when I heard something. This breathing. So I waited. To see if anything would be said. Was about to give up, but then I heard it. A voice. This uneven voice. One I never heard before, but still, somehow I knew she had the right number. And she asked me. She asked me this one thing. *(Pause.)* "Is your father happy?" *(Pause.)* I ain't say nothin'. I stayed quiet. I stayed. So, she asks again. "Is your father happy?" And the way she said it. So desperate. Soft. Like she. Like she was in love with you. Or needed to be in love with you. Sounded in need of something. She asks again. And this time, I was about to answer, but once I got strength up to… she hung up. She hung up. I've tried making sense of it. But it's a mystery. A total mystery. But those sort of things happen, I guess. Mysteries go unexplained. Phones get broken. I don't know what else to say. I don't know.

(Pause. R.P. pulls a piece of tape. He pieces together the phone.)

R.P.: Your brother finished his homework?

JAY: By now, I guess.

R.P.: *(Pause.)* He's failing.

JAY: Yeah.

R.P.: See to him.

JAY: Then?

R.P.: Then. You're free.

(R.P. looks to the phone. He picks up the receiver. He wiggles the cord. He listens. He hangs up.)

R.P.: This girl. Her parents. Have they seen you? Do they know?

(Nothing.)

What were you gonna say?

JAY: When?

R.P.: On the phone. When you was asked. "Is your father happy?" What were you gonna say?

JAY: I don't remember.

R.P.: *(Pause.)* See to your brother.

(Jay exits.)

(R.P. looks to the phone. He takes a drink. He picks it up and slowly dials six numbers. R.P. stirs his drink with his middle finger, clinking the ice gently. He sucks the liquor from his finger and finally punches the last number with it.)

Lights switch to Denny and Jay. Denny sits in a pool of papers. A math book lays close by. Jay stands over him, looking over a sheet.

JAY: This is no good.

DENNY: I meant it each time. Don't that count?

JAY: How long have you been doing this?

DENNY: Till my hand got tired.

JAY: Give me the book.

DENNY: My teacher has to understand.

JAY: I want the book and the page number.

DENNY: Did I spell it wrong? Is it just with one R?

JAY: Regardless of how you spell it.

DENNY: Is it with one or two R's? Just tell me.

JAY: This has to be done over. Done right.

DENNY: I can't do numbers, Jay. Every time. I feel like throwing up. All over the books. All over me.

JAY: Your teacher won't accept this.

DENNY: But I mean it.

JAY: She won't care.

DENNY: It's the only thing I could do. I know I'll be wrong. No matter what. So, I wrote it over and over. "I'm sorry." "I'm sorry." I wrote it clearly, right? You can read it. So, how can she not? How can she not care?

JAY: Give me the book and the numbers. I'll work them out. I'll do the work. You copy what I write afterwards.

DENNY: But I'm not a liar, Jay.

JAY: They're just numbers. You say numbers don't make sense, right?

DENNY: They don't.

JAY: You can't lie about what you don't understand.

(Pause.)

DENNY: But I know things, Jay.

JAY: Quiet. I need to focus.

DENNY: I know things about Dad.

JAY: No more talk.

DENNY: I don't want to be a liar, Jay. I don't.

JAY: Listen for footsteps.

Lights switch to Helen and R.P. R.P. hangs up the phone.

HELEN: Who was it?

R.P.: When?

HELEN: Just now.

R.P.: It was nothing.

HELEN: Nothing was on the phone?

R.P.: That's right.

HELEN: Can you call nothing back?

R.P.: We're gonna leave it alone.

HELEN: I can't.

R.P.: I don't feel like playing this out.

HELEN: *(Taking the phone.)* You don't got to dial.

R.P.: You should go wash your face.

HELEN: The number, R.P.

R.P.: I tellin' you what you need.

HELEN: *(Punching numbers.)* I'll just start punching buttons then. I got the patience. Don't think I don't.

R.P.: You look painful pale. It ain't natural. You wash your face, we can talk. But I can't look at you like this.

HELEN: So cruel. So cruel when I'm trying to concentrate.

R.P.: I'll rip the phone out.

HELEN: We got other phones.

R.P.: I'll rip those, too. I'll cut every cord in this house.

HELEN: Start with this one. Go ahead.

R.P.: That how you want this to happen?

HELEN: Maybe so.

R.P.: What do you want from me?

HELEN: I want to talk to nothing. I want to hear its voice. I want to say some words. I got plenty words for nothing.

(R.P. takes the phone. He dials. He holds the receiver to Helen. She stares at it.)

R.P.: C'mon take it.

(She does nothing.)

Say something. Ask a question.

(She does nothing.)

Talk.

(Helen takes a moment. Then takes the receiver. Then takes the whole phone. She opens the oven. She throws the phone in. She closes it and turns it on.)

(Silence.)

(Helen exits. R.P. stands alone. He opens the oven, looks in, and closes it. Enter Jay.)

JAY: *(Presenting the work.)* He's finished.

R.P.: All of it?

JAY: It's checked over. So, I'm going.

R.P.: Take your brother.

JAY: I can't.

R.P.: You need money?

JAY: Yeah.

R.P.: Take your brother.

JAY: He won't belong.

R.P.: Belong where?

JAY: Where I'm goin'.

R.P.: Then you ain't goin' the right places. Go get his shoes.

JAY: I don't want to take him.

R.P.: You get his shoes. You put them on his feet. When you tie them. You make sure they're tied tight.

JAY: I'm not going anymore. I decided. I don't want to.

R.P.: This ain't about what you want. *(Pause.)* There's a ten on the table.

JAY: I just need five.

R.P.: You keep the rest. You can take your time gettin' back.

JAY: I don't need it.

R.P.: You take the other five. You spend it slow.

> *(Helen enters.)*

R.P.: Go get your brother's shoes.

> *(Jay looks to his mother and then exits. Helen puts on oven mitts and opens the oven. She takes out the phone. She disappears with it. R.P. waits. She returns. She stands with her back to R.P.)*

R.P.: What are you doing?

HELEN: I'm through talking.

R.P.: Let me see.

HELEN: See what?

R.P.: Turn around.

HELEN: I don't want to.

R.P.: What kind of water?

HELEN: What are you talking about?

R.P.: On your face. What kind, warm or cold?

HELEN: *(Turning around.)* Are you serious?

R.P.: See there. The flesh on your face. I can see it now.

HELEN: I haven't been crying. That's not what this comes from.

R.P.: Come here.

HELEN: I heard Jay.

R.P.: You don't have to if you don't want to.

HELEN: He said he needed money. Did you give it?

R.P.: I'm asking you to, that's all. I'm asking.

HELEN: I heard you.

> *(Enter Jay and Denny.)*

JAY: We're gone.

HELEN: So, you're taking him with you?

DENNY: It hurts when I walk. Jay tied them too tight. He wouldn't let me do it on my own. It hurts.

HELEN: It'll get easier, Denny. It will.

(All is still a moment. Jay and Denny exit.)

HELEN: Where is he going?

R.P.: Where do you think?

HELEN: Did you talk to him?

R.P.: A bit.

HELEN: I told him to bring her. To bring her by.

R.P.: What for?

HELEN: Dinner or something. Sunday, maybe.

R.P.: She got a family of her own.

HELEN: It seems the thing to do.

R.P.: That what it seems?

HELEN: I think it would be good for her to see. Let her know what we are.

R.P.: She won't be around much longer. I'm sure.

HELEN: I don't even know what she looks like.

R.P.: He'll get tired. Boys get tired of these sorts of things.

HELEN: I know her smell.

R.P.: Just the way of the world.

HELEN: Have you been in Jay's room? Her perfume's all over.

R.P.: I know where she's been. I know where she's going. Where all of this is going.

HELEN: You sent Denny with him, didn't you?

R.P.: That's right.

HELEN: Why?

R.P.: We needed to be alone.

HELEN: So he won't go see her?

R.P.: I wanted to be alone with you.

HELEN: He shouldn't have to sneak around.

R.P. Why are you over there?

HELEN: It's not right. It says the wrong things.

R.P.: Come here next to me.

HELEN: I want them to see. To see what's possible.

R.P.: I'll come to you then. Is that what you want?

HELEN: She should see what happens when the world is right.

R.P.: Helen.

HELEN: Maybe she loves him, you know. Maybe that's the case.

R.P.: We're alone.

HELEN: Maybe they're like you and me.

R.P.: You want me to hold you?

HELEN: Our son could be loved. Don't that mean something to you?

R.P.: I don't want to talk anymore.

HELEN: He's you and me. And someone could love him. Everything that we've seen, that's been done, given up, to be here. That's who he is. And we owe him.

R.P.: We're alone now.

HELEN: You can't fall out of love with me, R.P. It's irresponsible.

R.P.: You hear what I said?

HELEN: If you do, that means she fell for nothing.

R.P.: We're alone.

(Lights up on Denny and Jay.)

HELEN: For nothing.

Later. Denny and Jay standing outside. The bus stop.

DENNY: The cold. It stings. Would you?

JAY: I'm tired right now.

DENNY: What am I supposed to do?

JAY: My back can't take it.

(Fade R.P. and Helen.)

DENNY: I can jump up and down, I guess. Keep my feet off the ground. But there's little rocks. Little rocks in the sidewalk. They sting me more.

JAY: You don't have to jump. The bus is comin'. Just wait.

DENNY: Don't know if I can.

JAY: It's your own fault, Denny.

DENNY: But the ground is smooth in the mall. Smooth and warm.

JAY: If you take them off, you have to look after them. Ain't that what I said?

DENNY: Do you have the bag?

JAY: Hmm?

DENNY: The bag. Or did I lose that, too.

JAY: I have it.

DENNY: They were impressed. The store ladies. That's the word they used. Impressed. Impressed at the way I asked them.

JAY: What did you say?

DENNY: The colors. I told them the color hair ribbons I wanted. That's what you said, right? Hair ribbons.

JAY: Did you say it was me? That I sent you in there?

DENNY: No.

JAY: Then what did you say?

DENNY: For my sister. Like you told me. Just like you told me.

No one thinks you're girlie, Jay. Not the store ladies. Not me. You're still a boy, I made sure. You're still a boy.

I only had five. The five you gave me so I picked the best ones.

JAY: All five. You spent all five?

DENNY: I needed all five. For the best ones.

JAY: I told you to save at least fifty. Fifty cents for the fare.

DENNY: But I wanted to buy the best for her. That's who they're for, right? The pretty one. So, I spent it all. The best. That's all I wanted.

JAY: What you want and what's expected, Denny.

DENNY: Huh?

JAY: Nothing.

DENNY: Is that where we're going? To go see the pretty one?

JAY: No.

DENNY: Then where we goin'?

JAY: We're just gonna ride.

DENNY: On the bus?

JAY: Yeah.

DENNY: But we ain't goin' nowhere.

JAY: That's right.

DENNY: Why would we do that?

(Nothing.)

Is it 'cause of me? That we can't see her?

(Nothing.)

I would've impressed her too, you know. Just like the store ladies. Impressed her even though I don't got shoes.

JAY: That's not where we're going. So, forget about it.

(Silence.)

DENNY: How does it feel?

JAY: How does what feel?

DENNY: How does it feel when she did that thing?

JAY: What are you talkin' about?

DENNY: You know, that thing she did with you and your, thing.

JAY: What you know about anybody's thing?

DENNY: I saw. Through the window. Outside. Between the curtains. (Pause.) Are you mad? I mean, if you want to hate me. You can.

JAY: Nobody hates you. But you shouldn't do things like that.

DENNY: I just wanted to know. The kind of things that happen in your room. I mean, after you looked. So new. I don't know if that's the right word, but... New.

I tried you know. So I wouldn't have to look. Tried to see what it's like. To be you. To be you and her. But it doesn't work. I yank and pull and nothing happens down there.

JAY: You shouldn't yank on it.

DENNY: The same things don't happen. It must be broke.

JAY: You didn't break anything.

DENNY: I don't know, Jay. Maybe when you get kicked.

JAY: What?

DENNY: When you get kicked down there.

JAY: Somebody kick you?

DENNY: No.

JAY: You just said.

DENNY: It must've been me, then. Maybe I kicked myself. I fall a lot. At school.

JAY: Don't lie to me.

DENNY: It's my shoes. The laces. They get loose and I fall. And I find myself kicked.

JAY: Tell me who.

DENNY: No one.

JAY: Who kicks you?

DENNY: It's all me, Jay. Me and my shoes. So it's good. Good I lost them. Kids will see that I'm not that smart. When they call me things. Yell them at me.

JAY: What things?

DENNY: They'll see that I'm stupid. That I don't understand what they're tryin' to do to me. I try showin' them my homework as proof. But they think I'm lyin'. They think I'm lyin' to them.

JAY: Are you?

DENNY: I'm not a liar, Jay.

JAY: But you know. You know exactly what they're sayin', don't you?

DENNY: Maybe. But I'm still stupid.

JAY: Quit sayin' that.

DENNY: Then why don't I understand? Why they call me those things. Why I keep getting kicked.

JAY: Do you cry?

(Nothing.)

Do you let them see you cry?

DENNY: I can't help what they see.

JAY: You can't let them have that. Hear me? You can't. You kick back, you swing, whatever. You got to be smarter, Denny. Than let them see you weak. You got to be smarter.

DENNY: You can't be smart and stupid at the same time. So, what am I supposed to be? In the middle of something so… wrong. Who am I supposed to be, Jay?

(Silence.)

Don't tell Dad. That I lost my shoes at the mall. He'll be so… ashamed.

JAY: I ain't gonna say anything.

DENNY: *(Pause.)* I almost did it.

JAY: What?

DENNY: A pair just like mine. In there. Sitting in front. Out in the open. I almost. I almost did it and ran.

JAY: You would've got caught.

DENNY: I know. That's why I didn't. But almost. I find myself almost a lot of things lately. *(Pause.)* Mom made hot dogs. Sunday morning. You were asleep.

JAY: I don't remember.

DENNY: I almost got you up. You really shouldn't miss breakfast. Especially on Sundays. When it's everybody. All of us.

JAY: There'll be others.

DENNY: I don't know, Jay. Sunday was special. I don't know if there'll be another one like it. I mean, you know, with hot dogs.

JAY: Maybe not.

DENNY: They were good. She split them. Split them with the big knife. And I almost. I almost then, too.

JAY: Almost what?

DENNY: When she put it down. She put it down and forgot it was there.

JAY: What would you do with a knife, Denny?

DENNY: Take it to school. Keep myself from falling. Cut my laces if I had to. Cut whatever. *(Pause.)* I'm not sad, Jay. Not sad at all. That you won't take me to see the pretty one. I understand why you would want to keep her to yourself. I know that I would want that sort of "new" to myself. Are you going to?

JAY: What?

DENNY: Bring her over. That would be special, I think. Sunday's got to have a way, to stay Sunday, you know.

(Silence.)

It stings. It still stings, Jay.

JAY: *(Pause.)* Alright.

DENNY: It's okay?

JAY: Yeah.

(Denny climbs up on Jay's back. They wait. The bus arrives.)

DENNY: Bus is here.

JAY: I see.

(They do not move. The bus leaves. They wait.)

DENNY: The next one?

JAY: Next one. *(Pause.)* Then home.

DENNY: Then home.

(Fade.)

Thursday Morning

Lights on Helen. She is dressed well. She carries a wrapped box in one hand, a ribbon in the other. She places the box on the table. She begins delicately garnishing the box with the ribbon, taking the proper time to get it right. Eventually she feels the presence of R.P.

HELEN: Early.

R.P.: Denny's coughin'.

HELEN: Is he?

R.P.: Runnin' around bare feet. Got him coughin', I guess.

HELEN: Mmmn.

(Silence.)

R.P.: You look nice.

HELEN: Thank you.

R.P.: That the reason?

HELEN: For?

R.P.: Why you left bed so early.

HELEN: I took some time to straighten the place up a bit. Sometimes a mess don't announce itself until there's the prospect of company. Funny how that happens.

R.P.: You really think he's going to ask her?

HELEN: Better safe than sorry, I suppose. Either way, it had me *into* things. I was rummaging.

R.P.: I know. I heard you. Makin' these…small rackets.

HELEN: Well, it only filled three-quarters. The pictures. The box they were in. Used to be full. And I checked. Looked for pieces, flakes of film or something. Thinkin' maybe they've corroded, wasted away. That time wasted… They go for so long unchecked. And in dark places maybe they just start fading. But I didn't see anything like that. No trace of something there that's going, just gone. Less than before, I find it strange. So, I had to take the time to find something more suitable. Bringing me here. To this box here. *(Pause.)* So, I wake you?

R.P.: Just said. Denny's coughing.

HELEN: That's right. You did. You said.

R.P.: Hacking something fierce. Figured I'd go ahead and face the inevitable.

HELEN: The inevitable?

R.P.: He's not going anywhere. School. Not with that sort of noise comin' from him. No. He's stayin' home.

HELEN: Maybe you should wait. Maybe it'll pass.

R.P.: Don't think so. All night I been in tune. Kept me up anticipatin'. Anticipatin' this morning. The mess when he wakes. Anticipatin' Denny the wakin' mess.

(Silence.)

R.P.: How many you think?

HELEN: What?

R.P.: You're suggestin' it's small, but it seems an awful lot. The box I'm saying.

HELEN: What about it?

R.P.: A good amount there. Pictures. Moments.

HELEN: I suppose.

R.P.: How many years' worth?

HELEN: Sixteen. Seventeen maybe.

R.P.: And you're taking the day. Just one day.

HELEN: Yes. One day.

R.P.: Even if you took the week. The month. The year. You think it'd be enough?

HELEN: Enough?

R.P.: To sit her down. One by one. And tell her. What each one means. Give her the proper understanding. Of what she's seeing. Who she's seeing. Why certain days. Or nights. Or whatever. Why they seemed worthy. To hold on to. To be reminded of. I just don't know if you can gift somebody that. Your history. Even if it does got a ribbon.

HELEN: Yeah. Well, it's tied so. So, it looks like I'm committed.

R.P.: Are you staying?

HELEN: I didn't go through all this trouble just to stand here.

R.P.: I'm sayin'. If she lets you in. You plan on stayin'?

HELEN: It's why I'm going isn't it?

R.P.: Stayin' for real. For awhile.

HELEN: Why?

R.P.: I think you should. Stay, I mean.

HELEN: What would keep me?

R.P.: If that's your gift. Then you should take the time. However long. To make her realize what she's been given. 'Cause it's such a long way, Helen. Just to end up feeling…foolish.

HELEN: Check Denny's forehead. Check it frequently. He fevers so easily.

R.P.: Just something you should think about.

HELEN: Make sure to see Jay off. He loves to oversleep.

R.P.: Did you hear me?

HELEN: Three to four hour trip. I'll have plenty of time. To think.

R.P.: No need to call. If the day ends. You're not here. I'll know.

HELEN: Fine.

R.P.: What now?

HELEN: I leave. *(Pause.)* Are you going to say good-bye?

(Nothing.)

Or have you been saying good-bye?

R.P.: I don't think so.

HELEN: Then what would you call it?

R.P.: Sayin' hello to something else.

(They look at one another. Helen exits.)

Lights up on Jay and Lorie.
Same morning. Outside. The woods. Jay stands. Lorie looks to the distance.

LORIE: Three minutes since. Three or four. Since the first bell. In case you didn't hear.

And there's ten, ten I think, minutes between first and late bell. In case you didn't know.

And you got to cut back through the gym. Through that alley. That adds

time. 'Cause you got to walk careful through there. I know. I've slipped
before. In case you were wondering.

I mean, if I knew. Knew I was gonna meet you. That out here meant, you
know, the woods. I would've prepared myself better. Wouldn't have worn
something so…delicate.

JAY: What is that anyway?

LORIE: What is what?

JAY: That you're wearing. Is that a skirt? Or they pants?

LORIE: Kind of like both.

JAY: What is it silk or something?

LORIE: I don't know. Some sort of cotton thing.

JAY: So, what do you mean by delicate?

LORIE: This color kind of begs to be dirtied, don't you think?

JAY: Didn't have to come if you didn't want to.

LORIE: What makes you think I didn't want to?

JAY: Your words. They got a tone.

LORIE: Just being out this far. Not exactly the smartest move, you know.
Might miss roll.

JAY: If you're so worried, feel free. Just know. You'd be risking it.

LORIE: Risking what?

JAY: Four I've felt. Counted each one. Four in a row. First, it was one every
few minutes. But now… Somethin's definitely on its way.

LORIE: You're counting rain drops?

JAY: Yeah.

LORIE: So, you have a sense? How close? The rain?

JAY: Yeah.

LORIE: Did you know I waited for you last night? From six to seven-thirty. I
waited. At the park. Did you know that?

JAY: I did.

LORIE: Did you know you didn't show up?

JAY: I'm aware.

LORIE: Do you want to keep going, or go back to ignoring it?

JAY: I wasn't ignoring it.

LORIE: What would you call it?

JAY: Getting up nerve I guess.

LORIE: For what?

   (Pause. He goes into his backpack. He gives her a plastic bag.)

JAY: You should keep it closed.

LORIE: Why?

JAY: There's colors inside. The rain. They'll bleed.

LORIE: What is it?

JAY: It's a gift. For you. You and your hair. *(Pause. Looks up.)* That's five. Five more. Five will turn into six. And keep going.

LORIE: Jay?

JAY: You'll get stuck here. You should go.

LORIE: What about you?

JAY: What about me?

LORIE: You're not coming to school?

JAY: Nope. Staying right here.

LORIE: You'll soak yourself.

JAY: I got cover enough. Besides. Too far to walk home.

(They stand. A moment passes.)

LORIE: I didn't say thank you. For the present.

JAY: You don't got to thank me.

LORIE: But I appreciate it. I do. The thought. You thinking of me like that. But that's not the reason, is it?

JAY: For?

LORIE: The woods. Your voice. Just doesn't sound right to me.

JAY: How does it sound?

LORIE: Unfinished.

JAY: *(Pause.)* Guess there's something else. Something else I was supposed to ask you.

LORIE: Then why don't you?

JAY: 'Cause if I did. You would have to answer. And I don't think you'd want to.

LORIE: You don't know that.

JAY: I'm pretty sure I do.

LORIE: Ask me anyway. And we'll see.

JAY: Alright then. Is it true?

LORIE: Is what true?

JAY: Lorie sucks nigger dick. *(Pause.)* That's what I heard. Lorie sucks nigger dick. Is it true?

(Pause.)

LORIE: I didn't.

JAY: Didn't what?

LORIE: I didn't expect that.

(Pause.)

JAY: I'm standing outside school yesterday. The sun shining. Shining like always. On everything, everywhere. I'm thinking about summer. Your green swoop and ribboned hair. Thinking so deep, I almost don't hear it. But I do. I most definitely hear.

LORIE: Who said it?

JAY: Does it matter?

LORIE: What did you do?

JAY: I got jealous. Angry jealous. On the hunt, wanting to know. Who this guy was. His name. And if he knew, knew about me and you. I mean, really, who the hell this nigger think he is?

(Pause.) You know, it only took half a second. For the answer to sink in. I've had this name my whole life. But it's like I never even heard it. Till then.

Suddenly the sun grows brighter. Hotter, harsher. A half-second later the world's different. That's what happens when a question and an answer come together, I guess. The world changes. It's an amazing thing the first time you realize that. You start listenin' for it to change all the time.

(Pause.) You do understand my question, right?

LORIE: I believe I do.

JAY: So is it? Is it true?

LORIE: What if I don't answer?

JAY: If you don't answer. That means you don't see me. That you never saw me. Then I'll have no choice. I'll have no choice but to hate you. To hate you deep. And that's not what I want to do. Out here. In the woods. The rain.

LORIE: Jay…

JAY: So much gets left unsaid in this world. So much. I need it to change. No matter what it looks like after. So, just tell me. Tell me the truth. Lorie sucks nigger dick. Is it true?

LORIE: *(Pause.)* Yes.

(Silence.)

JAY: Eleven. I counted eleven that time.

LORIE: I love you.

JAY: Thirteen. Fourteen. You should go.

LORIE: You think you could love me?

(Nothing.)

Jay?

(Nothing.)

Jay, I asked you a question.

JAY: Three o'clock. When the bell rings. I want you to find me. Come find me here.

LORIE: What then?

JAY: We can find somewhere else. Somewhere dark. You and me. In the dark.

LORIE: Then what?

JAY: I'll give you an answer. *(Pause.)* Too many to count now. *(Looking up.)* It's started.

(The two fade as a spotlight rises on Denny. He looks out the patio window.)

DENNY: So many things. So many bad things.

Late morning. Lights rise as Helen enters. Helen carries the box in her arms. She notices Denny.

HELEN: How you feeling, Sweety?

DENNY: Couldn't get up this morning. I got a cough.

(Helen places the box on the table.)

HELEN: You kept your father up.

DENNY: Didn't mean to.

HELEN: Of course you didn't.

DENNY: I never meant to.

(Helen takes off her raincoat.)

DENNY: It's raining hard out there, isn't it?

HELEN: What's that?

DENNY: So dark out there.

(Pause.)

HELEN: You okay, Denny?

DENNY: I left it open. The gate. When I went outside earlier, round back. I must've left it.

HELEN: The gate?

DENNY: And then the train came. It came, Mom. And there was nothing I could do. *(Pause.)* I think I need to go.

HELEN: Go where?

DENNY: It just happened. Maybe she's close. Maybe she didn't run that far, and I can catch her.

HELEN: Now just hold on a second.

(Denny slides open the patio door.)

DENNY: Our responsibility, I have to.

(Denny looks at his mother a second then runs out.)

HELEN: Denny get back here!

(Helen grabs her raincoat. R.P. enters. He says nothing. Helen notices.)

R.P.: You came back.

HELEN: What?

R.P.: The car. Your trip. You turned around.

HELEN: Yes. Well.

R.P.: So what was it? That changed your mind?

HELEN: I don't...

R.P.: Was it the rain? Must be sheets of it falling out there. Blocking your vision. Safest thing to do is come home, I guess. It's what needed to happen. It's what needed to happen. Not your fault. Ain't no one's fault.

HELEN: *(Pause.)* Are you telling me something?

R.P.: I'm saying. If you tell me it was the rain, then I'm willing to believe you.

HELEN: It wasn't the rain.

R.P.: Then what was it?

(Pause.)

(Helen makes her way to the table. She sits.)

HELEN: She's here, isn't she?

(Silence. R.P. moves to the window.)

R.P.: I was waitin' for him to do somethin'. React somehow.

HELEN: So, he saw her.

R.P.: Not for long. She was hysterical. I took her to the back.

HELEN: But still, he did. He saw.

R.P.: She arrived unannounced. He answered the door. She knocked and he answered. And we all stood there. Him, his father, and this strange woman. This woman that he knows isn't you. And she's looking at me. Waiting for her look back. But I'm too busy listening. Listening for him to ask me. Who this woman was. And why she was in our home. But he didn't. He didn't say a word.

HELEN: Maybe he was afraid.

R.P.: Of what?

HELEN: Of you.

R.P.: I'm not some monster, Helen. I'm just a man. I'm sure he could see that.

HELEN: Maybe he just decided not to see her. That he... that *I*, loved you enough not to see. It is possible, R.P. That you're loved that much.

R.P.: She's been here the whole time. The whole time. Something that obvious, it just can't keep itself unseen. It can't. So, I don't know. You really think that sort of love exists, Helen? Do you? *(Pause.)*

HELEN: Is she beautiful? The color of her eyes. Her skin?

R.P.: She's back there. Waiting. You should go see for yourself.

HELEN: And why would I do that, R.P.? Why would I want to see everything I'm not?

R.P.: *(Pause.)* 'Cause you have to.

(Silence.)

Ain't nothin' to be scared of anymore, Helen.

(Helen takes the time she needs. She exits to see for herself. R.P. stands alone. Denny stands in the open frame, soaking wet.)

DENNY: *(Pause.)* I messed up, Dad. I messed up big.

(R.P. walks over to his son and gently pulls him inside the house. He slides the glass door shut. He looks out to the rain. Helen re-enters. She looks to R.P., who is facing the window. R.P. turns around. They stand perfectly still. They look at one another.)

DENNY: She's gone too far. So, can we? Can we go looking? 'Cause she's out there. Out there helpless. We have to find her.

(Silence.)

We have to 'cause she's ours.

(Silence.)

She's ours.

(Silence.)

(Looking out.) She ran.

(Fade.)

END OF PLAY

Rembrandt's Gift
by Tina Howe

BIOGRAPHY

Tina Howe is the author of *The Nest, Birth and After Birth, Museum, The Art of Dining, Painting Churches, Coastal Disturbances, Approaching Zanzibar, One Shoe Off, Pride's Crossing,* and *The Divine Fallacy*. Most of these works can be read in her two collections published by the Theatre Communications Group. Major awards include an Obie for Distinguished Playwriting, a Rockefeller grant, two NEA Fellowships, a Guggenheim, the New York Drama Critics' Circle award, a Tony nomination and two honorary degrees. She has just completed a new translation of Ionesco's *The Bald Soprano* and *The Lesson* which is slated for production at the Atlantic Theatre Company in 2003. Ms. Howe has been a Visiting Professor at Hunter College since 1990.

HUMANA FESTIVAL PRODUCTION

Rembrandt's Gift premiered at the Humana Festival of New American Plays in March 2002. It was directed by John Rando with the following cast:

Polly Shaw	Penny Fuller
Walter Paradise	Josef Sommer
Rembrandt	Fred Major

and the following production staff:

Scenic Designer	Paul Owen
Costume Designer	Jane Greenwood
Lighting Designer	Tim Saternow
Sound Designer	Kurt B. Kellenberger
Properties Designer	Mark Walston
Stage Manager	Alyssa Hoggatt
Production Assistant	Nancy Pittelman
Fight Director	Rick Sordelet
Assistant Fight Director	Angie Figg
Photography Consultant	Tina Barney
Translator	Yolanda G.H. Gerritson
Dramaturg	Tanya Palmer
Assistant Dramaturg	Nancy Vitale
Casting	Jay Binder C.S.A.
	Jack Bowdan C.S.A.

CHARACTERS

POLLY SHAW, a photographer, 60s

WALTER PARADISE, her husband, an actor, 60s

REMBRANDT VAN RIJN, the great Dutch painter, 57

Author's Note: The following text includes a number of revisions that have been made since the play opened on March 30, 2002.

Josef Sommer, Fred Major and Penny Fuller
in *Rembrandt's Gift*

26th Annual Humana Festival of New American Plays
Actors Theatre of Louisville, 2002
photo by Larry Hunt

Rembrandt's Gift

SCENE ONE

Walter and Polly's top floor loft in downtown Manhattan. Towers of folded theatrical costumes, including hats, boots, swords and parasols rise to the ceiling, obscuring the windows and blocking out the light. They're slowly advancing into the room, pushing the sleeping, eating and living areas closer and closer together. Narrow footpaths wind through this maze, disappearing into other rooms that have already been swallowed up. Only one small corner has resisted the onslaught—Polly's studio. It contains a standing mirror, a field camera and a few samples of her photographs that transform minute areas of her body into brutal landscapes. A poster of Rembrandt's "Kensington" portrait advertising his latest retrospective at the Metropolitan Museum of Art hangs nearby. But none of this is visible, since it's the middle of the night and very dark. It's early spring. Polly and Walter are in bed. Walter's snoring.

POLLY: *(In a stage whisper.)* Walter? Walter?
 (Walter snores louder.)
 Are you awake?
 (He snores even louder.)
 (Polly speaks louder.)
 Sweetheart?
 (He snores louder still.)
 I can't sleep! *(In a sing-song.)* Walllllter? Oh Walllllter? *(Pause.)* WALTER?
WALTER: *(Waking with a start.)* Ugh! Ugh!
POLLY: I've been tossing and turning all night! *(Pause.)* Sweetheart?
WALTER: Uuuuugh…
POLLY: *(In a loud whisper.)* Are you awake? *(Pause.)* Darling?
WALTER: *(Groggy.)* I am now, thanks to you.
POLLY: *This is it!*
WALTER: Do you have any idea how many times I've been up tonight?
POLLY: The landlord's coming to evict us…
WALTER: Try, seven.

POLLY: With the New York Fire Department!

WALTER: No, make that eight.

POLLY: *La comedia est finita!*

WALTER: Fucking prostate!

POLLY: What are we going to do?

WALTER: I'd like to see *you* try and urinate with a prostate the size of an Idaho potato!

POLLY: Where are we going to go?

WALTER: I finally fall asleep after peeing my guts out half the night and what do you do?

POLLY: It's starting to get scary…

WALTER: Wake me up because *you* can't sleep!

POLLY: Very scary!

WALTER: You don't give two shits about my prostate!

POLLY: That's not true. I adore your prostate!

WALTER: Bullshit!

POLLY: I worship the ground it walks on.

WALTER: Prostates don't have legs!

POLLY: Alright, I worship the ground it… *dangles* over.

WALTER: *(Angrily heading to the bathroom.)* Yeah, yeah…

POLLY: Hey, where are you going?

WALTER: Where do you *think* I'm going? To pee. For the *ninth* time tonight, in case you're interested. You know the trouble with you? You always assume the worst! *(He exits, slamming the bathroom door.)*

POLLY: Assume? *Assume?* It's already happened. Did you hear what I said? *(Yelling.)* Wallllter? Oh WALLLLLLTER? *(Listening.)* What are you doing in there? You're not washing your hands again, are you? You already spent two hours at the sink this evening! Your skin will fall off if you keep this up! Walter? SWEETHEART…? *(Listening harder.)* Yoo hoo, are you still alive?

(Silence. Walter flushes and returns.)

POLLY: So, how did it go?

WALTER: I came, I saw, I conquered.

POLLY: Good boy.

WALTER: *(A game they play.)* Excuse me, but do I know you?

POLLY: I'm your wife.

WALTER: Ah…

POLLY: Polly. Polly Shaw.

WALTER: Ah…

POLLY: You remember, the slip of a thing you married a hundred years ago.

WALTER: Of course.

POLLY: Your sweet nothing, your delectable everything.

WALTER: Where did you come from?

POLLY: *(With a French accent.)* The brume.

WALTER: The broom?

POLLY: Not a broom you sweep with, but as in the French, *la brume*—mist, fog.

WALTER: Ah…

POLLY: *(Getting into bed.)* I'm everywhere and nowhere. A hunch, a presentiment, a toss of salt over the shoulder. *(Looking at him out of confused eyes.)* And you, oh mysterious one?

WALTER: Am Walter.

POLLY: Ahhh…

WALTER: Walter-the-Uncanny—man of a thousand faces and voices: tyrant, madman, lover or fool.

POLLY: Indeed.

WALTER: Just give me the role, and I'll play it.

POLLY: Do tell.

WALTER: Shakespeare, Sophocles, Strindberg… the whole fun-loving gang. Your wish is my command. *(He bows and then gets in bed beside her.)*

POLLY: Sing to me.

WALTER: Sing to you?

POLLY: It calms me down.

(Walter sings: "The Sidewalk is Laid out in Concrete Squares" like a baroque round. After several verses, Polly joins him in lovely harmony, then silence.)

POLLY: Thanks, I needed that.

WALTER: Anytime, anytime. *(Snuggling up to her.)* Mmmm, you're so warm… My little heating pad, my toaster oven, my sizzling hot plate…

POLLY: Hey, what are you doing?

WALTER: Adoring you.

POLLY: *(Pulling away.)* Sweetheart?

WALTER: Mmmmmm, you smell like nutmeg… Have you been rolling in the spices again?

POLLY: *I don't like this anymore!*

WALTER: Like *what?*

POLLY: *This!*

WALTER: Could you be more specific?

POLLY: *Our life!*

WALTER: Oh that.

POLLY: *(Leaping out of bed.)* You're burying us alive!

WALTER: Hey, where are you going?

POLLY: CRAZY!

WALTER: *(Grabbing her in his arms.)* There, there, something will come up, it always does.

POLLY: *(Trying to pull away.)* We've got to clean up!

WALTER: An act of God, a bureaucratic glitch, a man bearing gifts.

POLLY: *(Breaking down.)* Darling, *I'm begging you!*
(She struggles to get away, but he holds her fast. Blackout.)

SCENE TWO

Several hours later. The early morning sun dimly reveals the loft in its entire-ty. Polly's still asleep and Walter's checking and double-checking the locks on the front door. He wears a fur-trimmed kingly robe over his pajamas.

WALTER: *(In a breathy altered voice.)* One, two, buckle my shoe; three, four, lock the door; five, six, pick up sticks; seven, eight, lay them straight... Objects in the mirror are closer than they appear. By far, by far, by far, by far... Yet oh so near, so near, so near, so near... Boy oh boy oh boy oh boyo, we don't want any accidents here. No siree, Bob! No dead bodies piled up on this side of the road, thank you very much! And that means you, Eddie, Franz, Wilhelm and Pepe! Wrong! Wrong! Alphabetically, you asshole! You know the rules! Now you'll have to start all over again! *(Pummeling his head with each word.)* STUPID! STUPID! STUPID! STUPID! *(Picking up speed.)* One, two, buckle my shoe; three, four, lock the door; five, six, pick up sticks; seven, eight, lay them straight... Objects in the mirror are closer than they appear...

POLLY: *(Waking up.)* Sweetheart, is that you?

WALTER: *(Hitting himself and chanting.)* By far, by far, by far, by far, yet oh so near. Boy oh boy oh boy oh boyo, we don't want any accidents here. No siree, Bob!

POLLY: *(Getting out of bed.)* Walter, no... Not this morning, not today!

WALTER: No dead bodies piled up on *this* side of the road, thank you very much!
(Polly rushes to him and tries to pin his arms to his side. They wrestle.)

POLLY:
We've got to start
cleaning up. Comstock's
coming at six thirty.

WALTER:
And that means you,
Eddie, Franz, Pepe
and Wilhelm!

(She knocks him off balance. He falls.)

WALTER: *(Anguished.)* Now I'll have to start all over again. Once I start, I have to finish. You know that!

POLLY: *(Going to the closet.)* You are not checking those locks again!

WALTER: If I'm interrupted, it doesn't count!

POLLY: *(Returning with a recycling bag and heading towards a stack of costumes.)* Come on, sailor, let's get this show on the road.

WALTER: *(In an awful voice.)* DON'T TOUCH MY THINGS!

(Polly starts singing "There's No Business Like Show Business," as she stuffs costumes into the bag.)

WALTER: *(Grabbing her wrists.)* I said, don't touch!

POLLY: But you never wear them!

WALTER: *(Posing in his kingly robe.)* Excuse me.

POLLY: You haven't been on stage in over twenty years!

WALTER: I want to be ready when the call comes.

POLLY: The "call"? What "call"?

WALTER: The call to return.

POLLY: First of all, you're not going to get any call.

WALTER: *(Trying to drown her out.)* Peas and carrots, peas and carrots, peas and carrots *(etc.)*

POLLY: And second of all, since when do actors have to provide their own costumes?

WALTER: A bird in the hand is worth two in the bush. I happen to have one of the definitive costume collections in the country.

POLLY: This isn't a collection, it's an *aberration!*

WALTER: Who else had the foresight to acquire Olympic Rep's entire costume shop when the theater went belly up?

POLLY: ONE PERSON CAN'T POSSIBLY WEAR ALL THIS CRAP!

WALTER: It's not to wear, it's to *have!*

POLLY: What happened? You never used to be like this.

WALTER: I'm an actor Polly. These are the tools of my trade.

POLLY: But what about me and the tools of *my* trade?

WALTER: *Tools?* What tools?

POLLY: Some light would be nice… And a little room to move.

WALTER: What are you talking about? We have plenty of light.

POLLY: For growing mushrooms! I can't see my hand in front of my face. Which is something of a drawback if you're a photographer.

WALTER: *(Kidding around.)* You're a photographer?

POLLY: I was… A hundred years ago.

WALTER: Well, what do you know…

POLLY: *I have no room to work!*

WALTER: A photographer!

POLLY: My studio, if you can still call it that, has been swallowed up and my darkroom, such as it was, has disappeared without a trace! I'm a man without a country, a refugee without his fiddle.

WALTER: What about your latest ear lobe series?

POLLY: I'd like room to photograph more than my ear lobes!

WALTER: It's some of your best work.

POLLY: Forgive me for being crass, but do you see anyone *buying* it?

WALTER: What do dealers know?

POLLY: What *sells!*

WALTER: You've always been ahead of the curve.

POLLY: But I'm so buried under, I can't even *see* any curve! To say nothing about the rest of my body!

WALTER: Polly, Polly…

POLLY: *Plus…*

WALTER: Calm down…

POLLY: *Plus,* if there were a fire, the place would go up like a tinder box.

WALTER: If there were a *fire?* What *fire?*

POLLY: *Any* fire!

WALTER: I'm a custodian, a curator…

POLLY: You're a *hoarder* and you need help! *(She resumes stuffing costumes into a plastic bag.)* We're going to be evicted. Comstock's coming *with* the fire department. It's our fifth warning. This loft is a danger to the entire building, to say nothing of its threat to us—you and me—Mr. and Mrs. Walking Time Bomb.

WALTER: *(Pacing up and down, trying to drown her out.)* Peas and carrots, peas and carrots, peas and carrots, peas and carrots, peas and carrots…

POLLY: *(Stuffing more and more clothes in.)* This is it, Walter! The decisive moment! Either we clean up or we're out on our asses!

WALTER: *(Rushing at her.)* Stop it! Stop it! Put those back! I said put them back!

(They struggle. Polly breaks down.)

POLLY:
Sweetheart please...
I entreat you! I'm
begging you... Walter,
no...

WALTER:
Put those back right now!
Those are mine! *Mine,* I
say! You have no right...
It's my collection, mine!

(Rembrandt's self-portrait starts to glow. There's a brilliant explosion and Rembrandt suddenly appears in a pool of light, dressed as he appears in the poster. He's crouched on the floor clutching his palette and brushes in one hand and searching for an invisible object with the other. When he sees them he straightens up and stares at them out of terrified eyes.)

POLLY: Oh my God...

WALTER: Now just one minute...

POLLY: My God, my God, my God, my God...

WALTER: *(To Rembrandt.)* Who the hell are you?

POLLY: Sweetheart, do you see who that is?

WALTER: And how the hell did you get in here?

POLLY: I don't believe it!

WALTER: *I just checked the locks!*

POLLY: Look at his clothes...

WALTER: Answer me, how did you get through that door?

POLLY: The white hat, the lace dickey, the fur-trimmed coat...

WALTER: Of course! How stupid could I be?

POLLY: The palette and the paint brushes...

WALTER: *You came through the window!*

POLLY: It's Rembrandt!

WALTER: *(To Polly.)* He's a fucking second story man!

POLLY: Walter, it's *Rembrandt!*

WALTER: He climbed up the fire escape and then jimmied open the window.
Clever! Very clever!

POLLY: *(Pointing at it.)* Look at his self-portrait!

WALTER: Nice threads. Right out of a Restoration comedy. I like a man with
style, even if he is a thief. *(He bows from the waist. Rembrandt mimics him.
Walter executes a series of florid bows. Rembrandt mimics those as well.)*

WALTER: Clever, very clever. *(To Polly.)* He's quite a mimic.

POLLY: I can't breathe!

(They gape at him. Walter then does a bit of a soft shoe routine. Rembrandt

copies it to perfection. Walter pauses to think and then launches into a spirited tap routine.)

POLLY: *(Sotto voce to Walter.)* Honey, what do you think you're doing? *(Rembrandt executes it flawlessly.)*

POLLY: *(In a stage whisper.)* That's Rembrandt!

WALTER: *(Fast, trying to trip him up.)*
"Peter Piper picked a peck of pickled peppers;
A peck of pickled peppers Peter Piper picked.
If Peter Piper picked a peck of pickled peppers,
Where's the peck of pickled peppers Peter Piper picked?"

REMBRANDT: *(Twice as fast.)* "Peter Piper picked a peck of pickled peppers;
A peck of pickled peppers Peter Piper picked.
If Peter Piper picked a peck of pickled peppers,
Where's the peck of pickled peppers Peter Piper picked?"

POLLY: He speaks English! How does Rembrandt know English?

WALTER: *(In a grand voice.)* "Now is the winter of our discontent
Made glorious summer by this sun of York…"

REMBRANDT: "And all the clouds that lour'd upon our house
In the deep bosom of the ocean buried."

POLLY: And Shakespeare! He can recite Shakespeare!

REMBRANDT: "Now are our brows bound with victorious wreaths…
Our bruised arms hung up for monuments,
Our stern alarums changed to merry meetings,
Our dreadful marches to delightful measures."

POLLY: Well, why not? There were probably Shakespearean traveling companies all over Europe. One just never imagines *Rembrandt* doing "Richard the Third".

WALTER: *(To Polly.)* You're telling me this is *Rembrandt.*

POLLY: It's a miracle!

WALTER: And *I'm* supposed to be the lunatic around here!

POLLY: You said something would come along and save us—an act of God, a bureaucratic glitch, *a man bearing gifts…* *(She nudges Walter, eyeing Rembrandt's brush and palette.)*

WALTER: It was a figure of speech.

POLLY: *Well, here he is!*

WALTER: The resemblance is striking, I admit.

POLLY: *(With a flourish.)* Welcome to our humble home!

WALTER: The face, the hat, the palette and brushes…

POLLY: The pool of light...

WALTER: Pool of light?

> *(Rembrandt notices that he's standing in a spotlight. He takes several steps to escape it. It follows him.)*

POLLY: *(In a stage whisper.)* See, it follows him wherever he goes.

> *(Rembrandt moves around the room trying to shake it, but can't.)*

POLLY: Forgive my manners, we should introduce ourselves. I'm Polly Shaw, the photographer and this is my husband Walter Paradise, the actor.

WALTER: *She's* the famous one.

POLLY: Now, now...

WALTER: One woman shows all over the world...

POLLY: Please!

WALTER: Fêted by the greats and near greats...

POLLY: A thousand years ago.

WALTER: This woman redefined the limits of nude self-portraiture.

> *(Rembrandt is now doing vaudeville moves trying to escape the spot, but can't. He has a sudden coughing fit and staggers. Polly catches him and guides him to a chair.)*

POLLY: Sit, sit... The poor thing's exhausted.

> *(Rembrandt makes scary gurgling sounds.)*

POLLY: *(Crouching beside him.)* What is it? What's wrong?

> *(The gurgling sounds intensify.)*

WALTER: *(Backing away from him.)* Jesus Christ! He's probably got the plague! It wiped out half the population of Amsterdam during his lifetime.

POLLY: *(Terrified.)* The *plague?!*

WALTER: The guy's a carrier and now we've been exposed!

> *(They cover their faces.)*

WALTER: Thanks pal, thanks a lot!

REMBRANDT: *(Weakly.)* Prithee, calm yourselves, thou hast no cause for alarm. I suffer not from the plague, though those closest to me have succumbed to its ravenous grip. *(Suppressing a sob.)* My beloved wife, Saskia and our first three children, whilst still in their infancy: Rombertus, and our sweet Cornelias... two daughters within two years' time... Only Titus remains... 'Tis an irony most cruel that this old body has 'scaped its grasp. The oldest and most unworthy is spared... No, my complaint hath little weight by comparison. 'Tis as old and common as the earth itself— the relentless equalizer 'twixt man and beast, the Devil's handmaiden— hunger. Whilst wielding my brushes just moments ago, its pangs seized me with such intensity, I clumsily reached for a morsel of bread I had placed on the window ledge. But in my haste to seize it, I upset the plate it was sitting on and down it tumbled to the street below. I raced down the stairs to retrieve it before it disappeared down the gullet of some starving dog, my poor mouth watering in anticipation. But as I reached out to grab it, *mirable dictu*, I was suddenly here—dancing and speaking a language I know not... I have been visited by a host of wondrous dreams in my fifty-seven years, but this one... now, here with thee... 'Tis by far the strangest of them all.

(Silence as Polly and Walter gaze at him.)

WALTER: Jesus H. Christ...

POLLY: He thinks it's a dream.

REMBRANDT: Since my hunger doth naught but intensify, methinks the morsel of bread I was about to retrieve must lie nearby. I wager 'tis under foot, mocking these poor old eyes with its very proximity. *(He rises and starts looking for it.)*

POLLY: *(To Walter.)* Quick, get him something to eat.

WALTER: *(Bowing to her.)* Aye, m' lady.

REMBRANDT: *(Continuing his search.)* 'Twas merely a scrap, but 'twas almost in my mouth, and therein lies the agony.

(Walter exits to the kitchen.)

POLLY: *(Yelling to Walter.)* What would a Dutchman like?

WALTER: Something with a little *Hollandaise* sauce, get it? *(He roars with laughter.)*

REMBRANDT: 'Tis not merely the body that dances to hunger's tune, but the mind as well.

POLLY: How about a nice piece of gouda cheese?

WALTER: *(With an edge.)* I'm looking!

REMBRANDT: And therein lies the root of mine agitation.

POLLY: You don't have to snap!

WALTER: I didn't snap!

REMBRANDT: Reason hath deserted me.

POLLY: You most certainly did. *(To Rembrandt.)* Didn't he?

WALTER: Leave him out of this.

REMBRANDT: I am very like a specimen in an anatomy lesson whose brain hath been removèd.

POLLY: *(To Rembrandt.)* We'll get you something in a moment.

WALTER: Dream on.

POLLY: *(Yelling to Walter.)* How about some of that macaroni and cheese from last night?

WALTER: *(Yelling back.)* Nope! We polished it off!

POLLY: What about tuna fish? There must be a little tuna fish in there.

WALTER: Gone!

POLLY: Just bring whatever's there.

WALTER: It's pretty slim pickings.

REMBRANDT: My eyesight fails. 'Tis so dark I cannot see.

POLLY: Yeah well, we don't get much light these days.

REMBRANDT: Your windows appear to be obscured. Prithee, art thou in mourning?

POLLY: In a manner of speaking.

WALTER: *(Returns, spreading the contents of the refrigerator in front of Rembrandt.)* Half a bottle of seltzer, a head of wilted lettuce and a box of suppositories!

POLLY: That's it?

WALTER: We're down to two meals a day, if that. Food just isn't a priority anymore.

POLLY: No fruit?

WALTER: Plus, groceries are sky high. It would be cheaper to just eat the money. Toss a couple of bills into a frying pan and sauté 'em with a little garlic and olive oil. My mouth is watering just thinking of it. Add a couple of social security checks and IRS refunds... Mmm, mmm, good.

POLLY: *(Handing Rembrandt the head of lettuce.)* Eat, eat!
(Rembrandt tears into it like a starving animal. Polly and Walter watch him, appalled.)

WALTER: *(To Polly under his breath.)* I remember reading that he died in poverty, but I had no idea it was that bad.

POLLY: Tastes change. It's the fate of every artist. Look what happened to my, so called "career"... Sweetheart, why don't you get him some cereal?

WALTER: Great idea! I should have thought of it in the first place. *(He heads back to the kitchen.)*

POLLY: *(To Rembrandt.)* I was a trail blazer when I began, but then Walter went crazy and I lost my touch. It was probably inevitable. My work got a little... weird. Not unlike yours.

WALTER: *(Yelling from the kitchen.)* Here's something that will stick to his ribs, Mueslix. It's chock full of dried fruits and nuts and is so tasty, we eat it dry. Plus... it has very few calories, which is good for the old figure, such as it is. *(Returning with a spoon and bowl filled to the brim, handing it to Rembrandt.)* Dig in, dig in.

(Rembrandt lowers his face into the bowl and starts gobbling it up.)

WALTER AND POLLY: The spoon, use the spoon!

(Rembrandt switches to the spoon, greedily shoveling the cereal into his mouth.)

WALTER: What did I tell you? Delicious, isn't it?

POLLY: I like the figs, but Walter prefers the raisins.

(Silence as they watch him eat. When he's had enough, he dries his mouth on his sleeve.)

REMBRANDT: Would that mine stomach could speak, it would thank thee Sirrah, with words to melt thy heart. I have been praying of late for deliverance.

POLLY: Join the group.

REMBRANDT: From hunger, penury and above all—neglect.

POLLY: We're about to be evicted.

REMBRANDT: I am an agèd man in an unjust world.

POLLY: Tell us about it.

WALTER: Sons of bitches!

REMBRANDT: Vanity, vanity, all is vanity.

POLLY: What can you do?

WALTER: Fucking bastards.

REMBRANDT: Naught but the grave awaits!

POLLY: Please!

WALTER: *Cocksuckers!*

(Silence.)

POLLY: *(To Rembrandt.)* You don't know where you are, do you? You're at 103 Mercer Street. In Soho... *(Pause.)* "South. Of. Houston"... *(Pause.)* You know, in New York City, cultural capitol of the western world.

WALTER: YOU'RE IN THE UNITED STATES!

POLLY: The good old U. S. of A. America.

WALTER: WECOME TO THE NEW WORLD!

POLLY: In the year two thousand and two.

(Rembrandt starts to scream.)

POLLY: There, there, no one's going to hurt you.

WALTER: Easy, buddy, you'll wake the dead.

POLLY: You're safe with us.

WALTER: Wait a minute, if you're Rembrandt, you're already dead. *(He chuckles at his cleverness.)*

REMBRANDT: *(Sinking to his knees in prayer.)* "Almighty and most merciful Father, we have erred, and strayed from Thy ways like lost sheep…"

WALTER: Sorry, sorry, I wasn't thinking.

POLLY: Rembrandt… the greatest portrait painter who ever lived!

REMBRANDT: *(Rising.)* And so you call me by my name again. Prithee gentles, one question more.

POLLY: Walter said something would come along and save us—an act of God, a bureaucratic glitch, a man bearing gifts and here you are… *Rembrandt!*

REMBRANDT: I am most curious to learn how thou came'st to know my name.

POLLY: In our house, sitting in our chair, eating our Mueslix…

WALTER: For Christ's sake, Polly, let him speak!

POLLY: *(To Walter.)* Well, pardon me for living!

REMBRANDT: How do you know I am Rembrandt when I ne'er introduced myself?

POLLY: Easy. *(She points at his self-portrait. He sees it and gasps.)*

WALTER: She put me onto it, it's one of our favorites.

REMBRANDT: God have mercy on my soul!

WALTER: Not that the others aren't great.

REMBRANDT: 'Tis the very portrait I was working on!

WALTER: If you ask me, it's a toss up between this and your self portrait as the Apostle Paul.

POLLY: No, no, this is better, hands down.

REMBRANDT: *But 'tis not finished!*

POLLY: The sadness in his eyes, the valor about his mouth…

REMBRANDT: *(Rushing to examine it.)* Verily, it hath completed itself! God's blood, there is no trace of paint!

POLLY: It's a poster… You know, a photograph!

WALTER: *(To Polly.)* How could he possibly know what a photograph is, they hadn't been invented in his lifetime.

REMBRANDT: Prithee tell me how this came into your possession!

POLLY: I got it at the Met.

REMBRANDT: "IgotitattheMet"?

POLLY: *(Slowly.)* The Metropolitan Museum of Art. *(Pause.)* On Fifth Avenue and 82nd Street…

WALTER: The premier art museum in the country, if not the world.

REMBRANDT: 'Tis a dealer I am not acquainted with.

POLLY: A museum isn't a person, it's a *place!*

WALTER: A grand building where you go to see art—paintings, sculptures, armor, mummies…

REMBRANDT: Thou speak'st of the *Stadhouder's* gallery in the palace.

POLLY: You've been having a retrospective. You know, when a large body of an artist's work is assembled from all over the world.

REMBRANDT: Verily, I know it well. My "Passion of Christ" panels hang in that very place.

POLLY: "Rembrandt: Saints and Sinners". Forget the crowds!

WALTER: The pushing and wheelchairs…

POLLY: The crush at the gift shop…

WALTER: The children in strollers…

POLLY: The lines at the coat check…

WALTER: The lines at the *restrooms!*

POLLY: The blaring accusta-guides…

WALTER: The barking seals and hyenas…

POLLY: No, no darling, that's the zoo! We probably know more about you than you do! The Leiden years, the history paintings, the landscapes, etchings, engravings, portraits and self-portraits… It's all there. The whole kit and kaboodle.

REMBRANDT: "Thewholekitandkaboodle"?

WALTER: The whole nine yards.

POLLY: The whole ball of wax.

REMBRANDT: "Thewholeballofwax"?

POLLY: Almost every painting, drawing, etching and dry point you ever made!

REMBRANDT: They are in favor? They are seen?

WALTER: They are not only seen, you've become a fucking household word, my man!

POLLY: *(Sotto voce.)* Language, Walter, language!

REMBRANDT: Prithee, take me there at once!

WALTER: But we don't have tickets!

REMBRANDT: *(Grabbing her hands.)* If a hint of compassion stirs within thy breast, take me! I beg of you! That I may witness this miracle with mine own eyes. I am at the nether end of my years—bankrupt and ruin't. I survive—if this be survival—on scraps of bread and herring. Humiliation hath become my most constant companion.

POLLY: *(Pulling her hands away.)* Ow, you're hurting me!

REMBRANDT: Forgive me, Madame, but I have few students and fewer commissions. An important painting of mine was recently returned by the elders of the Town Hall, rejected for its… *(Suppressing a sob.)* bold chiaroscuro… Eager to please the town fathers, I cut it down and reworked it, only to have it returned yet again. I have become the laughing stock of Amsterdam. The "great" Rembrandt carving up his canvases like blocks of cheese. 'Tis the classical style that's in favor now—Vermeer and his pristine interiors which appear to mine eyes as having been *exhaled* onto the canvas, not painted... Verily, the artist's hand hath become invisible, so I no longer enjoy the reputation I once had. Gone are the anatomy lessons, the militia portraits and silk merchants with their plump wives! All that remains is this poor old face in its wretched moods. And so I pass my days scratching out my likeness 'til that happy hour when I return to the dust from whence I came... But soft, thou sayst thou hast seen my paintings of late, that they are displayed still at the Stadhouder's gallery...

WALTER AND POLLY: *(Correcting him.)* The Metropolitan Museum of Art!

REMBRANDT: *(Grabbing Polly's hands again.)* Prithee, take me there at once! I implore you!

POLLY: Aahhhh! God, you're strong!

REMBRANDT: *(Glancing at Walter's costumes.)* I will shed this tattered cloak for something more appropriate. *(He whips it off and pulls down a brocade doublet.)*

WALTER: Hey, what do you think you're doing?

REMBRANDT: *(Struggling to put it on.)* Uuugh... uughhh... I fear 'tis too small. *(He tosses it on the floor.)*

WALTER: *(Picking it up and putting it on.)* Watch it, buddy, I wore that in *Cyrano.*

POLLY: Walter was an actor, in case you were wondering.

REMBRANDT: *(Grabs a purple cape and puts it on, and striking a silly pose.)* I fear I resemble a large purple-throated thrush.

WALTER: *(Taking it from him and putting it on over the doublet.)* Oedipus the King... God, when was that? Twenty-five years ago? Thirty-five?

POLLY: *(To Rembrandt.)* He was the leading man at the Olympic Repertory Company for years, *years!*
(Rembrandt takes another robe and looks at himself in the mirror.)

POLLY: You should have seen him...

WALTER: *(Grabbing a crown and putting it on.)* Richard II. "For God's sake let us sit upon the ground and tell sad stories of the death of kings"...

POLLY: He was a god, a *god!*

REMBRANDT: *(Grabbing a feathered hat and putting it on.)* I am ready. And so like Agamemnon bound for Troy, let us set forth! *(Taking Polly's arm and heading for the door.)* Lead the way, O Queen.

WALTER: *(Blocking the door.)* Not so fast! Those are *my* costumes, from *my* personal collection! They do not leave this house!

POLLY: They're part of his stock pile. Don't ask... Also, we don't dress like this anymore.

REMBRANDT: *(Looking at Walter.)* But look you, Madame, *he...*

POLLY: Is crazy.

WALTER: Thanks, Pol.

POLLY: You know actors.

WALTER: Thanks a lot.

POLLY: These are his costumes.

REMBRANDT: Their multitude o'erwhelms me.

POLLY: He's a sick man.

WALTER: Please Polly, not now.

POLLY: He's got O.C.D.

REMBRANDT: O.C.D.?

WALTER: *(With a sigh.)* And she's off.

POLLY: You know, Obsessive Compulsive Disorder...

WALTER: *(Trying to drown her out.)* Peas and carrots, peas and carrots, peas and carrots... *(etc.)*

POLLY: When you're in the grip of a ritual and can't stop. Like washing your hands or checking the locks.

WALTER: Why not get a bull horn and announce it to the whole neighborhood!

POLLY: He's also a hoarder. He can't throw things out.

WALTER: A little louder please, we can't quite hear you!

REMBRANDT: Prithee, no more... 'Tis an affliction I know only too well.

POLLY: He tried medication and behavior therapy, but couldn't stick with it.

WALTER: *You* try those seratonin reuptake inhibitors and see how much you like them! Crippling sweats, dry mouth, ringing in my ears. I couldn't remember my lines.

POLLY: Walter records books on tape now. That is, when he's offered one.

REMBRANDT: There was a time when I too was a collector.

POLLY: How long has it been? Ten years? Twelve? Fifteen?

REMBRANDT: 'Tis oft said that my fondness for art and curiosities was the cause of my ruin. Seven years ago my creditors seized my worldly goods and put them up for auction.

WALTER: No...!

POLLY: I don't believe it!

REMBRANDT: I swear it on my mother's grave. *Everything* seized and scattered to the four winds. Verily, each and every treasure I had collected to add luster to my work. Everything, everything...

WALTER: Fucking bastards!

REMBRANDT: Forty-seven specimens of land and sea creatures... hides, antlers, minerals and shells... Antique weapons, helmets, swords and pistols... A large number of heads and hands cast from life... Harps, stringed instruments, a Turkish bow... Globes, chairs, mirrors and frames... Textiles, costumes, jewels and fans... And then my art collection, the envy of the Stadthouder himself... Works by Lastman, Lievensz, van Eyck and more... And my books, my books... Woodcuts by Van Leyden, engravings by Raphael, prints by Breughel, erotica by Bonasone, Rosso, and Carracci... Plus, of course, the inventory of mine own works... etchings, dry point...

WALTER: Stop, stop!

POLLY: How could they?

REMBRANDT: 'Twas the heirs of my beloved first wife that accused me of squandering her dowry. *Jackals!* They know naught of a painter's needs!

POLLY: But poor Walter's collection has spread beyond aesthetic consideration into pathology. He keeps acquiring *more!* So he'll be prepared... ready for the worst... It's become a health hazard! The landlord's about to evict us. Early this evening, as a matter of fact.

WALTER: Nice, Polly, nicely done! Is there anything else you'd like to share while you're at it?

POLLY: I was just trying to explain our situation.

WALTER: To a total stranger and an apparition, to boot! Unbelievable!

(A pained silence.)

I don't know about you, but I could use a change of mood.

(Polly goes to their C.D. player and plays Bach's joyful bass-soprano duet, "Mit unsrer Macht ist nichts getan" from his chorale, Ein Feste Burg, BWV 80.*)*

Ah, that's more like it!

REMBRANDT: *(Looking around the room, astonished.)* Prithee lady, where are the musicians?

POLLY: It's a C.D.

REMBRANDT: O.C.D.?

POLLY: No, C.D.

REMBRANDT: *(Parroting her.)* No, C.D.

POLLY: It sounds like O.C.D., but it's only two letters: C. D. For compact disc.

REMBRANDT: *(Understanding.)* Oh, C.D.

POLLY: You got it!

WALTER: We have the technology to capture music and play it back whenever we want to hear it.

POLLY: At home, in the car, at the beach, in the gym...

WALTER: Classical, jazz, rock and roll—you name it.

POLLY: I like Bach but Walter prefers Aaron Copland.

WALTER: Stand back!

(*He switches to "Hoe-down" from Copland's "Rodeo" and launches into an Agnes de Mille ballet, using unlikely objects as props.*)

POLLY: (*As an aside.*) He does this to let off steam. It's one of his things.

REMBRANDT: Pray, what do you call this dance?

POLLY: "Walter's Paradise".

WALTER:	POLLY:
That's my name, Walter Paradise!	That's his name, Walter Paradise!

REMBRANDT: Ah!

(*Walter's dancing becomes increasingly inspired.*)

POLLY: That's enough, dear he gets the point.

(*Walter winds down and collapses in a chair. Rembrandt applauds as Polly turns off the C.D. player. Silence. Rembrandt rises.*)

REMBRANDT:	WALTER:	POLLY:
Forgive my impatience, but I am most eager to visit this...	So, how would you like to see some of Polly's...	Maybe you could help us clear out some of this...

(*Silence.*)

ALL: Sorry, sorry!

(*Silence.*)

REMBRANDT:	WALTER:	POLLY:
If you could draw me a map and I will venture forth on my...	She's been documenting her body ever since she was...	Walter said something would come along...

ALL: Sorry, sorry!

REMBRANDT: I MUST GO! I MUST! (*He rushes to the door and tries to open it, but is stopped by all the locks. He tries to open them, grunting.*) Ugh! Ugh! Ugh!

WALTER: Hey, hey! What do you think you're doing?

POLLY: It looks like he's trying to leave.

WALTER: *(Grabbing him from behind.)* Hands off! Those are *my* locks! No one touches them! I don't care if you're Jesus Christ himself!

REMBRANDT: I am most anxious to visit this mausoleum wherein my paintings are displayed.

WALTER AND POLLY: Museum, *museum!*

REMBRANDT: To see that my work endures… 'Tis past imagining!

WALTER: Boy, is he in for a surprise!

POLLY: If we do go, you'll have to change your clothes.

WALTER: Now just one minute…

REMBRANDT: But these are the only vestments I have in my possession.

POLLY: Don't worry, Walter will lend you something.

WALTER: I will?

POLLY: *(Sotto voce, kicking him in the shins.)* Damn right you will! He's Rembrandt for Christ's sake!

WALTER: But…

REMBRANDT: Pray, allow me then to pay you for them, my lord. *(Fishing around in his pockets.)* Fortune smiles on me, for in my pockets are several guilders.

WALTER: Guilders? That's funny! *Guilders! (He starts laughing.)* Like the Pakistani at the newsstand is going to sell me a newspaper for a handful of… *guilders! (He laughs harder and harder.)*

POLLY: *(Embarrassed)* Darling?

WALTER: *(As if talking to the Pakistani.)* "Yes, I'll take a copy of the Times, that bottle of Poland Spring water and this pack of mints. Here you go… *(Handing over invisible coins.)* Here's 43 *guilders!"*
(Walter weeps with laughter. Rembrandt eyes him nervously.)

POLLY: *(To Rembrandt.)* Don't mind him. He has his own way of expressing himself. *(Pause.)* Walter! *Walter?!* PULL YOURSELF TOGETHER!

WALTER: *(Instantly calm.)* Sorry, sorry…

POLLY: *(To Rembrandt.)* Sit tight. I'll look in his closet and see what I can find.

REMBRANDT: Do not leave me alone with him!

POLLY: I'll just be a sec. *(She exits.)*

REMBRANDT: *(Reaching for her.)* Come back, dear lady. Come back!

WALTER: Forgive me, I don't know what came over me.

REMBRANDT: 'Tis passing strange that a handful of coins could provoke such mirth!

WALTER: Could I have a look at some of those… *(Trying not to laugh and failing.)* guilders! Sorry, sorry… I used to collect coins when I was a boy.

REMBRANDT: *(Handing him several.)* Good my lord, consider them yours.

WALTER: Holy shit, these are beautiful!

REMBRANDT: But worth precious little, alas.

WALTER: To you perhaps, but they'd fetch a pretty penny on the antique coin market. Maybe Polly's right. Maybe you really *are* Rembrandt!

(Polly enters with a baggy sweater and a pair of Walter's trousers.)

POLLY: Ta da!

WALTER: Look at these coins, Pol.

POLLY: Rembrandt's guilders…? *(She starts to laugh.)*

WALTER: It's not a joke, they're worth a fortune.

REMBRANDT: *(Fishing around in his pocket.)* But stay, I have another of greater worth. *(Pulling it out.)* Aye, here 'tis. *(Rubbing it on his sleeve.)* Rubens did giv'st me upon his return from Florence. 'Tis not a guilder, but a florin, giv'st him, in turn by Ferdinand de Medici as payment for his "Baptism of Christ". 'Tis exceeding rare, cast by the great Benvenuto Cellini himself. Marry, 'tis of solid gold and the detail, most wondrous fine. I have kept it lo these many years, as 'twas Rubens who op't mine eyes to the splendor of the Italians, above all, Caravaggio. In faith, I had never beheld such a whirlwind of… of… *(Words fail him.)* Rubens gave me this coin as a sort of… dare I say it? *Challenge!* (Pause.) "Perhaps, one day you too, Rembrandt, may stand alongside Carrivagio… Perchance e'en above him…" *(Placing it in Polly's hand.)* Prithee, accept it from me now.

POLLY: We couldn't possibly.

REMBRANDT: *(Closing his hand over hers.)* With my humblest thanks for thy many kindnesses.

POLLY: I don't know what to say.

WALTER: You might start with, "Thank you." *(Cuffing him.)* It's very generous of you.

REMBRANDT: *(Standing close to Polly, showing her the coin.)* On this side, Salome doth remove her seven veils for John the Baptist.

(Polly emits a little cry. Rembrandt turns the coin over.)

And on this, Bathsheba bathes in preparation for her wedding night.

(She emits another cry.)

Biblical scenes are much favored by the Italians, particularly those involving… *women.*

(And another.)

(Intimately.) Provocateurs of treachery and desire.

(Rembrandt looks into her eyes. She becomes increasingly smitten as they gaze at each other.)

WALTER: *(Feeling left out.)* Polly? *(Pause.)* Pol? *(Pause.)* Yooo hooo… *(In a whisper.)* The clothes.

POLLY: *(A million miles away.)* Clothes?

WALTER: My clothes you were going to lend his nibs.

POLLY: *(Waking up.)* Right, right. *(Handing them to Rembrandt.)* Here you go.

REMBRANDT: *(Bowing slightly.)* I humbly thank thee, dear Madame.

(Rembrandt removes his hat and coat and is about to take off his trousers, but stops.)

POLLY: Oh, don't mind lust. I mean *us!*

WALTER: He might like a little privacy, Polly.

POLLY: *(Laughing breathlessly.)* Right, right… Since this is a loft, we don't have desperate grooms, I mean *separate rooms!*

WALTER: *(Grabbing his arm.)* Here, I'll take you to the bathroom. You can change there.

(They exit.)

POLLY: *(Yelling after him.)* Now don't start washing your hands or we'll never get out of here!

(The moment they're gone, Polly lovingly picks up Rembrandt's coat and inhales its fragrance as Walter gives Rembrandt a tour of the bathroom.)

REMBRANDT: Marry, what is this?

WALTER: Indoor plumbing! Shower, sink and toilet. You bathe here, brush your teeth here and piss here. Go on, give it a whirl!

REMBRANDT: *(Flushing the toilet.)* I push this lever and lo, a whirlpool rises up. *(He flushes again.)* I push it again and it reappears! *(He does.)* And e'en once more! *(He starts laughing.)*

WALTER: I'll get out of here so you can have some privacy.

(Walter returns. Polly quickly drops Rembrandt's coat.)

WALTER: You ought to see him in here! He's like a kid on Christmas morning.

(Rembrandt keeps flushing the toilet and laughing.)

(Picking up Rembrandt's coat.) Look at this…

POLLY: *(Dreamily.)* Rembrandt's coat…

WALTER: It's threadbare! Well, the poor guy died a pauper. You heard him.

POLLY: *(Looking guiltily towards the bathroom.)* Shhh! Not so loud.

(Walter puts it on and starts striking poses.)

POLLY: *(In a whisper.)* Sweetheart, don't… Take it off…

(He grabs Rembrandt's brushes and palette as well.)

POLLY: What if he comes out and sees you?

(But Walter is gone. He reaches in his pocket and pulls out a pretend button.)

WALTER: *(Imitating Rembrandt.)* I wouldst like to present thee with this button. It looks like an ordinary button, but in truth, it fell off Michaelangelo's trousers as he was working on the Sistine Chapel... As he reached from his scaffold to fill in God's index finger, it popped, of a sudden off his fly and did'st spin most marvelously through the air. As fate would have it, I happ't to be strolling by when it landed at my feet with a tinkling, "Hey nonny, nonny!" Whereupon I picked it up and placed it in mine pocket. Marry, 'twas the only button that kept the poor man's modesty intact! God knows, how he got through the rest of the day. Methinks with a rope tied 'round his waist. But such are the vicissitudes of the artist's life... Prithee, allow me to present it to you now, dear lady... Or as we say in my country: "For you, my little Delft tea cup!" *(He mimes giving it to her.)*

POLLY: Walter, please... If we're going to the museum we ought to get moving!

WALTER: You were serious about going?

POLLY: How else did you expect him to get there?

WALTER: We're *taking* him?

POLLY: He's our guest.

WALTER: We're taking Rembrandt to his retrospective at the Met?

POLLY: How many artists get an opportunity like this?

WALTER: *But we'll be trampled to death!*

POLLY: No one will recognize him. He'll be wearing your clothes.

WALTER: I don't believe I'm having this conversation!

POLLY: That is, if they fit.

WALTER: I feel like Alice falling down the rabbit hole.

POLLY: Then stay home.

WALTER: What are you trying to do? *Kill* me?

POLLY: Nobody said you had to come.

WALTER: I find your disregard for my welfare dazzling.

POLLY: I know how to get to the Metropolitan Museum of Art.

WALTER: *Dazzling!*

POLLY: I'm perfectly capable of taking him by myself.

WALTER: You know what happens when I'm around crowds.

POLLY: In fact, it would make more sense if you *didn't* come. That way you could start cleaning up for Comstock.

WALTER: Now just a minute...

POLLY: You'll get a head start.

WALTER: *(Getting increasingly upset.)* First of all, no one's "cleaning up for Comstock!" And second, you're not going alone with him to any museum!

POLLY: We'll only be gone a couple of hours.

WALTER: Did you hear what I said?

POLLY: Even less.

WALTER: *I don't trust that man around the corner!*

POLLY: We'll be back before you know it. And he'll be able to pitch in.

WALTER: God knows what he's capable of—kidnapping, assault and battery... rape. I had my doubts about him when he first showed up, but now the guy's revealed himself. He's a scoundrel, a dog in the manger, a rank opportunist. He's not bearing any gifts, Polly—only disaster and the gnashing of teeth! Trust me on this.

POLLY: I'm going and that's that!

(Rembrandt suddenly appears in Walter's clothes. He's transformed into a modern man.)

REMBRANDT: *(Striking a pose.)* Ecce homo. *(He notices that Walter's wearing his coat and smiles.)* S'blood, thou art more Rembrandt than I myself!

(The three gaze at each other in amazement. Blackout.)

SCENE THREE

Four hours later. A bright mid-day sun vainly tries to seep through the block-aded windows. The loft is empty. Nothing happens for several moments, then we hear Walter struggling with his keys at the door as Polly and Rembrandt look on.

WALTER: Damned keys!

POLLY: Easy, sweetheart, easy...

WALTER: None of them fit! OPEN, FOR CHRIST'S SAKE... OPEN!

POLLY: Losing your temper won't help.

(Walter tries another key and shakes the door, roaring with frustration.)

REMBRANDT: Prithee, allow me.

WALTER: SON OF A BITCH!

REMBRANDT: My cousin Nicolaes Uylenburgh was a locksmith, so I am familiar with the physics involved.

(Walter tries another key and pounds on the door.)

POLLY: Come on, let him do it!

REMBRANDT: There was a time I considered being a professional thief.

POLLY: Give him the keys, Walter!

WALTER: OK, OK... Since you're the big genius around here, *you* open them!

(He throws the keys at him.)

REMBRANDT: *(Opening lock after lock.)* I used to fashion mechanical toys for my children—singing birds, juggling clowns and for Titus, an elephant that played a tune... When. You. Pulled. Its. Tail!

(He opens the door and they enter. Rembrandt's in the lead with Polly on his arm. He carries several shopping bags from the Metropolitan Museum of Art. He's a changed man, radiating confidence. Walter brings up the rear also carrying shopping bags from the museum.)

REMBRANDT: *(Suggestively to Polly.)* As with all procedures of a delicate nature, one must rely on observation—matching the configuration of the object one wishes to insert... into the cavity that awaits.

(Polly emits a little cry.)

WALTER: The guy can do anything! Paint, recite Shakespeare, open locks... Why don't we just ask him to move in with us. He could share our food, our toilet and our bed!

POLLY: *Walter?!*

WALTER: Thank God we're home. It was like being trapped in the ninth circle of hell! *(He overturns the first shopping bag. A blizzard of printed matter falls out.)*

POLLY: You didn't bring home more crap, did you?

WALTER: Guides and brochures about upcoming exhibits.

POLLY: *I thought we were trying to clean up!*

WALTER: *Plus...* *(Grabbing the second bag.)*

POLLY: *(Dropping her head in her hands.)* Sweetheart..?

WALTER: *Plus* extra copies of the literature that accompanied his show. *(He overturns it. Streams of pamphlets pour out.)*

POLLY: *Did you hear one word of what I've been saying?*

WALTER: Once it closes, it will be unavailable.

POLLY: WHO CARES?

WALTER: *I* care!

POLLY: But why so many? You have no sense of proportion.

WALTER: You never know when someone might need them. There are a lot of historians and archivists out there!

POLLY: *(Kicking through them.)* You're not responsible for keeping all of Western Civilization afloat!

WALTER: *(Trying to stop her.)* Hey, watch it! By tomorrow those babies will be collector's items.

POLLY: *(To Rembrandt.)* See what I have to put up with?

(A painful silence as Walter starts gathering them up and stacking them into neat piles.)

REMBRANDT: My gratitude to you knows no bounds... To see such a multitude of my works displayed... 'Twas as if I were the prodigal son, returned to sudden grace. My paintings, so maligned before were of a sudden embraced, admired, e'en revered. Though I was sorely distressed at the number of my pupils' works that were confused with mine—"The Polish Rider", "The Toilet of Bathsheba", "Christ and the Woman of Samaria".

POLLY: I just kept wishing I could tell everyone who you were. Think of the pandemonium if they'd known Rembrandt was actually *there*—in the same room with them!

WALTER: Well, the way you were falling all over him, it was clear you thought he was someone pretty special.

POLLY: "Falling all over him?"

WALTER: It was downright embarrassing! *(Imitating her.)* "This one's my favorite. No, *this* one... OH MY GOD, WILL YOU LOOK AT THAT ONE! They're all masterpieces. Every last one!" Good God, I forgot to double lock the door in all the excitement! *(Slapping the side of his head.)* STUPID, STUPID, STUPID, STUPID! *(Rushes to the door and starts incanting over the locks in his altered voice, as Rembrandt sinks to his knees in prayer, overlapping him.)*

REMBRANDT: "I returned, and saw under the sun that the race is not to the swift, nor the battle to the strong... neither yet bread to the wise, nor yet riches to men of understanding, nor yet favour to men of skill; but time and chance happeneth to them all."

WALTER: "One, two, buckle my shoe; three, four, lock the door; five, six, pick-up sticks; seven, eight, lay them straight... Objects in the mirror are closer than they appear. By far, by far, by far, by far... Yet oh so near, so near, so near, so near... Boy oh boy oh boy oh boyo, we don't want any accidents here. No Siree Bob! No dead bodies piled up on this side of the road, thank you very much! And that means you, Eddie, Franz, Pepe and Wilhelm. *(In a loop, overlapping...)*

POLLY: *(To Rembrandt, as Walter incants.)* Boy, you really know your bible.

REMBRANDT: I was raised within the tenets of the Reformed Church, but my mother, God rest her soul, was Roman Catholic. We are the envy of the world, for in Amsterdam, we practice religious tolerance. Calvinist and Catholic wed, Christian and Jew live side by side.

POLLY: Walter's Jewish, but I'm not. I'm nothing.

REMBRANDT: In faith, to be nothing is impossible. As Spinoza exclaimed, "Nature abhors a vacuum."

POLLY: I don't go to church.

REMBRANDT: But surely thou dost believe... In God's word... *(He takes off his sweater and is wearing a Rembrandt tee shirt from the museum.)*
(Walter's incanting intensifies.)

POLLY: Darling, please!

REMBRANDT: Prithee, Madame, what is he doing?

POLLY: Don't mind him, it's just one of his rituals...

REMBRANDT: He appears to be sorely distressed.

POLLY: Repeating nonsense phrases to ward off disaster. *(Lowering her voice.)* It's part of his... you know... If he says them enough times, it makes him feel safe.

REMBRANDT: In faith, I know only too well. When we remove our clothes at day's end, we search our bodies for signs of plague...

POLLY: *(Terrified.)* Plague? Did you say *plague?*

WALTER: *(Stops his incanting.)* What did I tell you? I knew he was a carrier!
(Walter and Polly back away in horror.)

REMBRANDT: Ne'er an inch of ground remains to bury the dead. Those who are interred are exhumed to make room for those freshly ta'en. Funeral bells peal night and day. We stagger under the devastation, checking groins and armpits for the fatal purple blooms... *(Launching into a dizzy checking ritual, examining and re-examining every part of his body. Singing a Dutch nursery rhyme.)* "Een twee drie vier/Hoedje van, hoedje van/ Een twee drie vier/ Hoedje van papier/ Als het hoedje dan niet past/ Zet het in de glazen kast/ Eeen twee drie vier/ Hoedje van papier" *(Walter returns to his incantations. They both get louder and louder.)*

POLLY: *(Suddenly screams.)* STOP, STOP, I CAN'T TAKE IT ANYMORE!
(Silence.)
Thank you.

REMBRANDT: Forgive me, Madame, I fear I quite forgot myself.
(Silence.)

REMBRANDT: *(Clasping his hands in prayer.)* "O praise the Lord, for it is a good thing to sing praises unto our God; yea, a joyful and pleasant thing it is to be thankful."

POLLY AND WALTER: *(Moved.)* Amen.
(Silence.)

REMBRANDT: Permit me to express my thanks for bestowing these gifts on me. They are wondrous strange indeed. *(He spills out the contents of his shopping bag, holding up an assortment of Rembrandt date books, calendars, coffee mugs, place mats and scarves.)* And each with this poor face affixed thereon.

POLLY: In your face, you make us see all faces.

REMBRANDT: 'Tis the only one available to me, alas. For I no longer receive the commissions I once enjoyed.

(A painful silence.)

POLLY: I've been documenting *my* body for over forty years now. *(Embarrased by her candor.)* Who said that?

WALTER: She's the best, the best! *(Handing him a lavish book of her photographs.)* Feast your eyes on this! It's a collection of all her photographs, published by the Museum of Modern Art.

POLLY: Back in the Stone Age.

(Rembrandt starts looking through it, becoming increasingly intrigued and aroused.)

POLLY: It wasn't out of vanity, I assure you… Oh, I was attractive enough, but hardly a beauty.

WALTER: Don't listen to her, she was a knockout, a *knockout!*

POLLY: I just got really curious as I started maturing into a… you know… *woman.* I'd always been this scrawny tom boy when suddenly these… *breasts* started to bloom… *(Handling them.)* It was astonishing! I mean, what were the chances? It was inevitable, of course, I just never imagined it would happen to *me*… You know, like falling in love or getting married… They were a total surprise. When I got in the shower, I couldn't keep my hands off them! They were so soft, yet firm… *(Handling them.)* So I took to striking dramatic poses to show them off. *(Doing it.)* Raising my arms over my head, clasping my hands behind my neck, arching over the back of a chair, getting down on all fours…

(Walter and Rembrandt stifle sobs.)

POLLY: I was staggered! I couldn't believe they belonged to me! So I got a camera and taught myself the rudiments of photography. Looking back on it, I was incredibly resourceful, managing to turn my closet into a make-shift dark room… I was barely fifteen, but desperate to document this… *metamorphosis!* Isn't that why we pick up a camera or paint brush in the first place? To fathom a mystery? The artistry and control come later… If you're lucky. There were plenty of guys doing female nudes—Stieglitz, Bill Brandt and Edward Weston—but who better than a woman to celebrate her own coming of age? And by the same token—her inevitable disintegration?

WALTER: *Polly?!*

POLLY: No, no, that's when things start to get really interesting.

REMBRANDT: Marry, 'tis true. The final years are the most...

POLLY: Provocative.

REMBRANDT: The most...

POLLY: Poignant.

REMBRANDT: And the most...

POLLY: Perplexing.

> *(Silence.)*

> When I began my entire body filled the frame, but as I matured, I started to narrow the focus. The *sum* of the parts no longer interested me. I wanted to isolate them, and in so doing, I opened up a whole new landscape—knees became mountain ranges, thighs, riverbeds and breasts, ancient burial mounds...

REMBRANDT: I faint, I swoon... These images ravish mine eyes, massing and dissolving, suspended twixt light and dark. They are naught of this world, but hath the lightness and transparency of dreams. *(He remains engrossed in the book throughout.)*

POLLY: But what with Walter's... difficulties, I've had to narrow my focus even more. I have no room to move! My studio has all but disappeared. Gone are the long shots of breast and thigh, now I must content myself with nostrils and earlobes—hardly promising subjects for transformation...

WALTER: Don't listen to her. It's her most daring work yet!

POLLY: But I do the best I can... I call them my "Curiosities"... Though "Monstrosities" would be more apt, since I haven't sold a one... Not that I can lay all the blame at his feet... I was on this shrinking trajectory to begin with. It's just now I have no choice. At the rate we're going, I'll have to get one of those miniature cameras, pop it my mouth and shoot my teeth and gums... I can see it now... Ending my career with slides of... "Polly's Dental Delights".

REMBRANDT: *(Putting the book down.) Instruct me!*

POLLY: I beg your pardon?

REMBRANDT: Prithee, instruct *me* that I might learn this art!

POLLY: How to take pictures?

REMBRANDT: I am an excellent student, I warrant thee.

POLLY: I'm sure you are, but...

REMBRANDT: Pray, *teach* me!

POLLY: How could I possibly teach... *Rembrandt?*

REMBRANDT: Show me your brushes and your paint, forthwith!

POLLY: But these aren't paintings, they're *photographs!* I use a camera.

REMBRANDT: Not a camera obscura! 'Tis a device of which Vermeer and his students are exceeding fond. The artist's hand is removed, nay amputated... replaced by a common lens which allows e'en a child to trace what lies before him and this tracing... this base *copying* is now called art... 'Tis the devil's work, I warrant thee. And now I learn that you employ this dastardly device as well...

POLLY: Not a camera *obscura*, but a camera that uses *film! (Pointing to her field camera.)* That baby cost over three grand!

REMBRANDT: I beg you then, instruct me in its use, forthwith.

POLLY: Now?

REMBRANDT: In faith, these pictures have filled me with an excitement I have not felt since I first beheld Caravaggio's great works.

POLLY: *(Impressed.)* Caravaggio?

REMBRANDT: 'Tis a new vision, lady; indeed, a new way of *seeing* itself!

POLLY: A new way of *seeing?*

REMBRANDT: Thou hast pierced the skin, revealing our very thoughts and desires. Prithee, give me instruction in this bewitching art. I know not how much time remains for me here.

POLLY: But I was hoping to try and clean up a bit before the landlord comes.

WALTER: If I told you once, I told you a thousand times, you are *not* touching my things.

POLLY: *(To Walter.)* But darling...

REMBRANDT: I fear 'tis all a dream that will shortly end.

WALTER: There will be no, what you so blithely call... "cleaning up" around here. You've already done enough.

POLLY: *Me?* What did *I* do?

WALTER: You mean I have to tell you?

POLLY: *You're* the one who made this mess.

WALTER: You turn our life upside-down in an effort to accommodate your... your... fancy flying Dutchman. I hate to say it Polly, but you're turning into a...

POLLY: Yes?

WALTER: Turning into a...

REMBRANDT: *(Reaching out to Polly.)* Have pity on me!

POLLY: I'm waiting.

WALTER: TURNING INTO AN I DON'T KNOW WHAT! *(Heading towards the bathroom.)* I'm going to the bathroom to wash my hands.

POLLY: *(Under her breath.)* Try to finish before next month!

REMBRANDT: *(Grabbing her book of photographs.)* Good my lady, of all the wonders I have beheld since my arrival here... This... these photopos...

POLLY: Photographs.

REMBRANDT: Fill me with such amazement, I cannot speak. Their beauty far exceeds mine own poor scratchings. Give me instruction in this wondrous art. Verily, 'tis my last and most urgent request. *(Seizing her hand.)* Teach me forthwith! Let me be your pupil!

POLLY: You're serious about this?

REMBRANDT: *(To himself in Dutch.)* If only my powers of speech were equal to my powers with a brush.

POLLY: I beg your pardon?

REMBRANDT: *(Falling to his knees.)* I will still my tongue, dear lady. I know when I am defeated. As with all my disappointments, I must accept my fate.

POLLY: O.K., O.K., I'll teach you!

REMBRANDT: Thank you, thank you. With all my heart. *(He suddenly grabs her hands and starts kissing her palms. Polly gasps, pulling them away, electrified by his touch. They look at each for a moment, then she heads over to her studio area. He follows her.)*

POLLY: Well, the first order of business is to show you my camera. This baby's called a field camera and like all cameras, is made up of your five basic components: *(Showing him.)* body, lens, shutter, view-finder and focusing mechanism. It's more cumbersome than a 35 millimeter, more primitive than a digital, but it can't be beat for portraits a) because of the size of the film it uses b) because it puts *you* in control, and c) because it's just so damned beautiful. Also, the whole hood thing adds a certain mystique... Like you're practicing black magic or something, when in fact, the process couldn't be more logical. *(Picking up speed.)* This is the front lens, the aperture ring, the shutter speed dial, the cocking lever, the cable release, the lens board, the focusing knobs, the bellows... *(Turning it around.)* The rear standard, the film gate, the focusing screen and the bubble levels... But before we start, it's a good idea to get some preliminary readings with a Polaroid.

REMBRANDT: Prithee, stay a moment, my poor brain can't keep pace with the speed of thy discourse. I am not accustomed to women who... who... who...

POLLY: Know cameras like me.

REMBRANDT: Who possess such lively powers of... expression.

POLLY: Why, thank you.

REMBRANDT: As well as being as... as well as being as... *(Long pause.)*

POLLY: As being as...?

REMBRANDT: *(Barely audible.)* Comely as thou art.

POLLY: *(Emitting a little cry.)* Comely...
  (Silence as they gaze at each other.)

POLLY: *(Trying to be business-like.)* As I was saying, you really should use a Polaroid first. You know, to get the *lay* of the land...

REMBRANDT: *(Moving closer to her.)* Thelayoftheland...?

POLLY: No, no, not "lay" as in ... "getting laid"... Oh boy, here we go again... It's a saying, an expression, like "While the cat's away, the mice will play!" *(A shower of laughter.)* For God's sake, woman, get a grip... *(Pause.)* Where was I?... Oh, yes... a Polaroid is like a blueprint...

REMBRANDT: A preliminary sketch?

POLLY: Exactly! Now hold still.

REMBRANDT: *(Starts to strike a commanding pose.)* I fear there's scant room to move.

POLLY: See what I have to put up with? Wait a sec, let me kick some of this stuff out of the way, so I can fit you into the frame. *(She makes a little clearing for him and puts him in place.)* There we go. Now I'll be able to capture you, from top to bottom!
  (She moves several feet away from him and snaps his picture, setting off the flash.)

REMBRANDT: *(Staggering around the room.)* S'blood! I am blinded, blinded!

POLLY: It was just a flash.

REMBRANDT: Darkness envelops me!

POLLY: *(Laughing)* I'm sorry, I should have warned you first.

REMBRANDT: Verily, I am like sightless Tobit in my etchings. *(He grabs a staff-like object and starts creeping around the room, with one arm outstretched.)*

POLLY: Hang on, you'll be O.K. in a minute.

REMBRANDT: *(Approaching her, speaking like an old man.)* "Tobias, my son, I hear thy voice, yet I cannot see thee!"

POLLY: *(Grabbing his hand.)* Gotcha! *(Holding up three fingers front of his face.)* Alright, how many fingers?

REMBRANDT: *(Squinting.)* A curtain of lace floats before mine eyes. Would'st there be three?

POLLY: You got it! *(Pulling the picture out of the camera.)* Ah here, it comes... *(Showing it to him.)* Take a look.

REMBRANDT: Sweet Christ who died for our sins!

POLLY: This is nothing. You should see what they're doing with digital cameras these days! Polaroids are passé. Here! *(She hands it to him.)*

REMBRANDT: *(Examining it.)* Look you how it darkens before mine eyes.

POLLY: Just look through here and push this button.

REMBRANDT: *(Looking through the viewfinder.)* Merciful God, the image is so clear!

POLLY: What did I tell you?

REMBRANDT: *(Gesturing.)* Prithee, stand there.

POLLY: You want me to *pose* for you?

REMBRANDT: *(Softly.)* 'Tis my most ardent wish.

POLLY: You want *me*... to pose for you... *Rembrandt?*

REMBRANDT: In faith, t'would make me the happiest of men.

POLLY: But what should I *wear?* I mean, would you like me in some sort of costume, like one of Walter's robes? *(She grabs one and strikes a heroic pose.)* Or something more "Dutch"— with a ruff at the neck... *(She pulls some paper towel off a roll and crinkles it up around her throat, putting on the face of a severe Dutch matron.)* I'll wear anything you like. Your wish is my... Oh God, you don't want me to pose um... *nude*, do you? *(A shower of nervous laughter.)* Not that I'm self-conscious in front of a codpiece... I mean a camera... It's just that *I'm* always the one holding it... The *camera*, that is... not the codpiece... God, what's wrong with me? *(Laughter.)* I have no trouble photographing myself nude, but the idea of posing for someone else... For *you*... to be terrific... I mean, specific... For *Rembrandt!*
(More laughter.)

REMBRANDT: Dear lady, you misunderstand. I would never presume such a...

POLLY: Of course once the pictures are hung, everyone sees me naked anyway, so what difference does it make? I can't tell you how many openings I've been to where all the men are gaping at close-ups of my who-ha while trying to carry on a normal conversation with me. It's kind of sweet how ill at ease they are. I actually enjoy it, to tell you the truth, but then I've always been a little, perverse that way. I like to make guys sperm... I mean, *squirm. (More laugher.)*

REMBRANDT: If thou could'st be still a moment.

POLLY: Sorry, sorry... *(She slaps her hand over her mouth, goes rigid and stops breathing. Several moments pass. She starts to totter and turn red.)*

REMBRANDT: Prithee, breathe, dear lady... *breathe!*

(Polly gulps for breath.)

Now look into mine eyes.

POLLY: *(In a little voice.)* Into thine eyes?

(She looks at him and blushes deeply.)

I can't. You make me blush.

REMBRANDT: *(Getting her in focus.)* And soft, what charming blushes they are... Polly.

POLLY: You said my name!

REMBRANDT: *(With feeling.)* Polly Shaw.

POLLY: *(Likewise.)* Rembrandt.

REMBRANDT: And at long last thou call'st me by mine.

(Silence as they gaze at each other.)

POLLY: *(In an off-hand voice.)* I've been meaning to ask, what do your friends call you?

REMBRANDT: Why Rembrandt, of course.

POLLY: It just sounds so... I don't know... Well I guess I never imagined actually... using it... With *you*, I mean.

REMBRANDT: *(Looking at her through the camera.)* Verily, the sun doth pale beside thee. Thou art like unto a starry night, a burning bush. I am blinded, Polly Shaw.

(He takes her picture, the flash goes off.)

POLLY: *(Covering her eyes, crying out in surprise.)* Oh God!

(The following should be like a dance in slow motion. Rembrandt approaches her. She pulls back. He gently peels her hands off her eyes. She looks at the floor. He raises her chin. She takes a deep breath and they gaze into each other's eyes. Rembrandt lowers his head and tries to walk away, but Polly puts her hand on his arm, stopping him. They look at each other again. Polly smiles, takes his hand and places it on her breast. She then covers it with her hand as in his "Jewish Wedding" portrait. They gaze at each other again. Rembrandt pulls her into his arms. They kiss and kiss.)

WALTER: *(On his way into the room.)* I finally finished washing my hands. Miss me? *(He sees their embrace and stops in his tracks.)* Polly...? What the hell is going on?

(Polly and Rembrandt spring apart. Dead silence.)

WALTER: SAY SOMETHING, GODDAMNIT! *SPEAK TO ME, WOMAN!*
  (The silence deepens.)
  I'm waiting.
REMBRANDT: Prithee sir, if thou would'st allow me to interject…
WALTER: *(Cutting him off.)* Excuse me, but I believe I was addressing my *wife!*
  (Silence.)
REMBRANDT: In faith, I'm loathe to surmise what black thoughts must be coursing through thy brain, I would'st…
WALTER: *Did you hear what I said?*
POLLY: *(To Rembrandt.)* Let me…
  (More silence.)
WALTER: *(Circling her like a wild animal.)* Yes?
  (The silence deepens.)
REMBRANDT: 'Twas merely a *pose.* She was…
WALTER: WILL YOU SHUT UP?!
POLLY: You don't have to yell.
WALTER: *(Dripping with sarcasm.)* Then how do you suggest I try to get through his numbèd skull, dear lady?
POLLY: Darling, please!
WALTER: Please *what?* Try not to notice that you were in each other's arms when I walked into the room?
POLLY: I can explain.
WALTER: I wish you would!
  (Polly tries to take Rembrandt's arm, but he walks to the other side of the room. She glowers at him.)
POLLY: Rembrandt?… *(Then to Walter.)* He said he wanted to try my camera, so I was showing him how it works and then, then… *(She trails off.)*
  (Silence.)
WALTER: Yes?
POLLY: He said he wanted me to pose for him. That I was like a rising sun, a starry night, a burning bush…
  (Rembrandt groans.)
WALTER: And…
POLLY: *(The words just pop out.)* I love him.
WALTER: *I beg your pardon?*
POLLY: I said, I love him!
WALTER: But he's not real!
REMBRANDT: Sirrah, one moment, I pray…

WALTER: He's a ghost, an apparition, a figment of your imagination.

POLLY: *I don't care what he is, I love him just the same!*

REMBRANDT: My arrival here is a mystery, I grant you. But I assure you I am very much alive, Sirrah.

WALTER: The name's *Walter!*

REMBRANDT: There is such a tumult in my blood, I feel the stirrings of ten thousand men!

(Polly swoons.)

WALTER: Yeah, yeah, I can just imagine the line you were feeding her. *(In Rembrandt's voice.)* "Thou art so much lovelier than my first two wives who also inspired my... *(With an erotic gesture.)* bursting *brush!* But thou, oh radiant damsel with the burning bush... thou wake'st my flesh in ways I ne'er dream'd possible... And after I finish these photographs, perhaps you might lend me a few thousand *guilders* to pay off some of my debts."

POLLY: *Walter?!*

WALTER: Do you know how many women this guy bedded and then fleeced?

REMBRANDT: Sirrah, you offend me!

WALTER: Unlike most people, I read all the crap that accompanies these shows. *(Grabbing one of his many brochures and shaking it in her face.)* Your friend here was very bad news! His first wife, who happened to come with a considerable dowry, wasn't even dead for a year when he took up with his son's nurse, Geertge Dircks...

(Rembrandt groans.)

WALTER: Next came eighteen year old Hendrickje Stoffels, his delectable new housekeeper. She didn't have any money, but oh, what she could do with a feather duster, if you get my drift...

(Rembrandt buries his head in his hands.)

WALTER: But how would he dispose of his loyal Geertge who had gotten used to the comfort of his bed? Why send her off to a house of detention. Which is exactly what he did.

REMBRANDT: *(Sputtering with rage.)* 'Tis slander most vile! Slander, I say!

WALTER: He kicked her out without so much as a "Goodbye" or "*Guten tag*" and took up with blushing Hendrickje and her ubiquitous feather duster... The art world was scandalized—the great Rembrandt bedding one serving girl after another. And who knew what was going on in his *atelier* with Amsterdam's most "liberated" women posing for him?

REMBRANDT: *(Lunging at Walter.)* Enough! I will still thy poisoned tongue!

WALTER: *(Grabbing a stage foil and slicing it through the air.)* Avaunt, knave and fight me like a man! *(He tosses one to Rembrandt.)*

REMBRANDT: *(Catching it and slicing the air just as impressively.)* Knave, you say? Thou call'st me *knave?!*

POLLY: *(Under her breath.)* He fences too!

WALTER: *(Lunging at him.)* Shit head!

REMBRANDT: Hedge hog!!

WALTER: Asshole!

(They launch into dazzling sword play.)

REMBRANDT: Spotted snake!!!

WALTER: Scum bag!

REMBRANDT: Dung beetle!!!

POLLY: *(Enjoying every minute of it.)* Boys, boys...

WALTER: This charade has gone far enough! Who do you think you are barging in here like some common thief?

REMBRANDT: My sudden appearance at your doorstep is as much a mystery to me, as it is to thee, Sirrah.

WALTER: How many times do I have to tell you? The name's *Walter!* Furthermore, you know *exactly* what you're up to, and I won't stand for it anymore!

(He lunges at him, setting off a new flurry of sword play.)

WALTER: You play the beleaguered innocent, but I see right through you!

REMBRANDT: Then your vision is keener than mine, my lord, for I ha' ne'er been so bewildered in all my days: C.D.s, O.C.D.s, retrospectives, gift shops, photographs... these strange clothes... I know not if I ha' been put here to play the prodigal son or the fool.

WALTER: From where I'm standing, I'd say *I'm* the one being played for the fool!

POLLY: They're fighting over me...

WALTER: You're trying to run off with my wife!

POLLY: *Me!*

REMBRANDT: But 'twas she who pursued *me*, placing my hand upon her breast as in my painting of "The Jewish Bride". 'Twas *she* who cast the net, I swear it!

WALTER: And what a net it is! Snagging all manner of prey in its shining folds— fish, fowl, man and beast. Don't think you're the first to be caught in its web, Rembrandt Van Rijn. It extends for miles... No ones knows its reach more than me, for no one loves her more than me; no one needs her more than me; and when she finally leaves—as she's bound to leave—no one will be more bereft than me. But who can blame her? *(Gazing around the room.)* Living like this… Once her prince, I've become her jailer… Only habit keeps her by my side. The rhythms of a long shared life—waking, eating, the occasional movie, dinner out and then back to sleep again. We finish each other's thoughts and complete each others sentences… It was only a matter of time before she'd dig her way out. But with you—a scoundrel and a rake… You call yourself an artist and indeed you are… *Sirrah!* A *con* artist of the first order!

(He drops his sword and lunges for Rembrandt's throat. They fall into an awkward wrestling match, biting and kneeing each other in the groin.)

POLLY: STOP IT, STOP IT! SOMEONE'S GOING TO GET HURT!

WALTER: That's the point my dear, to knock his fucking teeth out!

(They eventually lose steam and collapse on the bed, suddenly two old men, gasping for air.)

POLLY: *(Rushing to Rembrandt's side.)* Are you alright?

WALTER: Is *he* alright? What about *me?* I'm your *husband,* for Christ's sake!

POLLY: *(Taking Rembrandt's hands.)* Did he hurt you? *(To Walter.)* If you so much as scratched these hands, you're in big trouble!

WALTER: Not if he's making out with my wife!

(Walter lunges at Rembrandt again and starts choking him.)

POLLY: *That's it! I'm leaving!*

(The two struggle again. Rembrandt finally pries Walter's hands off his throat and retreats to a corner.)

POLLY: *(Heading for the door.)* Did you hear me? I said I'm leaving. I can't live like this anymore!

WALTER: Like what? *What?*

POLLY: With all your craziness!

WALTER: What craziness?

POLLY: *What craziness?* You mean I have to tell you? *(Pointing at his stacks of costumes.)* That! *(At all the locks on the door.)* And that! Your incantations and exhortations, your phobias and rituals, your rages and bellowing, your snoring and peeing…

WALTER: Now just one minute, I happen to have an enlarged prostate. And I bet your fancy admirer over there has one too! He just doesn't know it because the prostate gland wasn't discovered until 1803, by, by… Peter Prostate, court physician to William the Beside-Himself.

POLLY: Plus… *plus* Comstock's coming to evict us in a couple of hours and I'd just as soon not be here when he shows up.

WALTER: But I love you.

POLLY: Yeah, yeah…

WALTER: I do!

POLLY: Sure, you care about me in the abstract, but your obsessions take precedence.

WALTER: *(Upset.)* I have a disorder.

POLLY: Do tell.

WALTER: I can't help myself.

POLLY: Well, I can help *myself* and I'm getting out of here before it's too late.

WALTER: Where are you going?

(A pause as she considers.)

POLLY: *(Rushing to Rembrandt's side.)* With him!

WALTER: And where exactly might that be? Where he's *going*, that is… Back to 17th century Holland in the middle of a plague? That sounds like fun. Is that what you had in mind? Running sores, rotting flesh and bleeding at the mouth together… Of course, there's always staying put in the good old U.S. of A. Perhaps in this very neighborhood, except real estate prices have gone through the roof, which is why Comstock wants to evict us so badly, but with a little luck you could probably find something… Not in Manhattan, mind you, but maybe in the Bronx or Queens… And there's always Hoboken… Hell, you might even find a place with a little back-yard. You could have Sunday barbecues with Vermeer and the whole swinging crowd from Delft… S'blood! This is sounding better and better.

POLLY: *(Getting teary.)* I just want to be with him.

WALTER: *(To Rembrandt.)* But do you want to be with *her?* *(Lowering his voice.)* A woman of her age?

POLLY: *Walter?!*

WALTER: Don't worry, of course he wants to be with you. You're his green card, so to speak. But just wait 'til someone younger and more succulent comes along. Not that you don't have your succulent moments…

POLLY: I don't have to listen to this. *(Trying to pull Rembrandt towards the door.)* Come on, let's go.

WALTER: *(Blocking her way.)* I have just one question.

POLLY: Goodbye, Walter.

WALTER: Is this about wanting to go off with *him* or wanting to get out of *here?*

POLLY: What's the difference?

WALTER: All the difference, my love. Because if it's a change of scene you're after, I can do something about that.

POLLY: What? Get rid of all your crap? I've heard that before! *(Taking his arm.)* Come on Rembrandt, it's getting late.

REMBRANDT: *(Grabbing her camera.)* Verily, I will follow thee 'til the end of time, for thou hast op't mine eyes and pierced my very soul.

WALTER: *(To himself.)* And so the hour has come to don my kingly garb and play my final scene.

(Walter puts on a robe and starts tearing down the stacks of costumes as he recites from Shakespeare's Othello, *Act III, Scene iii.)*

WALTER: "I had been happy, if the general camp,
Pioners and all, had tasted her sweet body,
So I had nothing known. O now, for ever
Farewell the tranquil mind! Farewell content!..."
(To Polly.) You cannot leave, you are my wife!
"Farewell the plumed troop, and the big wars,
That make ambition virtue! O, farewell!..."
(To Polly.) We've been together almost fifty years. That's half a century!
"Farewell the neighing steed, and the shrill trump,
The spirit-stirring drum, th'ear-piercing fife,
The royal banner, and all quality,
Pride, pomp and circumstance of glorious war!..."
(To Polly.) Your heart beats in my chest and your gaze flows through my eyes.
"And, O you mortal engines, whose rude throats
Th' immortal Jove's dread clamours counterfeit,
Farewell!..."
(To Polly.) Give me a hand Polly, for you are my muse and my greatest joy.
"Othello's occupation's gone!"[1]
(To Polly.) Move, woman, Comstock will be here in less than two hours.
(Polly joins him in the destruction.)

POLLY: *(Singing.)* "London bridge is falling down, falling down, falling down; London bridge is falling down, my fair lady."

WALTER AND POLLY: "How then shall we build it up, build it up, build it up? How then shall we build it up, my fair lady?... Build it up with silver and gold, silver and gold, silver and gold; build it up with silver and gold, my fair lady..."

REMBRANDT: *(Overlapping.)* What will become of me now? Whither wilst I go? All have forsaken me.

(He sinks to his knees and starts to pray as they dismantle the room around him.)

"Our father who art in heaven,

Hallowed be thy name.

Thy kingdom come,

Thy will be done

On earth as it is in heaven.

Give us this day our daily bread.

And forgive us our trespasses,

As we forgive those who trespass against us.

And lead us not into temptation;

But deliver us from evil:

For thine is the kingdom

And the power and the glory,

For ever and ever. Amen."

(Blackout.)

SCENE FOUR

Two hours later. The loft is transformed. The bulk of Walter's costumes are gone and a golden setting sun streams through the cleared windows. Rembrandt has changed back into his original clothes. He stands as he first appeared in his Kensington self-portrait, holding his palette, maul stick and brushes as Polly photographs him. It's quiet except for the clicking of her camera which is attached to a tripod. She works with concentration and grace. Walter is nowhere in sight.

POLLY: I can't get used to this light... That it's coming through our windows... *our* windows. I'd completely forgotten about sunsets... well about any kind of sun for that matter. It's been like living in a dungeon. Now I know why all our plants died. It makes one wonder about the deleterious effects the darkness may have had on *us*... I saw this nature show on TV once about the various creatures that inhabit the sea and the ones that live on the very bottom, miles from the sun, in total darkness are all blind. And not only blind, but albino as well. They have no pigment in their skin, but are milky white. Milky white and blind... Part centipede and part shrimp, with millions of legs and long wavy antennae. They spend their brief lives scuttling around the ocean floor, struggling to survive... Bleached mutants... Like us. *(A prolonged shudder.)* It gives me the willies just thinking about them! So this sudden... bath of light makes me feel the color returning to my cheeks and hands and arms and legs... Look at me! I'm a rosy girl! And look at me, looking at you! My skin burning brighter still. I'm seeing again! Taking pictures again! *In the light of day! (She snaps several pictures and whoops with joy.)*

REMBRANDT: *(Starting to get restless.)* Prithee give me leave to break my pose. I ask for one moment, no more.

POLLY: I want to capture you as you first appeared to us.

REMBRANDT: Like a rotting timber, I fear I might topple to the ground.

POLLY: You'll never wear these clothes again.

REMBRANDT: My vision blurs...

POLLY: You'll blend into the crowd in modern dress. No one will know who you are.

REMBRANDT: Moths swarm before mine eyes...

POLLY: I've never done a portrait of anyone but myself.

REMBRANDT: *(Waving them away.)* Shoo! Shoo! Shoo!

POLLY: *(Gazing at his Kensington poster.)* Damn! Something's missing. Let's trade places a minute, maybe you can figure it out.

REMBRANDT: I stand before thee, yet feel I am breaking apart, like a raft, tossed on a stormy sea. And strangest of all, the sensation is familiar to me.

POLLY: We call those, "déjà vus". *(Going to him, taking his palette and brushes.)* O.K. Just pretend I'm you and tell me what's missing.

REMBRANDT: *(Breaking his pose.)* Finally! *(Heading towards her camera.)* Would thou *had'st* been Rembrandt in all thy loveliness!

POLLY: Don't focus on me, just tell me what's missing from the picture at large.

REMBRANDT: *(Looking at her through the camera.)* Had Rembrandt been a *woman!* 'Tis marvelous strange to think on!

POLLY: The background, the ambience... What is it?

REMBRANDT: Ah hah, I see't!

POLLY: See what?

REMBRANDT: The hemispheres.

POLLY: *Hemispheres?*

REMBRANDT: The two half-circles behind me.

POLLY: Of course!

REMBRANDT: Come, let me fill them in!

(He grabs his palette and a brush and expertly paints two perfect half circles on the wall.)

(As he works.) In faith, 'tis these very markings that pose the paradox. Peruse the portrait closely and you'll see mine hands to be a blur of activity, whereas the hemispheres they wrought are fix't and exact.

POLLY: Oh my God, you're painting two perfect circles, *free-hand!*

REMBRANDT: I compound the paradox by denying them the space to complete themselves. For all their precision, they are as unfinished as the hands that painted them.

POLLY: *(Yelling.)* Walter, come quick… Rembrandt's painting on our wall!

REMBRANDT: And therein lies the pact twixt artist and viewer. 'Tis the former who sets the scene, but the latter who must complete it—whether 'tis the sacrifice of Isaac, the blinding of Samson or fathoming this poor ruin. But hold, the pact becomes more complex still. For what in faith, doth the artist *see?* What does fashion decree he *reveal* and common sense suggest he *conceal?*

(Walter enters. He looks great. He's changed into a sports jacket and nice pair of pants.)

POLLY: *(Admiringly.)* Look at you!

WALTER: *(Bowing.)* Madame…

REMBRANDT: In faith, the silk merchant and his blushing wife present a most enviable pair as they pose, but do I record what I see? Are those flickers of pain that chase so fitfully 'cross her face? Hath she perchance contracted the plague? Are the deadly blooms spreading o'er her groin, as she gazes past her husband towards her grave? And from whence comes that hectic light in *his* eye? Is he perchance up to mischief? Bedding a rosy whore or stealing from his partners' till? Prithee advise me. Do I let the sour smell of humanity fill their lungs, or do I render them as they wish to be seen?

WALTER: Hey, where did those circles come from?

REMBRANDT: *(Tottering.)* Marry, I feel passing strange of a sudden.

POLLY: *(To Walter.)* That's what I was yelling about.

REMBRANDT: 'Tis very like the feeling I had whilst reaching for the scrap of bread that tumbled out the window this morning.

POLLY: He painted them.

REMBRANDT: As if I were here and yet not here.

WALTER: No way!

REMBRANDT: I fear 'tis all a dream…

POLLY: I'm telling you, *Rembrandt* painted on *our* wall! *(She resumes photographing him.)*

REMBRANDT: *(Starts staggering around the room.)* And I, poor fool, the hapless dreamer— struggling still to leave my mark—Rembrandt van Rijn, ninth child of Harmen Gerritsz van Rijn and Neeltgen Willemsdr van Zuytbrouk born the fifteenth day of July, 1606… I grow faint, I swoon, I break apart…

POLLY: Don't move, I haven't finished!

(The light around Rembrandt becomes increasingly intense.)

REMBRANDT: *(Staggering in circles, his arms outstretched.)* Hendrickje? Hendrickje…? Where art thou? I was on the stairs to retrieve my scrap o' bread when you vanished. Nay, 'twas *I* who vanished… In a dream most strange…

(There's an explosion and Rembrandt disappears in a brilliant flash of light.)

POLLY: Hey, wait for me! *(Running around the room, looking for him.)* I thought we were going together!

WALTER: *(Approaching Polly.)* Easy, easy…

POLLY: *(Starting to break down.)* Come back, come back…

WALTER: Let him go.

POLLY: *(Sobbing.)* But he promised…

WALTER: *(Wrapping his arms around her.)* He couldn't have taken you, no matter how much he wanted to.

POLLY: *(Struggling with him.)* Rembrandt… Rembrandt…

WALTER: And God knows he wanted to.

POLLY: COME BAAAAAAAACK!

WALTER: He's gone.

POLLY: But I loved him.

WALTER: Slippery son of a bitch!

POLLY: He inspired me.

WALTER: He inspires everyone! He's *Rembrandt*, for Christ's sake!

POLLY: He widened my focus.

WALTER: But who cleared the way?

POLLY: *(Succumbing to a fresh bout of weeping.)* Oh Walter…

WALTER: Though I shudder to think what might replace it—newspapers, phone books, restaurant menus, Styrofoam food containers… As good old Spinoza said, "Nature abhors a vacuum."

POLLY: He left, he left…

WALTER: You'll recover.

POLLY: You think so?

WALTER: You have no choice.

(Silence)

POLLY: *(Spying something on the floor.)* What's that?

WALTER: Oh my God…

POLLY: *(Picking it up.)* It looks like a piece of bread.

WALTER: It can't be…

POLLY: *(Sniffing it.)* Yes, it's bread.

WALTER: It's the scrap of bread he dropped out the window!

POLLY: And it landed here!

> *(Silence as they gaze at it. Polly suddenly pops it into her mouth.)*

WALTER: Polly, that's over three hundred years old!

POLLY: Mmm, not bad…

> *(There's a knock on the door.)*

POLLY: *(Freezing)* It's him! He came back!

> *(The knocking gets louder.)*

COMSTOCK: Open up! It's Comstock!

WALTER AND POLLY: *(Looking at each other, panic-stricken.)* Comstock!

COMSTOCK: With the New York Fire Department!

WALTER AND POLLY: *With the New York Fire Department!*

ANOTHER VOICE: Alright, you two. We know you're in there, so why don't you just open the door and save us all a lot of trouble.

WALTER: *(In a falsetto voice.)* Just a minute… *(Rushing to the C.D. player while doing a riff as Blanche Du Bois.)* A girl wants to look her best when company comes. I just stepped off the streetcar, Mr. Comstock and haven't had a chance to freshen up. Why, I haven't even bathed or powdered my nose. I want to look fresh and pretty for you, is that a mortal sin?

POLLY: Darling, what are you doing?

WALTER: I'm giving you something to photograph, *someone* to photograph.

COMSTOCK: *(Banging on the door.)* WHAT'S GOING ON IN THERE?

WALTER: *Art, Mr. Comstock! Art is being made!*

> *(He rushes to the C.D. player and turns on the dreamy "Saturday Night Waltz" from Copeland's* Rodeo *and launches into an Agnes de Mille type ballet.)*

COMSTOCK: OPEN THE FUCKING DOOR!

WALTER: Go Polly! Do your stuff!

POLLY: *(Starts photographing him.)* Yes! Yes! Yes! Yes!

COMSTOCK: DID YOU HEAR WHAT I SAID?

> *(Walter's dancing becomes more inspired.)*

POLLY: *(Following him, snapping away.)* Yes! Yes! Yes! *(etc.)*

ANOTHER VOICE: OPEN THE DOOR OR WE'RE BREAKING IT DOWN ON THE COUNT OF THREE.

POLLY: Go on, you get it.

WALTER: But you're closer.

POLLY: No, I want you to get it.

WALTER: You want me to open the door... Just like that?

POLLY: Just like that. On the count of three. *(Pushing him towards it.)* Go on, you can do it. Just undo the locks and let them in.

(Walter drops to his knees and looks at them, trying to resist their power. He can't.)

WALTER: *(Lowering his head, incanting in his altered voice.)* One, two, buckle my shoe; three, four, lock the door; five, six, pick up sticks...

POLLY: *(Shaking him.)* No, Walter... Stop it! *Stop it!* That's over. Just turn the knobs...

COMSTOCK: ONE...

WALTER: Seven, eight, lay them straight... Objects in the mirror are closer than they appear. By far, by far, by far, by far...

POLLY: *(Trying to restrain him, overlapping.)* You don't have to do that anymore. You're safe. You got rid of everything! No one's going to throw us out! You cleaned up! You finally did it! After all these years! You got rid of your crap and came back to the land of the living! You're alright now! You're safe!

COMSTOCK: TWO...

WALTER: *(Overlapping her.)* Yet oh so near, so near, so near, so near... Boy oh boy oh boy oh boyo, we don't want any accidents here. No Siree, Bob! No dead bodies piled up on this side of the road, thank you very much! And that means you, Eddie, Franz, Pepe and Wilhelm...

COMSTOCK: THREE!

(Polly quickly pulls Walter out of the way. She shelters him in her arms as the door is pushed in with a mighty crash. They bow their heads as a blinding light floods over them.)

AND THE CURTAIN QUICKLY FALLS

Classyass
by Caleen Sinnette Jennings

BIOGRAPHY

Caleen Sinnette Jennings is Professor of Theatre at American University in Washington, D.C. She teaches acting, playwriting, and theatre history among other courses. She also directs for the mainstage and is a two-time recipient of a Kennedy Center/American College Theatre Festival award for Meritorious Achievement in Directing. She is a two-time nominee for the Charles MacArthur Award for Outstanding New Play (Helen Hayes Awards), and in 1999 she received a $10,000 grant from the Kennedy Center Fund For New American Plays for her play *Inns & Outs*. Her play *Playing Juliet/Casting Othello* was performed at the Folger Elizabethan Theatre in 1998. Four of her plays have been published by Dramatic Publishing Company, and two of her children's plays have been published by New Plays, Incorporated.

HUMANA FESTIVAL PRODUCTION

Classyass premiered at the Humana Festival of New American Plays in April 2002. It was directed by Rajendra Ramoon Maharaj with the following cast:

Ama . . . . Jason Cornwell
BigB . . . . Nikki E. Walker
Miles . . . . Robert Beitzel

and the following production staff:

Scenic Designer . . . . Paul Owen
Costume Designer . . . . John White
Lighting Designer. . . . . Paul Werner
Sound Designer . . . . Colbert Davis
Properties Designer . . . . Doc Manning
Stage Manager. . . . . Heather Fields
Assistant Stage Manager . . . . Debra A. Freeman
Dramaturg . . . . Timothy Douglas

CHARACTERS

AMA: or Amadeus. Black college freshman.

BIGB: or Belinda. Black woman, 20, dressed like a street person.

MILES: White college senior and radio station manager.

Nikki E. Walker and Jason Cornwell
in *Classyass*

26th Annual Humana Festival of New American Plays
Actors Theatre of Louisville, 2002
photo by Larry Hunt

Classyass

A small room that serves as a modest campus radio studio at Bellmore College. Ama speaks into the mic with a suave broadcaster's voice.

AMA: Okay you Bellmore boneheads, that was Tchaikovsky's *1812 Overture*, bet those cannons busted a couple of you dozers. Perfect for 3:47 a.m. on a cold, rainy Thursday in finals week. It's the end of the time at the end of the line. Study on, people. Bang out papers. Cram the facts. Justify that exorbitant tuition and make Bellmore College proud. I'M FEELING Y'ALL! Especially those of you studying for Calc 801 with Professor Cobb. Call me if you have a clue about question #3 on page 551. You're listening to "Casual Classics," because you don't have to be uptight and white to love classical music. This is WBMR, the radio station of Bellmore College. Miles Morgan is your station manager. Ama here. That's Amadeus Waddlington, with you 'til 6 a.m. Guzzle that warm Red Bull and cold Maxwell House. Here's music to squeeze your brains by. It's Dvořák's *New World Symphony* comin' atcha. *(He puts on the CD, grabs a beer and a huge textbook, and sprawls out on the floor. A bold knock interrupts him. He shouts.)* Go to hell, Miles. I like *New World*! *(Another knock.)* Okay, okay. I'll play Beethoven's *Symphony #1* next. Lots of strings, okay? *(Persistent knocking.)* Damn!
(Ama strides to the door and opens it. BigB strides in, carrying shopping bags and waving several faxes.)

BIGB: You messed up, boy!

AMA: Excuse me?

BIGB: And your smart-assed faxes made it worse!

AMA: Do I know you?

BIGB: *(Examining the mic and CDs.)* I want a public apology.

AMA: Don't touch that! Listen, whoever you are…

BIGB: Whomever!

AMA: Whatever!

BIGB: You ain't got a clue who I am.

AMA: A fabulous person, no doubt, but you've got to go. This is a classical music show and I've got a killer calculus final tomorrow.

BIGB: Color me compassionate. You're shorter than I thought. But I figured right about you being a dumbass. I told you right here…

(BigB shows Ama the faxes and he realizes who she is.)

AMA: Oh my God…you're…BigB! I thought you were…

BIGB: …a brother, I know, 'cause I ain't hearing none of your bullshit. Well, I thought you was a white boy, and I was right.

AMA: Look, I don't know what you want…

BIGB: How long I been faxing you, moron? You said the "Gloria" was by Fauré…

AMA: …As I told you one thousand faxes ago, "Gloria" is by Poulenc and when I played it, I said Poulenc…

BIGB: …Fauré!

AMA: …Poulenc!

BIGB: I know what I heard, you arrogant shithead.

AMA: Does that BigB stand for "bitch" or "borderline psychotic"?

BIGB: I ain't even 'pressed by you trottin' out them tired SAT joints. I'm down at the Palmer Street Shelter, which you knew by the headin' on the fax, and you just figured I didn't know shit about classical music.

AMA: BigB, I'm truly flattered that you even listen, but you don't…

BIGB: My crew at the shelter want to come up here and kick yo ass.

AMA: Whoa, whoa there. I'm sorry about our misunderstanding, okay?

BIGB: And that s'posed to float my boat?

AMA: Let's be calm, B?

BIGB: BigB to you, and I know you ain't s'posed to be drinkin' beer up in here.

AMA: You never saw that.

BIGB: Now I got two things on ya. This gonna be what they call an interesting evening. *(Thumbing through his calculus book.)* This the shit probably got your brain too messed up to know your Poulenc from your Fauré. *(She sips Ama's beer.)*

AMA: Don't do that. Suppose I have a social disease?

BIGB: Ha! Bet you still a cherry.

AMA: Suppose YOU have a social disease?

BIGB: I'll just call your Dean and tell him I caught it sippin' outta your freshman-ass beer can.

AMA: What do you want from me?

BIGB: You made me look stupid in front of my crew.

AMA: Look, I'm just a nerd playing dead white men's music. Why do you even listen to my show?

BIGB: So a sister like me ain't s'posed to be a classical music affectionado.

AMA: The word's "afficionado"…

BIGB: Boy, I'm feelin' better 'n better about bustin' yo ass.

AMA: This is like something out of Scorsese. If I apologize for the thing I DID NOT DO, will you go?

BIGB: Maybe. Or maybe I'll stay and watch you work awhile.

AMA: It's against the rules.

BIGB: Lots of things against the rules, freshman boy. Don't mean they ain't delicious to do.

AMA: If my station manager comes in…

BIGB: Tell him I'm studyin' witcha, that we putting the "us" in calculus.

AMA: Well, you don't exactly look like a student.

BIGB: Well, you don't exactly look like a asshole, but you the poster boy. Where you get "Ama" from anyway?

AMA: Wolfgang *Amadeus* Mozart. My dad's a classical musician.

BIGB: Oh yeah? Where he play at?

AMA: He sells insurance. No major symphony'll hire him.

BIGB: I know that's right. Oughta be called "sym-phoney," like phoney baloney, right?

AMA: *(Patronizingly.)* That's very clever, BigB, but I've got a lot of work to do. How about I give you and your people at the shelter a, what do you call it, a "shout out." Right in the middle of Dvořák. How would you like that? *(Ama goes to the mic, but BigB stops him.)*

BIGB: How you gonna interrupt *New World Symphony* and mess up everybody's flow? You crazy, Amadeus Waddlington. You also a lucky bastard. BigB like you. She gonna take it easy on you.

AMA: Why does your use of the third person chill my blood?

BIGB: Take me to dinner and we cool.

AMA: What?

BIGB: Over there to the Purple Pheasant, where the President of Bellmore College eat at!

AMA: …Are you crazy? I don't have that kind of…

BIGB: …an' buy me a present…

AMA: …a present? I'm broke!

BIGB: …somethin', how they say it, "droll." Yeah, "droll" and "ironic"! Like a CD of "Dialogues of the Carmelites" by *POULENC*. I can see you 'n me sittin' up in the Purple Pheasant, chucklin' over our little in-joke, sippin' a half-ass California *pinot grigio.*

AMA: Who the hell writes your material?

BIGB: And pick me up in a shiny new car.

AMA: Hello? Freshmen aren't allowed to have cars.

BIGB: Beg, borrow or steal, my brother, but you better have yo ass waiting for me at the shelter tomorrow night at 7:30. And don't shit in your khakis. My boys'll watch your back in the 'hood.

AMA: You're delusional.

BIGB: Oh, you insultin' BigB, now? You don't wanna be seen with her?

AMA: I'd love to be seen with her...you! I'd give my right arm to have the whole town and the President of Bellmore see me escort you into the Purple Pheasant. Hell, I'd even invite my parents. But I'm a scholarship student with five bucks to my name.

BIGB: *(Sniffing him.)* Ya wearing cashmere and ya reek of Hugo Boss. Don't even try to play me, boy.

AMA: Maxed out credit cards, BigB. I'm just a half-ass, wannabe freshman with a little gig, trying to make some headway with Mr. Mastercard. I'll apologize on air. I'll stamp your name on my forehead, I'll run naked down the quad and bark like a dog...

BIGB: ...anything but take me out. You're a snob, Amadeus Waddlington. You a broke-ass, cashmere-wearin', shit-talkin' loser who don't know his Poulenc from his Fauré... *(BigB finishes off Ama's beer.)* ...and drinks lite beer! My crew was right. Ya need a beat down.

AMA: BigB, please...

BIGB: See, I be down at the shelter, diggin' on ya voice early in the mornin'. People say you ain't shit, but you gotta way a soundin' all mellow an' sexy. And when you spank that Rachmaninoff, oh yeah, baby! So when you screw up the Poulenc I send a friendly fax to point out yo error and help yo ass out...

AMA: And I appreciate...

BIGB: But you had to get up in my grill wit that, "what-do-you-know-about-classical-music-you-stupid ass-homeless-crackhead" kind of attitude. *(She starts to leave.)* Well, Palmer Street crew will be very happy to whup yo behind.

AMA: *(Stopping her.)* I didn't mean to give you attitude. I'm sorry. I'm broke, I swear! I'll show you my bills, I'll show you my bank statements. Isn't there anything else I can do, BigB? Please!

(Pause. BigB looks Ama up and down, to his great discomfort.)

BIGB: Kiss me.

AMA: What did you say?

BIGB: I'm gettin' somethin' outta this deal. Kiss me.

AMA: But...

BIGB: Not one a them air flybys, neither. Gimme some tongue!

AMA: Oh God.

BIGB: *(She advances on him.)* Lay it on me, Amadeus Waddlington. Kiss me or kiss yo ass goodbye.

AMA: *(Backing away, near tears.)* This isn't Scorsese, it's John Woo.

BIGB: Come on classyass, pucker up!

> *(BigB tackles Ama and plants a long, deep kiss on him. When she lets him go, Ama steps back, looks at her, touches his mouth, and faints. BigB kneels calmly beside him. Her entire demeanor changes. Her voice is rich, cultured, her grammar impeccable. She sits him up and gives him a few light slaps.)*
>
> Hey! Hey! Ama? Damn it, Amadeus Waddlington, wake up!
>
> *(Miles Morgan enters drinking a beer.)*

MILES: Who are you, and what the hell did you do to Waddlington?

BIGB: He fainted. Get something cold.

> *(Miles pours cold beer on Ama's head. Ama comes to.)*

BIGB: Have you sufficiently recuperated Mr. Waddlington?

MILES: *(To BigB.)* Hey, you look familiar...where do I know you from? ...in the paper...from the shelter. You're... Man you sure look...different! Oh my God...You're not going to tell your father about the beer, are you? I'm a fifth-year senior trying to graduate...

BIGB: Just make sure he's okay.

> *(Miles bends down to Ama who grabs him by the collar. They whisper urgently, while BigB thumbs through the CDs and eavesdrops, greatly amused.)*

AMA: Oh God. Oh God! I kissed her!

MILES: Way to go, man!

AMA: I'm gonna die!

MILES: She's that good, huh? Bet she's a knockout under all that stuff she's wearing. You all going to a costume party or something?

AMA: Don't you get it, Miles? I kissed her!

MILES: Lucky bastard! Kickin' it with Dean Stafford's daughter.

AMA: *(After a beat.)* What did you say?

MILES: That's Belinda Stafford, Dean Stafford's youngest daughter! She dropped out of Bellmore to work at the shelter. It was all in the papers and everything.

BIGB: *(Handing him money.)* Thanks for the beer and the amusement, Mr. Waddlington.

AMA: Is this true? Are you really…?

BIGB: *(Removing her dirty garments and putting them in a bag.)* I work night shifts at the Palmer Street Shelter. You can imagine that some of the women find it hard to sleep. Your music and your incredibly boring commentary usually do the trick. Everything was fine until you responded so rudely to my fax. You assumed because it came from the shelter…

AMA: No…I just…I didn't…

BIGB: You're an arrogant, ill-informed elitist, Amadeus Waddlington. I've known guys like you all my life. It broke Daddy's heart when I dropped out of Bellmore, but your faxes reminded me exactly why I did it. So, I decided to teach you a lesson. You're not going to die from my kiss, but I hope you won't forget what it felt like to think that you were. *(She scatters the faxes over his head and starts to exit.)*

MILES: Now, uh, Ms. Stafford, you wouldn't mention this to your father…

BIGB: I've got people without winter coats on my mind.

AMA: *(Rushes to her.)* BigB, I mean Belinda, I mean, Ms. Stafford, please wait. I get a lot of shit from people about this show and I thought you were just another brother hassling me. I don't have an attitude about the shelter because I've got too many poor folks in my own family. I'm sorry about the vibe. Can I make it up to you? Maybe put in some hours at the shelter?

BIGB: If you think you can hack it. I picked out some CDs for you to play. My people sleep well to Debussy. I'll be checkin' you! *(She puts on her headphones as she exits.)*

MILES: And you won't mention this to… *(Miles exits calling after Belinda. Ama suddenly remembers he's on air. He runs to the mic.)*

AMA: Yo, my people, was that dope? Bet the *New World Symphony* woke yo asses up! Hey, I'm still waiting to speak to anybody with a clue to #3 on page 551 in Cobb's calculus class. Anybody? It's 3:59 on WBMR the voice of Bellmore College. I'm Amadeus Waddlington and this is "Casual Classics," because you don't have to be uptight and white to love classical music. You don't have to be a snob either. I wanna give a shout out to my girl BigB. I think I'm in love, people. Yo, B, I apologize. "Gloria" was, is, and always will be Poulenc. I dig the lesson… *(He touches his lips.)* …and I dig the way you taught it. I'll be down to lend a hand, you better believe that. And for the folks listening at the Palmer Street Shelter, here's a little Debussy to soothe you to sleep. Better times ahead, my people. Better times ahead. *(Lights dim as sounds of Debussy come up.)*

END OF PLAY

Nightswim
by Julia Jordan

for Tonya Christianson

BIOGRAPHY

Julia Jordan's plays include the ten-minute *Mpls./St. Paul* and full-lengths *Smoking Lesson, Tatjana in Color, 3 1/2 Catholics* and *Boy*. She has written the books to the musicals *Sarah, Plain and Tall* and *The Mice*, which was included in Harold Prince's *3hree*. She is a former playwriting fellow at The Juilliard School.

HUMANA FESTIVAL PRODUCTION

Nightswim premiered at the Humana Festival of New American Plays in April 2002. It was directed by Rajendra Ramoon Maharaj with the following cast:

Rosie . . . . Kate Umstatter
Christina. . . . . Stacy L. Mayer

and the following production staff:

Scenic Designer . . . . Paul Owen
Costume Designer . . . . John White
Lighting Designer. . . . . Paul Werner
Sound Designer . . . . Colbert Davis
Properties Designer . . . . Doc Manning
Stage Manager. . . . . Heather Fields
Assistant Stage Manager . . . . Debra A. Freeman
Dramaturg . . . . Steve Moulds

CHARACTERS

ROSIE: Seventeen years old.
CHRISTINA: Seventeen years old.

Stacy L. Mayer and Kate Umstatter
in *Nightswim*

26th Annual Humana Festival of New American Plays
Actors Theatre of Louisville, 2002
photo by Larry Hunt

Nightswim

Lights up outside Christina's house. It is midnight and her parents are asleep. Her bedroom window on the second floor is dark. Rosie is in the front yard.

ROSIE: *(Whispers loudly.)* Christina. Christina! *(Christina, dressed for bed in a ratty old T-shirt and underwear, comes to the window. She has not been sleeping.)*

CHRISTINA: What?

ROSIE: Come out and play.

CHRISTINA: We're too old to play.

ROSIE: Wanna do something?

CHRISTINA: What?

ROSIE: I don't know, something.

CHRISTINA: Like what?

ROSIE: Wanna go climb the railroad bridge? Cross the river?

CHRISTINA: We're too old to climb the railroad bridge.

ROSIE: Go skinny-dipping in the old man's pool?

CHRISTINA: He's always watching.

ROSIE: So?

CHRISTINA: It's undignified.

ROSIE: We'll go to the lake.

CHRISTINA: The police will catch us.

ROSIE: They haven't all summer.

CHRISTINA: We haven't gone all summer.

ROSIE: So they won't expect us.

CHRISTINA: It's cold.

ROSIE: That'll make the water feel warm, like swimming in velvet.

CHRISTINA: There's no lifeguard.

ROSIE: So we can swim naked.

CHRISTINA: What if we drown like the Berridges' boy? Our bodies would get caught under the weeping willow in the water. No one would find us for weeks.

ROSIE: We won't go anywhere near that tree.

CHRISTINA: But there's no lifeguard.

ROSIE: You forgot how to swim?

CHRISTINA: No.

ROSIE: Let's go.

CHRISTINA: I'm tired.

ROSIE: Skinny-dipping is like resting itself.

CHRISTINA: What if that rapist with the moustache and the beady eyes is out there?

ROSIE: He's in jail.

CHRISTINA: There could be another one. Beady-eyed rapists are a dime a dozen. A copycat crazy.

ROSIE: Black water, black night. He won't even see us.

CHRISTINA: Our skin glows like 60-watt bulbs at night.

ROSIE: The water will cover us.

CHRISTINA: He'll come in after us.

ROSIE: Rapists can't swim so good.

CHRISTINA: He'll get us on the beach.

ROSIE: You can run, can't you?

CHRISTINA: He has a fast car.

ROSIE: You can hide, can't you?

CHRISTINA: He carries a flashlight. He senses fear. He'll find me.

ROSIE: You can fight, can't you?

CHRISTINA: He's bigger than me.

ROSIE: You can scream, can't you?

CHRISTINA: No one will hear me.

ROSIE: I'll hear you. Two against one.

CHRISTINA: What if there are two of him? Or three? Or a gang of crazies hiding under the weeping willow tree waiting for us.

ROSIE: We won't go anywhere near that tree.

CHRISTINA: What if there are two?

ROSIE: What if there are none?

CHRISTINA: I can't.

ROSIE: You're scared?

CHRISTINA: Yes.

ROSIE: Admit it.

CHRISTINA: I do.

ROSIE: Say it.

CHRISTINA: I'm scared.

ROSIE: Don't be.

CHRISTINA: Why not?

ROSIE: 'Cause it's a beautiful night for a swim.

CHRISTINA: It is?

ROSIE: The water will be like swimming in black velvet because the air is cool. The lake will be all ours because everyone is locked up in sleep. We will swim naked because there is no lifeguard. And there won't be any crazies because I have a feeling. *(Beat.)* It's a beautiful night for a swim.

CHRISTINA: The police.

ROSIE: It won't be the same ones.

CHRISTINA: What if it is?

ROSIE: They change their beats.

CHRISTINA: What if they haven't?

ROSIE: That was last summer.

CHRISTINA: I saw them, a picture of them, in the paper today.

ROSIE: I saw it, too.

CHRISTINA: They saved a mother's little girl. CPR. She called them heroes.

ROSIE: It's good they saved her girl.

CHRISTINA: Heroes.

ROSIE: They're heroes.

CHRISTINA: Heroes can do anything they want, you know. They give them the key to the city and stuff like that. They could catch us swimming naked and take our clothes and make us leave the water all naked and shine their flashlights on us and hold our clothes above their heads and laugh and say, "Jump." You'll cry.

ROSIE: I will not cry.

CHRISTINA: I won't know what to do. I'll jump and they'll laugh and I won't know what to do. I'll jump.

ROSIE: I promise you, on my honor, I will not cry.

CHRISTINA: What will you do if those heroes come?

ROSIE: I will hide under the weeping willow branches that grace the lake.

CHRISTINA: You said we wouldn't go anywhere near that tree.

ROSIE: I'll swim to the middle of the lake and tread water until they leave.

CHRISTINA: Your legs will tire. You'll drown like the Berridges' boy.

ROSIE: I'm a strong swimmer.

CHRISTINA: They'll come in after you.

ROSIE: They won't get their uniforms wet. It'd tarnish their medals.

CHRISTINA: They could take off their uniforms.

ROSIE: Then they wouldn't be cops.

CHRISTINA: They could take off their medals.

ROSIE: Then they wouldn't be heroes.

CHRISTINA: They could take our clothes and drive away in their police car. Sirens and lights and them laughing.

ROSIE: We'll drive home naked.

CHRISTINA: Our moms will catch us.

ROSIE: They've seen us naked before.

CHRISTINA: What if it's our Dads?

ROSIE: That won't happen.

CHRISTINA: What if it does? Naked? *(Beat.)*

ROSIE: *(In a father's voice.)* "NO MORE SKINNY-DIPPING BEHIND OUR BACKS—SNEAKING AROUND—DOING WHATEVER YOU PLEASE—FOR YOU, YOUNG LADY."

CHRISTINA: Those are your favorite jeans they'd be driving off with. You'd never get them back.

ROSIE: I don't care.

CHRISTINA: Took you two years to break them in.

ROSIE: I'll hide them in a tree.

CHRISTINA: There's only the weeping willow.

ROSIE: I know.

CHRISTINA: They'll find our clothes again and they'll know they've got two naked girls again. And one will shine his flashlight on you and one will shine his flashlight on me. And the water that maybe was like swimming in black velvet when we were alone and moving will be cold when we're still and wondering what to do. And they will order us out and we will be naked and shivering and your tan skin will turn white and frightened. They'll see right into us. Your eyes will fix on them and you won't look at me. You won't tell me what to do and I'll be so cold. They'll say, "Come on out now, girls." And the water will fall away from your body with only hands and wrists, white elbows and arms to cover you. Your arms look so breakable. And I'll follow you watching the water run down your back. The flashlights will glare down our faces, down our legs. They'll shine their flashlights one for each of us. They'll smile at us trying to cover ourselves. They'll hold our clothes above their heads and smile at us naked and say, "Jump." And you'll cry and I'll cry and I'll jump.

ROSIE: We'll walk out of that lake like we've got nothing to be ashamed of and we'll look them right in the eye.

CHRISTINA: We won't cry?

ROSIE: We will not cry.

CHRISTINA: When they hold our clothes above their heads and won't give them back and say, "Jump"?

ROSIE: We will not cry. You will not jump.

CHRISTINA: When they say with grins on their faces and our clothes in their hands, when they say…

ROSIE: *(Cutting Christina off.)* "Lucky for you."

CHRISTINA: "Lucky for you it was just cops that found you and not some crazy sicko."

ROSIE: "Murderous Peeping Tom."

CHRISTINA: "Rapist."

ROSIE: "What are you two thinking about swimming at this hour with no lifeguard?"

CHRISTINA: "What if a storm came up all of a sudden and lightning struck the lake?"

ROSIE: "Why, you could be electrocuted!"

CHRISTINA: "What are you thinking about swimming with no clothes on?"

ROSIE: "You could catch a chill and die of pneumonia!"

CHRISTINA: "It's cold at night with no sun!"

ROSIE: And when they say, "Run along home now, girls."

CHRISTINA: "Before we call your parents."

ROSIE: We'll just stare at them, but we won't say a word.

CHRISTINA: We won't?

ROSIE: We won't stoop to their talk, talking nonsense. We'll just press them with our knowing eyes and they'll know that we know better.

CHRISTINA: We know all about skinny-dipping at midnight.

ROSIE: Warm, black water, black sky, no flashlights to trash the darkness, one moon, some stars, and a weeping willow tree. A perfectly beautiful night for a swim.

CHRISTINA: Standing there naked we will not cry.

ROSIE: We will not.

CHRISTINA: I can't.

ROSIE: Why?

CHRISTINA: The floorboards creak, they'll wake up.

ROSIE: Tiptoe.

CHRISTINA: My parents have radar.

ROSIE: Climb out the window.

CHRISTINA: There's nothing to climb.

ROSIE: Jump.

CHRISTINA: It's a long way down.

ROSIE: Bend your knees when you land.

CHRISTINA: Catch me.

ROSIE: You're too old for catching.

CHRISTINA: *(Christina climbs into the window frame.)* Just jump and bend my knees?

ROSIE: I don't like to swim alone.

CHRISTINA: It is a beautiful night for a swim.

ROSIE: C'MON JUMP.

(Christina jumps. Lights out.)

END OF PLAY

Limonade Tous les Jours
by Charles L. Mee

BIOGRAPHY

Charles Mee's play *Big Love,* inspired by Aeschylus's *The Suppliant Women* and directed by Les Waters, premiered at the 2000 Humana Festival and was performed during the 2001–2002 season at the Long Wharf in New Haven, Berkeley Rep, the Goodman in Chicago, and the Next Wave Festival at Brooklyn Academy of Music in New York. *True Love* opened at the Zipper Theatre in New York in November 2001. And *First Love* opened at New York Theatre Workshop in September 2001. Among his other plays are *bobrauschenbergamerica,* which performed at the 2001 Humana Festival at Actors Theatre of Louisville, and *Vienna Lusthaus (Revisited),* which opened at New York Theatre Workshop in May 2002. His complete works are available on the Internet at www.charlesmee.org.

His work is made possible by the support of Jeanne Donovan Fisher and Richard B. Fisher.

HUMANA FESTIVAL PRODUCTION

Limonade Tous les Jours premiered at the Humana Festival of New American Plays in March 2002. It was directed by Marc Masterson with the following cast:

Jacqueline	Christa Scott-Reed
Andrew	Tom Teti
Waiter	Josh Walden

and the following production staff:

Scenic Designer	Paul Owen
Costume Designer	Katherine Hampton
Lighting Designer	Tim Saternow
Sound Designer	Vincent Olivieri
Properties Designer	Mark Walston
Stage Manager	Heather Fields
Assistant Stage Manager	Debra A. Freeman
Music Supervisor	Kimcherie Lloyd
Video Designer	Valerie Sullivan Fuchs
Dialect Coach	Lilene Mansell
Dramaturg	Tanya Palmer
Assistant Dramaturg	Carrie Nutt
Casting	Orpheus Group Casting

CHARACTERS
JACQUELINE
ANDREW
WAITER

SETTING
Paris, in the springtime.

TIME
The Present.

Tom Teti, Josh Walden and Christa Scott-Reed
in *Limonade Tous les Jours*

26th Annual Humana Festival of New American Plays
Actors Theatre of Louisville, 2002
photo by Larry Hunt

Limonade Tous les Jours

Outdoors.
A hundred slender young chestnut trees. Late spring.
Blue, blue sky.
A café table.
Jacqueline, a young French woman,
sits at the café table.
Andrew, an American man in his fifties, enters,
looking out of place,
a video camera in his hand.

JACQUELINE: Are you Andrew?

ANDREW: Oh, well, yes, I am.

JACQUELINE: I am Jacqueline,
 I am a friend of your friend you were going to meet but
 he cannot come
 because for some reason.

ANDREW: Ah.

JACQUELINE: You will have a limonade ou un café with me?

ANDREW: Oh, yes, certainly,
 thank you very much.

JACQUELINE: Pascal sends his apologies but
 you know?
 It can't be done
 so
 he will hope to be in touch with you tomorrow.

ANDREW: And you are: Jacqueline, did you say?

JACQUELINE: Yes.

ANDREW: Jacqueline, right.
 I'm happy to meet you.

(As he sits.)
>And you and Pascal:
>you are a couple?

JACQUELINE: Oh, no, he's much too old for me.

ANDREW: Of course.

JACQUELINE: I think he's forty.

ANDREW: Ah.

JACQUELINE: You can understand.

ANDREW: Of course.

JACQUELINE: I mean, not that I have anything against older men
>quite the opposite in a way
>only I was married to an older man
>and he took such a patriarchal position
>and then I
>I found I liked it
>I invited it
>so we had almost a sado-masochistic relationship
>which I found I just loved
>he had other lovers
>he treated me like dirt
>he wanted always to handcuff me to the bed
>and it seems I not only fell into a sort of dependent role
>but I had sought it all along
>so now
>I'm trying to go straight
>you know
>grow up
>have a relationship with another grownup person
>as a grownup person
>if I have any relationship at all
>and at the moment I don't have one at all
>and don't want one
>because I'm still recovering
>and you?

ANDREW: Oh, yes, well, I am recovering, too.

JACQUELINE: From a love?

ANDREW: Right. Of course. What else?
>I came to Paris to forget.

JACQUELINE: I don't know.
Maybe this is not the place to forget about love.
ANDREW: Right. Well. But now it's too late. Because, here I am.
(As they talk a waiter brings a limonade to them and leaves again without speaking.)
JACQUELINE: Or else maybe it's a nice place to remember how it is to be alone
and to be starting out in a new world
where anything could be possible again
where you don't know what might happen next.
ANDREW: Right.
JACQUELINE: Because when you come to the end
you need to get back on the horse.
ANDREW: Right.
JACQUELINE: I have moved into a new place
which I love.
Of course, I am very lonely
because after you live with someone
you are used to not being alone
even if you hate him and he is disgusting
and picks nothing up from the floor
so that even when you get out of bed in the morning
you slide on a pile of magazines and fall to the floor
and hit your head on the edge of the bed.
But my new place,
it is all mine.
Very simple.
I have a fireplace
a shaded lamp
a box of stationery
a lounge with a mess of cushions of all sizes
a very simple bed in a separate room
and of course my coffee table
made from an old pheasant trap.
Do you know what a pheasant trap is?
ANDREW: No.
JACQUELINE: No, neither do I.
It looks like a large
what would you say?

A foot locker
two foot lockers together
but made of wood
with little bars, like a wooden bird cage
where you can keep your pheasants
I don't know why
maybe to keep them there
until you set them loose so you can shoot them
I don't know.

And then that delicious feeling of being alone
when you are alone in your new home
and lonely
that feeling that feels sometimes like soaring freedom
at other times like retribution almost,
do you know?
You are being punished for what you did wrong
or didn't do quite right
and sometimes it is a heavy crushing feeling
that makes you want to hit your head against the wall.

So you are looking for a young woman
half your age?
ANDREW: No, no, not at all.
I am not looking for a woman of any sort
because, frankly, I'd like nothing so much as to have a little rest.
JACQUELINE: And then?
ANDREW: Well, and then, if I ever do recover,
I am going to look for a woman my own age
because my wife
my former wife
was ten years younger than I am
and I came to think, finally,
that it might have been the difference in our ages
for her to somehow know in her bones
just where I was in my life
biologically almost
but certainly emotionally

what I was thinking about
how I felt
and for me, too,
she being younger and at a different stage of life
you would think ten years would not make such a difference
but somehow, we felt as though we were from two different generations.
So now, if I am looking for anyone,
I am looking for someone my own age
or older
so that I can just relax
and feel I am with a friend.
JACQUELINE: I understand, yes.
And probably part of the problem was
you're a little bit of a stuffed shirt.
ANDREW: I am?
JACQUELINE: Just a little around the edges.
I like a stuffed shirt
but many people find it boring.
ANDREW: They do?
JACQUELINE: Just a little bit.
I find it a little bit relaxing
because I don't feel so threatened.
With most men you know what they want
they are like animals with their appetites
they have only one thing on their mind
and you always know what it is
so you have to be all the time vigilant
and if they are exciting
well, that makes it harder to stay vigilant
but if a man is a little bit boring
then you can let down your guard and relax
because you know at least you yourself are not going to make trouble.
ANDREW: Oh, good. Good.
JACQUELINE: So.
We can have dinner.
ANDREW: What?
JACQUELINE: We can have dinner together.
Because

I'm starving.
Everyone here, they wait until nine o'clock to have the dinner,
so I am always hungry
is that what you say?
ANDREW: Hungry?
JACQUELINE: Dinner?
ANDREW: Oh. Yes.
JACQUELINE: Do you want?
ANDREW: Yes, yes, of course.
JACQUELINE: And then you will come to hear me sing?
ANDREW: How do you mean?
JACQUELINE: I am a singer.
   I sing in the nightclub
   to make my living.
   So
   after dinner
   we can go to my nightclub
   and I will sing for you.
ANDREW: Oh, oh, well: wonderful.

   (The lights sweep to darkness.
   Music: the first few bars of an intro to a song.
   A spotlight.
   Dim, smoky light.
   A microphone.
   Jacqueline steps up to the microphone and sings.)

JACQUELINE: If the sky should fall into the sea
   and the stars fade all around me
   all because what we have known, dear
   I will sing a hymn to love

   We have lived and reigned we two alone
   in a world that seemed our very own
   with its memory ever grateful
   just for you I'll sing a hymn to love

I remember each embrace
the smile that lights your face
and my heart begins to sing
your arms—
your eyes—
and my heart begins to sing

If one day we had to say goodbye
and our love should fade away and die
in my heart you will remain, dear
and I'll sing a hymn to love.

(When she finishes the song,
she turns,
steps out of her dress,
and gets into bed with Andrew.
The lights go to darkness
and rise to bright morning light in a single cue.

The bed is now in the midst of the hundred trees.
And the trees have moved just a little.

As they talk, she is getting dressed quickly.
And he follows her lead, more slowly and uncertainly.)

JACQUELINE: Well, you see, this was a mistake.
ANDREW: What?
JACQUELINE: I don't mean to say I didn't have a wonderful time.
 In fact, with you, the sex:
 I'll say no more.
 Because I like to be kissed
 what do you say?
 All over.

I had a wonderful time.
I'll say no more.

But, to be honest, this was not a good idea

except for the kissing
or unless one thinks it was not serious.
If one thinks it was just an escapade
ANDREW: An escapade.
JACQUELINE: A fling.
ANDREW: A fling. Yes.
JACQUELINE: And then, too, not just the kissing
   let's be honest
   but still
   I'm not ready even for a fling.
ANDREW: No, of course not.
   Well, I don't think I am either.
JACQUELINE: You liked making love with me?
ANDREW: Yes, I did. I certainly did.
JACQUELINE: So, that's no good.
   We are damaged goods
   both of us.
   With the experiences we have had
   we can't be with anyone just now.
ANDREW: No.
JACQUELINE: The point is: we can't trust anyone.
ANDREW: So.
JACQUELINE: This is crazy.
ANDREW: You could find yourself suddenly in a relationship with someone
   all over again
JACQUELINE: and you don't know anything about him
ANDREW: so you are just falling into the old patterns
JACQUELINE: because you are doomed
   to repeat who you are over and over again
ANDREW: because
   probably
JACQUELINE: you don't know who you are.
ANDREW: Right.
   (Silence.)
JACQUELINE: So, forget about it.
   I am going to take you somewhere
   and drop you off.
   Where do you want to go?

ANDREW: Well, I don't know.

JACQUELINE: It seems you are a little bit helpless.

ANDREW: Well, I just arrived, you know,
  and then
  well
  things happened so
  I don't actually know quite where I am.

JACQUELINE: How does this happen?
  You think I am promiscuous?

ANDREW: No. Certainly not.

JACQUELINE: Do you think I just sleep with any man the moment I meet him?

ANDREW: Certainly not.

JACQUELINE: Why not?

ANDREW: I don't know.
  It's not the sense I have of you.
  I mean I even thought possibly
  for you
  there was something about me in particular.

JACQUELINE: You did.

ANDREW: Well, yes.

JACQUELINE: And you?

ANDREW: And me?

JACQUELINE: Are you just sleeping with everyone
  and spreading death by virus wherever you go?

ANDREW: No, certainly not.
  I've been...
  I haven't been interested in any sort of intimacy of any kind
  since I separated from my wife.

JACQUELINE: You've been celibataire?

ANDREW: Celibataire?

JACQUELINE: You speak no French at all?

ANDREW: Almost none.

JACQUELINE: And then why did you come to Paris?

ANDREW: I didn't think about speaking French.

JACQUELINE: This is a French-speaking town.

ANDREW: Yes, I suppose it is.

JACQUELINE: Because you are from America
  you expect everybody to speak English?

ANDREW: I didn't think about it.
  Probably I do.
JACQUELINE: This is the trouble with Americans
  they don't need to think about anything any more.
  Is English the only language you speak?
ANDREW: And a little bit of Greek
  some Serbo-Croatian
  Sanskrit
  you know, the usual,
  German, high and low German,
  Italian, old Italian and modern Italian
  Arabic
  a couple of tongue-clicking languages
  and Creole.
JACQUELINE: So, nothing but English.
ANDREW: Right.
  So you could say: here is a stupid person,
  parochial and arrogant.
  Or else you could say:
  here is a wonderful person
  stepping out into the unknown
  taking a chance
  not afraid.
JACQUELINE: And yet
  the man I loved
  would say to me from time to time
  don't you think you should go home now for a while
  to visit with your parents
  because he didn't think where he and I lived was our home
  and because he wanted to have a fling
  and even to have his fling in the bed we slept in

  because he, too, was not afraid of anything

  and sometimes I would come home—because it was home to me—
  and he would be there with a mistress
  and I was expected to make conversation with her
  and I did because—what did she know?

She must have been as confused as I was—
and sometimes he would even expect me to take his mistress out for a walk
because he was expecting another lover
and so his mistress—is this what you say,
these days still: his mistress?—
ANDREW: Yes. You could.
JACQUELINE: His mistress and I would go for a long walk
and sit in a café drinking coffee
while my husband was making love with someone else
who could do this now that you think back on it?—
Why would I live like that?
But the one thing that is for sure is
if I am so untrustworthy a person
so unable to look out for myself
for sure I don't want to get mixed up with another man
before I know what I am doing
and what just happened if it wasn't that?
ANDREW: I understand.
Absolutely.
And I myself: in the same way
I married a person because I fell in love
but I don't know with whom or what.
She was very beautiful and smart and quirky
and she seemed stable
not a crazy person
because I had had some hot romances before
but with women who were crazy
because I like a passionate person
JACQUELINE: Of course.
ANDREW: and it turned out I was always falling in love with crazy people
who would fly off the handle and curse and scream and throw things
JACQUELINE: I do that myself.
ANDREW: and, of course, sometimes it must have been my fault
because, partly, I was cool and rational
in a way that would drive any normal person crazy
JACQUELINE: Right.
ANDREW: but also I think I chose people who were erratic and unpredictable
because I was so rational

and I wanted someone who would take a sudden turn
you know and take me to some surprising place
and then only later did I discover that people who did that
are often crazy people
JACQUELINE: Oh, yes.
ANDREW: they take these unexpected turns all the time
JACQUELINE: Yes.
ANDREW: and you don't always appreciate it
you wake up in the morning
and find a note on the pillow saying
"I'm going to see Ulu, going to see Ulu,
going to see Ulu Skrebenski"
and you don't know whether it's a poem of a kind
or she is just feeling really light-hearted
or she is already drinking at seven o'clock in the morning

and then when we stayed in a hotel
and she ripped up the pillow cases so we could take turns
tying one another to the bedposts

and she had her period so she made sure she got blood on her fingers
and reached back up behind the headboard of the bed
and streaked the wall with blood

or sometimes when she was just happy
she would throw dishes
dish after dish against the wall
just because she felt a little bit happy.
JACQUELINE: Oh.
ANDREW: You'd like to do that.
JACQUELINE: Well. Yes.
ANDREW: Unh-hunh.
So when I found a stable person at last who was also sexy
I thought: ok, at last, I've found a person I can marry
and that was the fatal thought, I think,
"I've found a person"
which is to say, I'd found a kind of person
a category of person I felt good with

JACQUELINE: Ah.

ANDREW: not always sitting on the edge of my chair
wondering what might happen next
someone I could just feel
OK, this is going to be a quiet evening at home
and so I married her

JACQUELINE: Oh.

ANDREW: and it's still not clear to me if my mistake was thinking categorically
or, on the other hand,
if the mistake was just that the category was wrong:
stability

JACQUELINE: Yes.

ANDREW: or if the mistake was just thinking at all
instead of following my instincts
because I think sometimes I think too much
and not always very clearly or intelligently
and I'd be better off just to say:
oh, right, good, okay, hot, go for it

JACQUELINE: Right.

ANDREW: and live life moment to moment
without thinking about the consequences
weighing and balancing
trying to use a lot of forethought
because that kind of thing always puts you living in the future
which we can't predict
and know nothing about
and simultaneously takes us out of the present
where we are living
and might know something about it if we only paid attention.

So, as you can see,
I don't think I'm a person
who ought to be getting involved with anyone else either.

JACQUELINE : Right.

ANDREW: I mean, my intentions are not so clear either.

JACQUELINE : Right.

ANDREW: And it's no good to be involved with someone
whose intentions are not clear.

JACQUELINE: No.
ANDREW: Although, I have to say,

if we were involved with one another

I don't think I'd ever tell you you ought to go home.
(Silence.)
JACQUELINE: So
we are saying goodbye.
ANDREW: Yes.
JACQUELINE: So, I'll drop you off
at Pascal's
so you don't get lost.
ANDREW: Pascal's?
JACQUELINE: Your friend you were going to meet.
ANDREW: Right, of course. Pascal.
Good.
Thank you.
And maybe on the way
we could take a walk in the park
just so
parting from each other
it isn't so abrupt
so even it almost seems so rude
so catastrophic.
JACQUELINE: OK. Yes. We could do that.
ANDREW: Just have another limonade or a coffee
and then say goodbye.
JACQUELINE: OK. Good. Yes. We could do that.

(Music.
Charles Trenet, the French Sinatra, sings.

A video is projected, filling the whole rear wall
and spilling over onto the proscenium arch or side walls:
a hand-held movie—
we see Jacqueline, in a café;
and then we see Andrew in a café,

close-ups of her, then of him,
back and forth
as, obviously, they have passed the video camera back and forth,
little bits of things—the waiter, and other tables,
and, disconcertingly, all of it done extremely amateurishly:
a bit of a shoulder, a foot on the sidewalk,
the corner of a café table with an arm,
the camera moving so quickly that the person is a blur,
pictures of the two of them together
where Andrew has held out the camera with one hand, unsteadily,
and tried to point it back at them both,
getting bits of them together here and there
on the Bateau Mouche on the Seine,
at a flea market, walking in the streets—
panning up on a building into the sky
and then staying on the sky for a long time—
increasingly relaxed and enjoying themselves—
in scenic spots.

At the end of the movie,
Jacqueline and Andrew are in a very expensive restaurant,
white linen table cloths.

There are a dozen beautifully set tables
amidst the hundred trees.
And the trees have moved just a little.

The video camera is on the table.)

JACQUELINE: The thing is
    when I was a girl
    my father was dying of alcoholism
    and my mother took me away from him
    and married another man
    and I grew up without my father
    missing him
    so that when he died
    I ran away from home

and I lived in a car parked next to his grave
and mourned for him and missed him

but when you think this might be an explanation for things
that happened later in my life
you can always think of one or two or three big reasons for anything you do
and then probably you have a hundred little reasons
you can't even remember them all
but they come back to you
in different clusters
so that finally you have so many explanations for things
you can't know anymore what is true
and your own inner self
like the inner selves of everyone else
just remains a mystery.

Sometimes a woman will want the love of an older man
she is captivated by an older man
she wants to be a daddy's girl
this is so common
you might almost consider it normal
even though it's wrong.

One time when I was nineteen years old
riding home in a cab with an older man
I found myself begging him to kiss me.
ANDREW: When you were nineteen.
JACQUELINE: Yes,
    and he
    he thought I was too young to know what it was I wanted
ANDREW: Well....
JACQUELINE: and so I became so jealous
    the next thing I knew I was in a rage
    accusing him of wanting to get rid of me
    so that he could go off to sleep with his other lovers
ANDREW: Oh, that was...
JACQUELINE: of course he denied it
    and said he had no other lovers

and then I knew he wanted me
you know, because he lied
and this is how you tell about a man
if he lies to you then he wants you.

ANDREW: Really?

JACQUELINE: Oh, yes.
So I said to him:
I need a friend, I need a lover
because autonomy it takes such a toll on me
it exhausts me and exasperates me
and I feel I've been looking all my life
now I have no doubt of it
I have been looking for a master.

I said to him:
I don't know what I'll do if you won't have me
which of course just aroused him.

ANDREW: Yes, well, of course.

JACQUELINE: He said, again, but the difference in our ages
and I put my fingers to his lips
and I said don't you know
there are a thousand thousand young girls
who dream of being the plaything of an older man.
It is their secret and their ugly desire
that they can expiate only by fulfilling it.

You see how wrong this is?

He slapped me, then,
so that I put my hand to my cheek
and felt it burn
and felt my love for him burst into flame
and I knew
this relationship is all wrong.
(The waiter again.)

WAITER: Madame?

JACQUELINE: What will you have?

ANDREW: I'll just have a salad.

JACQUELINE: And then?

ANDREW: I don't think anything else.

    You go ahead.

    I'll just have a salad.

JACQUELINE: You can't have just a salad.

ANDREW: It's all I want.

JACQUELINE: No, no, no.

    That's no good.

    You can't go through life having just a salad.

ANDREW: Why not?

    Sometimes that's all I have. I like it.

JACQUELINE: Not here, I don't think.

    Not in France.

ANDREW: Why not?

JACQUELINE: That's the rule in France.

ANDREW: It's a rule?

JACQUELINE: Of course, look on the menu.

    At the bottom, do you see?

    "No salad as a meal."

    That's all.

    It's not right.

    Monsieur, il aura le steak frites.

    Et moi, le canard confit.

    Merci.

WAITER: Merci, Madame.

    Et du vin?

JACQUELINE: Ah. Oui. Bien sur. Le Bordeaux—ici.

WAITER: Une bouteille?

JACQUELINE: Oui, ca va?

WAITER: Oui, ca va bien. Merci, Madame.

    (He leaves.)

JACQUELINE: So.

    He said he would drop me at home….

ANDREW: This is the man who slapped you?

JACQUELINE: Yes.

ANDREW: The man in the taxi still.

JACQUELINE: I said to him: it's you I want to go home with
   you only want to drop me off
   so that you can go to your lovers
   the ones you love
   but they don't love you
   and they will leave you
   I know you're going to sleep with them
   and kiss them, even kiss them on the mouth
   and who's going to kiss *me?*
ANDREW: You said this.
JACQUELINE: Yes.
   And then I said to him:
   Why don't you want me
   at least for your daughter?
ANDREW: You said this?
JACQUELINE: I should have been your daughter, I said,
   your friend, your lover
   everything, everything
   there's no one in the world for me but you
   I could feel the muscles trembling in his arms
ANDREW: Right.
JACQUELINE: and I could see
   even in the darkness in the back seat of the cab
   I could see that he was pale
   because he knew it was all wrong, too
ANDREW: Really.
JACQUELINE: and then he leaned his head down to me
   and kissed me slowly on my cheek.
ANDREW: My God.
JACQUELINE: I struggled and leaned back
   so that I didn't know whether I was resisting him or yielding
   and he kissed me on my eyes, my hair,
   under the ear just where it makes you shudder
   and at last he kissed me on my hot mouth
   I gave my lips to him
   what could I do?
ANDREW: Oh.
   Well.

JACQUELINE: And then at once he pulled back away from me
    and said
    please
    I'm a poor dazzled man
    completely swept away by you
    don't tempt me any more
ANDREW: Right.
JACQUELINE: and I said you are
    someone who is everything all at once to me
    someone who if he goes away
    leaves a widow and an orphan and a friendless person
    because you are a miracle to me
ANDREW: Oh.
JACQUELINE: and I could see a tear come from the corner of his eye
ANDREW: Yes.
JACQUELINE: he couldn't help himself
ANDREW: No.
JACQUELINE: I put my arms around his neck
    and I asked him if I had hurt him somehow
    if I had made him unhappy

    and he held me in his arms
    and he said to me
    oh, please, don't give me time to be ashamed of what I'm doing
    I'm keeping you
    I can't do anything but keep you.
ANDREW: Men are terrible.
JACQUELINE: Women, too.
ANDREW: Yes.
JACQUELINE: You see I don't have the problem with men
    what I have a problem with is the older man.

    If I am to be with a man
    OK
    I like sex
    this is OK
    I am not against it
ANDREW: I see.

(The waiter again, putting things down.)

JACQUELINE: but to be the child

　no

　I don't think so

　I don't like to give up the control

ANDREW: No.

JACQUELINE: why should it be I give up the control?

　No thank you.

ANDREW: Of course.

JACQUELINE: You want to touch me?

　Not there

　no, not there

　why?

　I don't like it

　you want to touch me?

　Touch me here

　touch me here

　I'm not against the touching

　I'm against where the touching is

　who controls this.

ANDREW: Right. Of course.

　And yet, even so,

　not necessarily in the context you describe,

　because of course that was

　I mean, a person does not want to repeat that

　necessarily

　or even at all

　not at all

　but possibly in a different context,

　if you don't give up the control

　then how can you be surprised?

JACQUELINE: Surprised?

ANDREW: Yes.

JACQUELINE: I have to be surprised all the time?

ANDREW: Not all the time

　but sometimes

　it could be fun

　don't you like to be surprised?

JACQUELINE: No.
　　I don't think so.
　　No.
ANDREW: About anything?
JACQUELINE: No.
ANDREW: A surprise party?
JACQUELINE: That's the worst.
　　All these people.
　　If I wanted to see them I would call them.
　　Suddenly they are there
　　and I would never have them all at once
　　I would have this person and that person
　　but not together
　　and not today.
　　Not this evening
　　I am just getting into bed to read a book
　　and suddenly here are all these people?
　　No, thank you.
ANDREW: Or: here's a present!
　　Do you like a present for a surprise?
JACQUELINE: That's different.
ANDREW: How is it different?
JACQUELINE: Because I always like a present.
ANDREW: It's a surprise.
JACQUELINE: I can't help it.
ANDREW: And if you never give yourself up to another person
　　how can you I don't know
　　how can you love someone.
　　Because isn't that what it is?
　　To reach that moment
　　we all long for
　　having put ourselves completely in the hands of another human being
　　when we are completely defenseless
　　feeling the excitement and danger of that
　　and the pleasure when it turns out we have been safe after all
　　when we have been most helpless.
JACQUELINE: Helpless.
ANDREW: Yes.

JACQUELINE: I don't think so.

ANDREW: You don't want to be helpless.

JACQUELINE: No. No, thank you.

ANDREW: You don't want that moment when you don't know where you are anymore
you've just lost yourself in some other place
you can't get to in any other way
you don't know where your body is
that moment of you know I think that's what they mean when they say ecstasy.

JACQUELINE: I don't need that moment.
Because what does this mean?
It means the man will want to kiss you and lick you
up one side and down the other
and turn you over
and have his way with you
upside down and backwards
and in the armpit
and the small of your back
and put his hands everywhere
and his tongue
and fingers fingers all over the place
and you are supposed to love it
it makes me feel creepy
the only worse thing is sticky.
(The waiter again, refilling the glasses.)

ANDREW: Sticky?

JACQUELINE: I don't like to feel sticky.

ANDREW: For a man, too,
he has to surrender.

JACQUELINE: He never does.

ANDREW: He should.

JACQUELINE: He never does.

ANDREW: In just the way you say about your home
you surrender to it
you give yourself up
and live in it
that's the pleasure of it.

JACQUELINE: I never see the man who wants to give up.
    I see the man who wants to have it his way
    who tries to have it his way
    and if he doesn't have it his way
    he sulks
    he gets gloomy
    he doesn't speak to you
    and then he yells at you
    and then he tells you not to yell at him
    and then he tries to explain to you
    how you were wrong
    or even he will explain to you
    if he is very devious
    how he was wrong
    so that if you will only agree
    then he will have his way
    and this is what you call giving up?
    I don't think so.
ANDREW: No, well, this was not what I meant.
JACQUELINE: With a woman
    it is unconditional surrender
    nothing else will be accepted
    and the man he will work at her and work at her
    until he gets it
    or
    if he doesn't
    he will dump her
    and try it with someone else
    this is how it is to be a man.

    Especially: an older man.
    Why?
    I don't know.
    (The waiter again.)
ANDREW: You know:
    don't think I want to be your father
    I mean, I am somebody's father
    and that's enough fathering for me.

JACQUELINE: You are a father?

ANDREW: Of course I am.

(He takes out his wallet to show pictures to her.)

I have a boy and a girl

no longer a boy and a girl

JACQUELINE: And you haven't mentioned this?

ANDREW: a young man and a young woman

both grown up

with their own lives.

If I had my way I would see more of them all the time

but they are gone, you know

to their own lives

one of them in California, one in Texas

Texas!

You have to let them go whether you want to or not

if they didn't leave home you would have failed

everyone knows that

so I have done my fathering.

JACQUELINE: They are older than I am.

ANDREW: Yes. Yes they are.

At least probably my son is older than you are I don't know.

JACQUELINE: I can't have a son older than I am.

ANDREW: No, of course not.

I mean, was I suggesting you should be his mother?

Was I ever suggesting that?

No. No.

Frankly, I don't need to be committing incest either.

I mean with someone young enough to be my daughter.

I don't know how this came about.

Probably because I wasn't thinking

I was just following my instincts

which clearly are all wrong!

I mean, from my point of view:

I certainly don't want to be anybody else's father.

JACQUELINE: No. No.

And yet, the point is:

you have a family.

ANDREW: Yes?

JACQUELINE: You have a family and a history and a whole
apparatus!
A whole life
more past than future in your life really
and I am a young woman
I need a fresh start in life
a new adventure
where anything is possible
even if I don't want some things
to not have the possibility of them
to have those possibilities shut down already
by definition
this is a death sentence.

ANDREW: Yes. Yes. I understand.
I see.
I understand completely.
I apologize.
I don't know what I was thinking.
I was being selfish.
I was taken by you
smitten, you know
or even more, or worse
I thought: oh, my God
what a chance in life
that's only normal
but I tried not to
because I understand I am much too old for you
and then, I was only trying to be a human being
I mean, to be honest about it
that I find you a wonderful person

JACQUELINE: Thank you.

ANDREW: what am I supposed to do
say you are a disgusting person?

JACQUELINE: That's very considerate,
because I have some feeling myself
and if you had said that
it might have been difficult for me.

ANDREW: No, you are lovely
   you are adorable
   but, in fact,
   that has nothing to do with me
   because I am saying that at the same time I am saying goodbye
   because if I feel any true feeling for you
   for example, if in fact what I feel is really love
   which I think it may be
   then that alone makes me want to step back
   and let you be free to find a life with a younger man
   because I wish for your happiness above all.
JACQUELINE: Right.
ANDREW: I am not necessarily looking for someone who would wear
   nothing but a slip, a slip and nothing else
   to the opening night of a play
   or someone who wants to lift up her skirt
   and have sex in the middle of the afternoon
   in front of that diner on the coast road near Malibu
   you know
   just before the road up into that canyon
   whatever the name of that canyon is.
   Plus
   it is not as though I don't have health issues after all
   the next thing you know
   I will probably have a heart attack
   or a stroke
   I will be sitting in a chair leaning over sideways
   drooling
   my left arm dangling by my side
JACQUELINE: Oh my God.
ANDREW: and you are still a child
   well, not a child
   a grown woman
   but a person with a whole life ahead of you
   do you think I want to marry you
   and then live with you by my side
   making me feel wretched that you are still young
   while I am falling apart in front of my own eyes?

I'll be farting and shitting in my pants
and all of your friends will be out at discotheques!

JACQUELINE: Now here you should slow down
because my friends are not so stupid that they are always at the discotheques
and sometimes I, too, read a book
you don't need to think
I cannot enjoy an evening by the fire.

ANDREW: Of course. Of course.

JACQUELINE: But what do you think,
do you think I want to be with your friends
and they are looking at me and thinking
look at this little bimbo he got for himself
she is a brainless piece of ass
she must fuck like a fire truck
(The waiter again. Andrew looks at the waiter; he is uncomfortable to be having this conversation with the waiter present.)
all the women your age
looking at me with contempt
what is it with her:
she is not a liberated woman?
She is a candy doll
do you think they will speak to me?
No.

ANDREW: Well.

JACQUELINE: I will go to a dinner party with you
no one will speak to me
because they will know that you and I
we are wrong!
Wrong!

ANDREW: I don't know...

JACQUELINE: And who could be more hostile
than your liberal friends
with all their tolerant ideas
except for me
every pent-up wish they have to be intolerant
finally
could be dumped on top of me

ANDREW: I don't think...

JACQUELINE: because I would be wrong
this much we know
and you!
You would be double wrong
all wrong
and we have all known for years how wrong you are
and this would be frankly
humiliating to me.
ANDREW: No.
JACQUELINE: So, what will I do?
You think I can introduce you to my friends?
And they are going to think
he must be amazingly rich
she fucks this old hulk
what kind of slut has she turned out to be?
ANDREW: Oh, I don't...
JACQUELINE: And then what would happen if it turned out that I did love you
which I don't
so then when I'm thirty or thirty-five
I would watch you die?
What?
You would get weaker and weaker
and I would weep and weep
what is the point of that?
And then I am a widow at thirty-five
and never able to have another relationship with another man
as long as I live
anyway what does it matter
because by then you would be impotent for most of the years I know you
anyway
even beyond the help of any drugs and suction pumps
and so what do I have in the end?
ANDREW: Plus, anyway, in the meanwhile,
from my point of view,
I should be with an older person who will understand
what the other person is feeling
without even talking about it
oh, you miss your children, oh yes so do I

and so forth
you share this feeling
without having to explain anything
feelings you would never understand
because you are still someone else's child who is missed
not someone who is missing you
and so forth.

JACQUELINE: Yes, I understand.

ANDREW: And then the fears of mortality
or simply the regret of having not so many years ahead
on the good days no fear at all
just the relishing of each day
because finally one has learned to relish them
and knows they are few and precious

JACQUELINE: Yes.

ANDREW: whereas you, you are just starting out,
you are oriented to the future
not the past or the present

JACQUELINE: This is true.

ANDREW: and so what do you know of relishing a day

JACQUELINE: *(Disagreeing.)* Well, I don't know about that.

ANDREW: or feeling you are losing your powers

JACQUELINE: This is true.

ANDREW: it's a subtle thing perhaps
but one can feel it
as a sea change

JACQUELINE: Yes.

ANDREW: so what would we have in common, you and I
we would live in different emotional landscapes
it would be like taking a walk in the woods with a dog
the man is going from sight to sight
oh, there is a beautiful flower, look at the color, the delicacy
look at the sunlight through the leaves falling onto the ground
the fading light, how beautiful
and his dog is going oh, my God, here's an amazing smell
oh, over there, over there, there's another incredible smell
my God, let's sniff that up
so the man and the dog are on a walk together in the woods

but they are walking in two entirely different worlds
the man sensing nothing that the dog senses
and the dog oblivious to all that the man is seeing.
JACQUELINE: And I am the dog in this.
ANDREW: It was just an example.
JACQUELINE: Still, you immediately cast me in the role of the dog.

This is the thing women object to, you know,

and perhaps you can see why.

(The waiter brings the check.)
ANDREW: I was trying to make an example.
JACQUELINE: But you can see how a woman might object to being a dog.
ANDREW: Yes, yes, of course.

I apologize.
JACQUELINE: Fine. OK.

Then you be the dog.
ANDREW: OK I am the dog then.

A woman takes a walk in the woods with her dog.
JACQUELINE: OK.

Come on. I'll take you for a walk.
ANDREW: *(Looking at his watch.)* Probably I should get on over to Pascal's.
JACQUELINE: I'll drop you there.
ANDREW: OK.

(Street music: an accordion player.

Another video:
this time we see Jacqueline, terrifically happy,
running toward the camera in the Tuilleries or the Luxembourg Gardens;
but the video is made in such super-extreme slow motion,
like the video installations of Bill Viola,
so that we can see a thousand emotions flicker across her face
within this happiness are also anxiety, terror, disgust—
whatever the camera catches.

When the video ends,
Jacqueline and Andrew are sitting on a park bench.

Andrew has a sailboat in his hands,

of the kind that is sailed on the Luxembourg pond,
and he is fixing its rigging.

Again, the bench is set amidst the hundred trees,
which have moved again just a little.)

JACQUELINE: Do you shop?
ANDREW: You mean, for groceries?
JACQUELINE: I mean for things you don't need.
    For dresses or lingerie.
ANDREW: Oh, no.
JACQUELINE: Oh, well, you need to do that.
ANDREW: Why is that?
JACQUELINE: Otherwise, how do you let your imagination run free?
    You see a dress, you think:
    oh, I can see her in that
    she moves toward me
    the breeze ruffles the skirt
    it is silk
    it is so sheer
    I see the shape of her leg
    I see even the contour between her legs
    I can think: OK, now, how would I get her into bed?
    I take her to a café
    and then I am thinking
    we are in bed making love
    I smell her perfume
    and so, yes, the next thing
    you go to a perfume shop
    you get some perfume
    you give it to her
    she puts it on
    it fills your senses
    you don't know where you are any more
    you are in heaven
    the world has disappeared
    and you are living in eternity with love.
ANDREW: I don't know
    it seems wrong to me.

JACQUELINE: How can love be wrong?
ANDREW: But really a fantasy of sex
    of seeing a woman as a sexual creature
    or even object.
JACQUELINE: So?
ANDREW: Well, I don't know.
    I mean, also
    you are a whole person.
JACQUELINE: Of course I am a whole person.
ANDREW: And not just an object of desire.
JACQUELINE: Yes, of course.
    I am a person.
    But also I hope I am a desirable person.
ANDREW: Also, frankly,
    I don't think I am going to discover myself
    and set my imagination free
    by becoming a sort of reckless consumer
    sort of find myself by shopping.
JACQUELINE: How will you do it?
ANDREW: I don't know.
    I will go to museums.
JACQUELINE: Are things there for sale?
ANDREW: Of course not.
JACQUELINE: So you can look
    but you can't touch
    you can't have
    you can see these things as part of someone else's life
    but not part of your own life
    that's the real art
    when it becomes yours
    you take it into your own life
    and it transforms your life
    how you feel
    how you live.
    Of course, if I could afford it
    I would buy what?
    Andy Warhol.
    But if I can't
    I buy a skirt.

ANDREW: It seems wrong to me
that's all I'm saying.
JACQUELINE: You know, where I've lived, in my country
in my lifetime
I've seen much worse.
And just because you buy a skirt
and live during your life
doesn't mean you can't do the right thing and be a voyeur too
and look at Picasso all you want.
I like to look at Picasso.
How is your home?
ANDREW: My home?
JACQUELINE: Yes. How is it?
ANDREW: Well. It's fine.
JACQUELINE: What is it
some orange crates with a lot of books in them
a mattress on the floor
you need a lot of pillows in a home, you know,
and rugs with many kinds of red and yellow and blue
little designs that make you dizzy
and some mirrors
and a nice big couch with inlaid wood of little scenes of hunters
and some velvet
and gold leaf on the frames
pictures on the walls
and puppets from India
and a Zulu fighting stick
do you know those fighting sticks
all painted with bright designs
and you can hit someone in the head with it
and break their skull
do you like to make a home?
ANDREW: Well, I don't know.
Do you?
JACQUELINE: Yes. I love to make a home.
A place to live in
to have it fill your dreams
to feel soft and you can drift in its arms forever

that's it: a home
where you live
and then, after you have lived there for many many years
you can look at it and say
I have had a life here on earth.
I had a place.
I was not a mosquito who floated over a swamp here and there
and don't know where I've been or what I'm doing here
but this was my place
for as long as I was blessed to have it.
ANDREW: Right.
JACQUELINE: You buy things for your home
or not always buy them
friends can give them to you
or you find them on the street
it doesn't need a million dollars
you get the beautiful things from the world
and bring them to your home.
Acquiring things:
this is a good thing to do
like a squirrel
like a rat
it's OK
people can do this, too
and they like it
you could do it.
You and I
we could have a whole relationship
based on shopping.
ANDREW: We could?
JACQUELINE: Of course we could.
ANDREW: I am maybe more of a Buddhist
you know, I like a bare floor
and even just a mat on the floor
and a few books
a cup of tea
I don't buy things
I never have.

JACQUELINE: Maybe you're just a cheapskate.
ANDREW: Maybe I am.
JACQUELINE: Or maybe you have a philosophy.
ANDREW: I thought I did.
JACQUELINE: That's an interesting thing to me.

(A rack of clothes amidst the trees.
They are shopping for a dress.
She steps right out of her dress and lets it fall to the floor,
puts on something from the store,
looks at herself in it,
steps out of that dress,
tries on another,
and so forth,
so that a succession of dresses
just falls to the floor like autumn leaves
as she goes from dress to dress
and they talk.
Each time she sheds a dress, however,
it stops him in mid-sentence;
he can't speak or concentrate for a moment,
and then he resumes.

The waiter is in attendance;
he is the shopkeeper,
and occasionally he will stoop down and pick up a dress
very delicately and tentatively.)

ANDREW: It seems to me,
the trouble always begins with love.
People always say the trouble is differentness
or even hatred or prejudice
or some such bad thing that is the root of all troubles
but really it's love that always disrupts everything.

Once you've set love loose in the world
anything can happen

if human beings give free rein to love
—and, if they don't, you can hardly call it love—
JACQUELINE: How is this?
ANDREW: Very nice. Very nice. I like it.
   (She takes his faint praise for condemnation
   and immediately slips out of it.)
And love pays no attention to what is useful or considerate
then we throw the world into turmoil with every breath we take
not just love of another person
but love of the earth
love of trees
love of the country
of little green farms
and fenced-off tracts of wild quince with great pink flowers
the blue air chill but full of the new and subtle warmth of spring.
JACQUELINE: How is this?
ANDREW: I don't know about the color.
JACQUELINE: You don't know about the color?
ANDREW: I don't know.
   (She lets it slip to the floor.)
All these things we cherish and covet
and protect from the intrusions of others
love of one's own country
of one's own friends
of the familiar ways our friends have
their manners and the way that they are dressed
and then
love of wine
   (Jacqueline through this is putting on dresses and letting them slip off,
   he stopping each time she does,
   and then resuming when she is buttoning another dress
   or fixing the straps on her shoulders.)
love of pleasure
of a picnic in the woods
and sweet red peppers with a pinch of thyme
love of music
love of riches, of speed, of power
all the things that we desire

and even love of sorrow
love of tears
love of heartache
love of anguish
love of exhaustion of sleep of solace
love of warmth, love of pain
love of lasting longer than we think we can
love of loud noises and of cheering
of marching steps
of martial music
of causing death

with all these kinds of love
what need is there of hatred?

Hatred is just the kerosene put on the fire.

This must be why there's nothing to be done about it.
You cannot eradicate the human heart itself.

Because it's not the worst in us that leads us into trouble
it's the best.
(Silence.)
JACQUELINE: Do you think you could....
(She has a button snagged in her hair,
or can't button a button at the back of her dress;
he stops talking and gives full attention to the button
for several minutes:
this is several minutes of complete silence,
the only such silence in the play,
while, in a perfectly tender and solicitous way,
with no agenda other than helping her—
nothing flirtatious or lascivious about it—
he helps her.
At the end she stands back.
He looks at her.)
ANDREW: Oh, that's beautiful.

*(The waiter, a castrato, steps forward
and sings a heartbreaking aria,
Handel's "Pena tiranna" from **Amadigi**
Handel's "Pena tiranna" from **Amadigi**
Handel's "Pena tiranna" from **Amadigi**
Handel's "Pena tiranna" from **Amadigi**
Handel's "Pena tiranna" from **Amadigi**
Handel's "Pena tiranna" from **Amadigi**
Handel's "Pena tiranna" from **Amadigi**
Handel's "Pena tiranna" from **Amadigi**
Handel's "Pena tiranna" from **Amadigi**
Handel's "Pena tiranna" from **Amadigi**
Handel's "Pena tiranna" from **Amadigi**
Handel's "Pena tiranna" from **Amadigi***

*And, while he sings,
Andrew picks Jacqueline up in his arms
and lifts her high above his head
so that she is a flying angel*

and they dance

her dress flows out in the breeze of their movement

*and the dance is almost entirely
his lifting her into the air so that she flies*

*the castrato might put several park chairs in a row as he sings
and Andrew lifts her as her toe touches first one, then another, then another
of the chairs
as she flies to a bench
and flies from there again
to touch the ground lightly
and be picked up in his embrace.*

*At last, her dress drops to the ground
and Andrew puts her down into a bathtub
as the aria ends*

and then he joins her in the tub
amidst the hundred trees.)

JACQUELINE: What I had in mind was
 I would come to Paris and make a life
 because I grew up in the country
 so I made my hair red
 and tied it in a fountain on the top of my head
ANDREW: Right.
JACQUELINE: and I didn't know what I had in mind
 I came to the Sorbonne
 and there I was
 a young person going from day to day
 thinking of what I did
 of singing
 of the clothes I wore
 of where I was living
 that's all
ANDREW: Right.
JACQUELINE: thinking of some friends I made
 of the bookshop I meant to go to
 the book I meant to pick up there
ANDREW: Your mind just drifting.
JACQUELINE: and of the little basket I might buy to keep ribbon in
 there was a room in a little hotel in Provence
 where I once stayed
 with its faded yellow walls
 and the shutters opening out onto the interior courtyard
ANDREW: It's like a dream.
JACQUELINE: the white arum lilies, purple irises,
 a hundred little tulips with pointed cups,
 and pittosporums whose scent paralyzes the will
 I thought I would have pittosporums in my Paris apartment
ANDREW: Right.
JACQUELINE: and then I met this man in a café
 who was very intelligent
 and not at all handsome
 because I thought if he is handsome I cannot trust him.

ANDREW: You can't trust a handsome man.

JACQUELINE: No.

> And I guess I thought
> if he is ugly I can trust him
> which was my first mistake
> and then he had a book that he was reading
> which of course, for a student
> is right away a good thing
> and he was an editor at a publishing house
> very distinguished, a literary person already
> I was so flattered
> and I could see he just licked me up with his eyes
> so I liked that even though I knew it was wrong

ANDREW: Right.

JACQUELINE: and pretty soon

> in this world I was carrying around in my head
> he would drift in and out
> and sometimes I thought he was living there
> and I was living with him
> so that my thoughts of my world took form around him
> and it seemed quite natural
> so that I never made a decision
> I just moved into my life all the time I was thinking
> I am a young woman
> just trying on my own life

ANDREW: Right.

JACQUELINE: seeing what it is to have a life in a big, beautiful city

ANDREW: Right.

JACQUELINE: I couldn't possibly think of having a life that involves another
person as a couple

ANDREW: No.

JACQUELINE: it has nothing to do with my life that I am living

> and yet, how can I not,
> what if I should let the choices of my life slip past me
> so that I have no life at all
> and so I married him

ANDREW: Oh.

JACQUELINE: is this the way people get married these days?
    I don't think so.

ANDREW: I don't know.
JACQUELINE: Other people think about it so much more
    and so much more clearly
ANDREW: Well…
JACQUELINE: but there I was
    and I didn't know at all how I had gotten there
    and then it turned out
    he was a prick.
ANDREW: Ah.
JACQUELINE: Who knew?
ANDREW: Right.
JACQUELINE: Well, it may be everyone knew but me
    men are pricks.
ANDREW: You mean…
JACQUELINE: It seems to me all men
    this is how it seems to me now
    of course I know this is wrong
    I try not to make a sweeping judgment
    but how else can I judge?
    In my experiences this is how it is
    and I look through the brown-colored glasses that I have
    and this is how I see men.
ANDREW: Oh.
JACQUELINE: You know what it is with a man?
    They are there, they are there, they are there
    all the time they are pursuing you
    and then,
    once they have you
    they are gone.
    You turn around
    all of a sudden they are gone.
    You can't count on a man
    because
    just when finally you decide OK I can count on him
    that is the moment

he just disappears
and you never see him again.
And what you have left is just a big dearth.
Is that what you say?

ANDREW: A dearth?

JACQUELINE: Yes.

ANDREW: Yes. You could.

(Silence for a moment.)

When I met my wife for the first time
she was riding a bicycle
a friend of mine introduced us
we said hello
nothing special
until she said she was on her way somewhere
and she turned around
and got onto her bicycle
it was a boy's bike
and as she got on
and swung her leg around over the seat
to sit on the bike
she was wearing blue jeans
a little bit tight
and I saw her back
her hands and arms and shoulders as she took hold of the handlebar
and the small of her back
and her butt
and I thought then that
I wanted to marry her.

JACQUELINE: Because of her butt?

ANDREW: Yes.

What I always had in mind was a real friend
so we would share feelings
and be coming from the same place
this is such a complicated thing
because people come from different places
I mean to begin with if they are a man and a woman
their lives have been so different
and then if they are different ages

JACQUELINE: Even generations.
ANDREW: even generations
   how can you bridge such a gap
JACQUELINE: Then they come from different countries
ANDREW: and one from this town, one from that
JACQUELINE: different families
ANDREW: one had brothers the other sisters whatever
   the thousands and millions of minuscule things
   that make us so different from one another

   and if it is hard for just anyone
   you can imagine how hard it is for someone who comes from Serbia
   and someone who comes from Montenegro
JACQUELINE: how can two people then ever share the same feeling exactly
ANDREW: and without effort
JACQUELINE: with comfort even
ANDREW: easily
JACQUELINE: so that they can relax together
ANDREW: and feel
   there is someone in the world who really understands me
JACQUELINE: really knows who I am in the deepest sense
ANDREW: where we both look at a piece of beach and say:
   oh, how beautiful
JACQUELINE: or—at the same moment we both feel:
   what an ugly place
ANDREW: so that these two people can go arm in arm through life
   knowing they have someone who will always be there for them
   because they know exactly how it is for you
JACQUELINE: even sometimes they are there already before you've gotten there
ANDREW: so
   you face some trouble?
   No problem
   I know exactly how you feel
   and we will come through this together.
JACQUELINE: Right.
ANDREW: Do you think this can never happen?
   That two people can never really know one another?
   Or really feel the same?

This is just a romantic wish
no one ever feels it
it's just not possible
that's the tragedy of life
we are all alone.

JACQUELINE: I don't know.

ANDREW: No. Neither do I.

(MC Solaar sings French rap music.

Another slow motion video:
this time amidst the carnival entertainments in the Tuilleries
emerging from a scary tunnel ride—
again the slow motion so extreme
that we see a thousand expressions in one:
this time it is not the anxiety that pops up through the happiness
but vice versa,
the relief and pleasure and exhilaration
that pops up through the terror of the tunnel ride.

They are in a café amidst the hundred trees.
They are having dessert.)

ANDREW: You'll have a limonade?

JACQUELINE: Yes, bien sur.
   (He looks around for a waiter.)
   You see,
   we've had a good time together.
   This has been a nice little romance after all.

ANDREW: Yes. Yes, it certainly has.

JACQUELINE: We were afraid to have a fling
   I won't speak for you,
   I was afraid
   but it turns out it was OK.

ANDREW: Yes.

JACQUELINE: And I hope, when you go back home,
   you will keep me in a good place in your heart.

ANDREW: Yes, I will.

I certainly will.

JACQUELINE: You know, in France,
    this is how it is
    you have a lovely time
    you hold your life with a light touch
    and it's not a tragedy.

ANDREW: Right.

JACQUELINE: All we did was talk about how we can't get together
    and all the time we got together anyway.

ANDREW: Right.

JACQUELINE: Because we liked it.

ANDREW: Yes.

JACQUELINE: We thought
    we are too damaged
    we can't do this
    because of our histories
    they hold us in a grip and
    we can't go on
    but then we do.

ANDREW: Yes.

JACQUELINE: We don't go on to be together, of course,
    because still
    when we are just being quiet and considerate with each other
    still we know
    it's not right for us
    because we are grown-ups.

ANDREW: Right.

JACQUELINE: Because we are different in age.

ANDREW: Yes.

JACQUELINE: And because we still do have our histories
    they don't go away all at once
    a person cannot suddenly
    all over again become a different person.

ANDREW: Yes.

JACQUELINE: And because you are still a little boring.

ANDREW: I know.

JACQUELINE: And you have some ways of being I don't know
    I won't say I don't have some ways of being that aren't wrong

but with me
these ways of being are passing things
because I am young
and maybe I don't know any better
Or anyway I will learn
because I will see what these bad ways of being get me into
and I won't like it
and I will have other ways of being.

ANDREW: Yes.

JACQUELINE: But you,
    I don't mean to say:
    after all, you are a nice person, I think

ANDREW: Thank you.

JACQUELINE: and I think you still have the capacity to learn

ANDREW: I hope so!

JACQUELINE: and nothing is to be said against a person
    who is so considerate
    a real gentleman I think

ANDREW: Thank you.

JACQUELINE: but still
    with you, you have some ways of being that you have
    because they are so old
    and you haven't gotten over them
    and even if I wouldn't care
    because I would love you
    you know
    I would see right through your ways of being to you yourself
    and say, well, so what
    he's a little stupid
    but he's a nice guy underneath it all
    even so, after I would do all that
    still the things I think are fun
    you think are silly
    and what you find interesting
    to me is just incredibly tedious.

ANDREW: That could be.

JACQUELINE: So finally you would bore me to tears
    I wouldn't be able to stand it

I would be feeling guilty about it
because here you would still be
being considerate and supportive and generous and loving
and I would just want to hit you in the face with a frying pan
so it would be wrong
it would be bad
that would be no fun for you.

ANDREW: No.

JACQUELINE: So, if we have had our little fling
and you go back to America
and I go back to my life
maybe we think of each other

ANDREW: Yes.

JACQUELINE: and we think of each other in a way of warmth
and affection

ANDREW: Yes. I know I will.

JACQUELINE: and I think
OK maybe a man is not such a bad thing
and I could have a life with another man

ANDREW: Right.

JACQUELINE: and you could think maybe a woman is not such an evil species
and you will find someone
or you will have your old friend
because an old friend is a good thing
and when you get to be your age
probably this is more important than anything else.

ANDREW: A friend?

JACQUELINE: Yes. And solace
and, you know, getting ready to calm down
to enjoy being in the twilight of your life
wallowing in that a little bit so you don't miss it
and you don't have some frantic bimbo
trying all the time to get you out of the house.

ANDREW: Right.

JACQUELINE: You can have your grandchildren.
And they will play around your feet
next to the dog

and you will doze off in the afternoon sunlight coming through the
window
I think this will be good for you.

ANDREW: You do.

JACQUELINE: And me, I am at the beginning
I want some excitement, you know,
I am going to want to travel quite a lot
and maybe even have sex with a lot of guys
who knows?
Or maybe not
because I am not so wild
or just looking for the thrills
but to be free to be with whoever it is I want
to have the adventures
it's a little bit, you know,
with each person
you enter into their world
you live in their world for a while
it is like a trip to the moon

ANDREW: Yes.

JACQUELINE: to step into their lives for a while
it is to have another entire life for yourself

ANDREW: Yes, it certainly is.

JACQUELINE: and a person wants these things
to have many lives in one life
not a thousand lives maybe
because then you don't notice any one of them
but to have some lives
since you won't have another chance if you only have one life yourself.

ANDREW: Yes.

JACQUELINE: Or you might say
why can't you find all people in one person?

ANDREW: Right.

JACQUELINE: This is what a man I once knew used to say
I was interested in him
in a romantic way
and I tried to seduce him
I have to admit it

and he was in love with another woman
and I said to him
how can you just be faithful to her
isn't this a little boring
because if you would be with me, too,
then it's another whole world for you to live in before you die
ANDREW: Yes.
JACQUELINE: and he said
yes, but,
with this woman I love
I find all the women of the world in one woman
and I thought
oh, yes, well, this could be what people want
and they never find it.
ANDREW: Right.
JACQUELINE: So
you are leaving.
You wish I would drop you at Pascal's?

ANDREW: I can find my own way.
Thanks.
JACQUELINE: I'll say goodbye then.
Probably I won't ever see you again.
Probably not
not for a million years.
ANDREW: Right.
Well.

Goodbye then.

(Do they shake hands or kiss goodbye?

The lights sweep at once to darkness.
Music: the first few bars of an intro to a song.
A spotlight.
Dim, smoky light.
A microphone.
Jacqueline steps up to the microphone and sings.

A French cabaret love song
A French cabaret love song
A French cabaret love song
A French cabaret love song
A French cabaret love song
A French cabaret love song
A French cabaret love song
A French cabaret love song
A French cabaret love song
A French cabaret love song
A French cabaret love song
A French cabaret love song
A French cabaret love song
A French cabaret love song
A French cabaret love song
A French cabaret love song

At the end of her song,
she turns, and Andrew is standing there
with his hand out to her.
She takes his hand.)

JACQUELINE: Oh.
    (Silence.)
ANDREW: How time flies.
    (Silence.)
JACQUELINE: Yes.
    (He leads her back into the darkness
    as the lights fade to black.)

END OF PLAY

The Mystery of Attraction
by Marlane Meyer

BIOGRAPHY

Marlane Meyer's plays include *Etta Jenks*, *Kingfish*, *The Geography of Luck*, *Why Things Burn*, *Moe's Lucky Seven*, and *The Chemistry of Change*. She's been produced at the Los Angeles Theatre Centre, The Women's Project, Playwrights Horizons, The Joseph Papp Public Theatre, The Royal Court Theatre and South Coast Repertory. Her plays have received many awards including The Joseph Kesselring Award, The Susan Smith Blackburn Prize and The Pen Center Award for Drama.

HUMANA FESTIVAL PRODUCTION

The Mystery of Attraction premiered at the Humana Festival of New American Plays in March 2002. It was directed by Richard Corley with the following cast:

Ray	Steve Juergens
Warren	David Van Pelt
Denise	Claudia Fielding
Roger	Robert Ian Mackenzie
Larry	Lee Sellars
Vicky	Laura Masterson

and the following production staff:

Scenic Designer	Paul Owen
Costume Designer	Christal Weatherly
Lighting Designer	Tony Penna
Sound Designer	Martin R. Desjardins
Properties Designer	Mark Walston
Production Stage Manager	Paul Mills Holmes
Assistant Stage Manager	Leslie K. Oberhausen
Dramaturg	Tanya Palmer
Assistant Dramaturg	Nancy Vitale
Casting	Orpheus Group Casting

CHARACTERS

RAY
WARREN
DENISE
ROGER
LARRY
VICKY

SETTING
Carson, California

TIME
The Present

Claudia Fielding and Steve Juergens
in *The Mystery of Attraction*

26th Annual Humana Festival of New American Plays
Actors Theatre of Louisville, 2002
photo by Fred Furrow III

The Mystery of
Attraction

Eleven o'clock at night. A sparsely furnished living room; couch, two chairs, coffee table, lamps. An exterior door can be seen Down Right. Two interior doors can be seen at either side of the stage. A bottle of scotch and an ice bucket are on the table Down Center. The entire upstage wall is glass doors behind which can be seen a beautiful tropical garden. It is lit for night viewing. Vicky stands staring out the window. Ray and Roger stand downstage, Left and Right, at either side, watching her.

ROGER: She's like a daughter to me, but she's not my daughter, she's my fourth wife's daughter. I raised her after the wife was killed in an avalanche. She is nothing like the mother, the mother was a monster. But the girl is sweet, docile. For years such an idyllic relationship exists between us that I'm on the verge of taking her as my bride when suddenly she is always in trouble. Escalating calamity as she matures. Disappearing every other weekend, lowlifes shaking me down, shoplifting, drug abuse and a string of accidental homicides. *(Ray looks at Roger.)* She says accidental and I believe her.

RAY: Who did she kill?

ROGER: Let's talk about who she killed this time.

RAY: Okay.

ROGER: Let me first say this. I've spent a lot of money keeping her out of jail. But does she appreciate it? No. She sees life as an experiment. A series of adventures. So this time, she confesses. *(He watches her.)* She wanted to see, from the inside, how the justice system works. So, she confessed. The cops have the knife. Her prints are on the knife.

RAY: Who did she kill?

ROGER: I think she's doing it to spite me. That's right, isn't it? *(Vicky ignores him.)* She's in a rebellious phase… Who did she kill? This guy named Vince, ex-fighter, stunt man, loser, doper… They came to the house in

Palos Verdes one time and when they left so did the silver. I'm talking sterling, at least twenty thousand dollars worth of sterling and you know what they did with it? They sold it at a swap meet out of the trunk of their car. A dollar a spoon, a dollar a fork. For sterling silver flatware. What are you going to do with a kid like that?

RAY: How about lock her up?

ROGER: For stealing silverware?

RAY: For murder. I'm saying that maybe it's right that your daughter do time. Time is not the worst thing that can happen to a person who is testing the limits of morality.

ROGER: For one thing I no longer think of her as my daughter, I think of her as my fiancée, and the second thing is the penal system is a whore house. Guards sexually abuse the females under their protection on a regular basis. Don't you read the newspaper?

RAY: No.

ROGER: You don't read a paper.

RAY: I don't need a newspaper to tell me that evil flourishes, all I have to do is wake up, stay here, and people like you come to see me.

ROGER: My object in coming here is to see that she keeps from slipping through the cracks.

RAY: I understand that.

ROGER: But also that she gets the help she needs.

RAY: Okay.

ROGER: Because I don't want you to think for a moment there won't be retribution, just not at the hands of the state.

RAY: The law should be the same for everyone.

ROGER: But it's not.

RAY: I think the best thing you can do is to let discipline be administered. Bad dog.

ROGER: That's not why I'm here. *Counselor.* That's not what's happening here. Discipline the *dog.* She is not a dog, she's a delicious gumdrop. She kills zeroids. Nobody ever wonders what happened to them. Nobody ever publishes an article questioning what happened to all the John Does? Okay, granted, she might have problems with socialization. But she's my responsibility and I love her and I have to do everything I can for her.

RAY: I'm giving you my best advice.

ROGER: I think you're trying to shake me down.

RAY: Not at all.

ROGER: Because I have a lot of money.

RAY: I said when you called I didn't know if I could help you or not.

ROGER: Look. The situation is that when she goes to trial I want her to get off. Can this be done?

RAY: This is America and there are two types of justice, one for the rich and one for the poor. Which are you?

ROGER: What do you think?

RAY: Then it can be done.

ROGER: Are you the man to do it?

RAY: No, I am not.

ROGER: I know you have connections in the system.

RAY: I don't know what you're talking about.

ROGER: I happen to know you need money.

RAY: Anybody who looks at my shoe leather knows that.

ROGER: I also know you have a problem.

RAY: A man without a problem is not a man.

ROGER: You are in trouble with the animals and the animals are about to open you up and take a piece out.

RAY: But nobody knows which piece.

ROGER: I do.

RAY: *(Shaken, he laughs.)* You know which piece? Really... you know which piece they're taking?

ROGER: Do you have children?

RAY: Supposedly, I have a daughter in Phoenix I've never seen.

ROGER: Well, at least you'll have the one child then.

RAY: *(He lets it sink in.)* So you're saying they're going to... *(Beat.)* They wouldn't do that.

ROGER: Oh really...?

RAY: It's a shitty little twenty grand note!

ROGER: Getting bigger everyday you don't pay.

RAY: Look, let's... you go, please... I don't want to be rude but, this is... good night.

ROGER: Ray, may I call you Ray?

Ray, you seem more concerned about doing the right thing than saving your own dick.

RAY: Roger, may I call you Roger? Roger, I believe there is a balance and order in the world that we will all have to reclaim for ourselves one day, and Roger, if that is indeed your name? Today is my day. Good night.

(Roger takes out his checkbook and tears off a check, leaves it on the coffee table.)

ROGER: I'm leaving you a check for the amount of your debt.

RAY: I wish you wouldn't.

ROGER: And then some. If you cash it, and I'm assuming you will, then you'll handle our problem. If you don't… Well, I can only assume you're not as bright as you seem. *(Exiting.)* Victoria, come.

(Vicky walks past Ray, she stops, turns, starts slowly back toward him when…)

ROGER: *(Sharply, heightened.)* Vicky? Leave him alone!

(Vicky stops, turns and exits. Ray locks up for the night. He looks at the check. He can't bring himself to tear it up. He hides it in a stack of magazines. He turns off the interior lights. He moves to the garden window, looks out, turns off the lights outside. A moment. He turns the lights back on. His brother, Warren, can be seen in the garden. He opens the door.)

WARREN: Hi.

RAY: How long have you been out there?

WARREN: I saw that you had company and I just waited out here.

RAY: Come in.

WARREN: What time is Denise home?

RAY: It's her late night.

(Warren enters. An awkward moment.)

WARREN: You want a drink?

RAY: I was going to bed.

WARREN: Uh, if you want to go to bed we'll just make it a short one.

(Ray pours a drink.)

RAY: I thought you were off the sauce.

WARREN: I am, I'm quit, just, you know, now and then.

RAY: Me, too.

WARREN: So. Who's this guy.

RAY: He's a client, was going to be, maybe but… not my kinda thing.

WARREN: What's he doing here at the house in the middle of the night?

RAY: Well… *(Beat.)* I had to let go of my office and I was busy all day doing fuck all…

WARREN: You let go of the office?

RAY: Don't tell Denise.

WARREN: Okay.

RAY: *(Changing the subject.)* So. What's up, Bro?!

WARREN: Nothing, you know… I just dropped by. Haven't been by in awhile, in the neighborhood and saw your lights.

RAY: In the neighborhood. You live in Marina Del Rey, I live in Carson.

WARREN: Ray? Do you think there's something wrong with me?

RAY: Yes.

WARREN: Really?

RAY: Yes.

WARREN: Because I don't remember there always being something wrong with me but NOW there is. You know? Before I was married I didn't think about myself the way I do now. I think about myself all the time now. And I think there's something wrong.

RAY: Why don't you go home and talk it over with Sharky?

WARREN: She started all this and now she doesn't want to listen to me anymore. She tells me to put a lid on it.

RAY: Are you two fighting again?

WARREN: If my heart is breaking open and the words are coming out all I want is to be held… to be held and reassured, not told that I'm a mama's boy or that I have a Peter Pan Complex… And what's wrong with having a Peter Pan Complex anyway? Who doesn't want to sail away to Never Never Land and have Wendy take care of the details?

RAY: It's the Wendys of the world who write those books.

WARREN: The point is, I don't want to be fixed.

RAY: Then you shouldn't be married.

WARREN: I never thought there was anything wrong with me and now I don't trust myself anymore, I find myself lying to retain my privacy, I don't like to lie.

RAY: It's not a perfect world, but there are trade-offs, unnegotiated trade-offs we silently assent to.

WARREN: Like what?

RAY: How about cooking?

WARREN: I do all the cooking.

RAY: What about the shopping?

WARREN: Since I cook I do the shopping.

RAY: Cleaning up?

WARREN: I do that too, since I'm home more… *(Irritated.)* NOW.

RAY: What about paying the bills and dealing with the auto insurance and giving advice about rashes and cuts and splinters and calling in sick for you and making hot tea, etc.

WARREN: She never does any of that for me and you left out sex.

RAY: I don't like to think about you and Sharky having sex.

WARREN: We don't have sex anymore, Ray, why is that?

RAY: Jesus, Warren, I don't know.

WARREN: Have you ever hit your wife?

RAY: No. I am not a cave man. I have cultivated myself, I have cultivated my responses. I'm a civilizing influence, and to be that you must be civilized.

WARREN: Uh huh...

RAY: Stuff like wife beating only happens at night. You shouldn't stay up so late.

WARREN: Up late is the problem.

RAY: For some.

WARREN: Don't you think that at this point in time men and women should be able to talk to each other? But we can't because women don't listen. No, I take that back, they are listening, they are listening for a way to present their agenda which is to fix what's wrong with you.

RAY: That's not all women. Some women, well, they have a life.

WARREN: A life of the mind?

RAY: Sometimes, yes.

WARREN: We're not attracted to those women.

RAY: Yes, we are.

WARREN: No, we're old now... and we can be honest. That type of woman scares us.

RAY: I've dated women lawyers that were...

WARREN: Very smart and you dated them a few times and you took them to bed but it didn't last because you couldn't relax.

RAY: What, are you in my head?

WARREN: Tell me I'm wrong.

RAY: The chemistry was off. This was right after the divorce and I was having a hard time relaxing with anyone.

WARREN: Shit.

RAY: I think we both pick bright women.

WARREN: But we don't think they're brighter than we are until it's too late. We think we have the upper hand, they let it happen, they let us believe in our superiority, and then wham... one day you're going through the mail and you find the *Mensa Newsletter*.

RAY: What are you talking about, Sharky's been a member of Mensa for years, she never goes to the meetings.

WARREN: *I* never knew that.

RAY: What difference does it make?

WARREN: It's huge. Knowing she's got these… I.Q. points makes me feel like I have to answer all her questions. And when I do, she analyzes everything I say. But more than that, she analyzes everything I DON'T say, I mean, who cares what it means when you're late AGAIN.

RAY: So you were late again?

WARREN: I don't have to be anybody's boy on time!

RAY: You know you should call.

WARREN: You know, Ray, when God invented woman he did not say I am making you an equal, he said I am making you a helpmate. But like most men poor old Adam's not listening because Eve's wearing not a stitch so he's in a fugue state most of the time thinking about all the ways he wants to do it to her. So when she says "Hey, daddy, reach me that fruit," he says without thinking, "Sure, baby, whatever you want," and boom, there they go on their midnight ride to nowheresville. And for all eternity we're not only totally hung up on food, we can never seem to get enough sex, have you noticed that? But I ask you, what woulda happened if Adam had just said, "Woman, get that fruit outa your head." You think we'd be in the mess we're in now? No way. We'd be living in a place that looks a lot like… *(He looks at the garden and says with feeling.)* Well, a whole hell of a lot like your backyard, Ray. I think it's one of the most beautiful spots on earth.

RAY: Thank you.

WARREN: I mean it.

RAY: Look, for one thing that is not a real story, Adam and Eve.

WARREN: How do you know?

RAY: It's a fable that attempts to explain the genesis of human suffering.

WARREN: Women are the genesis, Raymond!

RAY: You consider the times, Warren, men were trying to stamp out the goddess culture that was six thousand years old, it's pure politics.

WARREN: I don't always trust how you talk, it's not masculine.

RAY: One person cannot be the sole cause of human suffering.

WARREN: Unless they are a woman.

RAY: You've stopped reading and you're watching too much TV.

WARREN: No.

RAY: Yes, you are, because you're talking like an idiot.

WARREN: Have you, Ray, son of God, ever hit your wife?

RAY: I told you… *(Beat.)* Okay, what do you mean by hit?

WARREN: Punch, slap, kick, shake, trip, pinch, pull, squeeze. Push.

RAY: Okay, I might have pushed her to keep her from hurting herself one time.

WARREN: To keep her from getting hurt you pushed her.

RAY: She was coming at me with a knife and I pushed her away, not hard, just a little shove but we were gassed and I guess she lost her balance and fell into this glass table and that was kind of a mess… stitches and bleeding and all kinds of dirty looks from nurses at the emergency room wondering if she wanted to call the cops which she did not, of course, since she was, unbeknownst to me at the time, running that credit card scam that eventually got her popped for grand larceny.

WARREN: *(Incredulous.)* This happened with Denise?

RAY: No! Not Denise, I wasn't talking about Denise, I was talking about Sharky.

WARREN: Ray, you haven't been married to Sharky in years.

RAY: Seven years, Warren. Seven years, four months, twenty-three days.

WARREN: *(Beat, realizing.)* I meant the current Mrs. Potato Head.

RAY: No. I never hit Denise. After Sharky I told myself, never again.

WARREN: What are you saying?

RAY: Sharky drove me nuts, you know that. We used to chase each other around trying to kill each other.

WARREN: You're not in love with Denise like that?

RAY: Correct.

WARREN: *(Amazed.)* You're not?

RAY: Don't sound so surprised, it's not like I don't have feelings for Denise… but it's more like she's my friend. The sex is friendly sex… accommodating… but not impossible to imagine stopping entirely at some point and not missing, and in fact, it's actually been quite awhile now that I think of it, I mean, we sleep in separate rooms, she's there, I'm here.

WARREN: Separate rooms.

RAY: She complained about my snoring so I moved.

WARREN: What about in the beginning? The initial attraction, the courtship, the heavy petting, the public sex…?

RAY: Her body is not… I don't know, she's not my type. Can I say that…?

WARREN: She's stacked.

RAY: Yeah, but I never liked that big boob thing.

WARREN: I love that.

RAY: And she has a smell about her that's... I don't know what it is, some kind of skin oil, musk. Look, I don't want to say anything against her, she's one of the finest people I've ever met and I'm glad, no, I'm grateful she's my wife... really. I mean, when Sharky took off...

WARREN: She didn't take off, you turned her out.

RAY: I asked her to leave when she told me she was in love with you, Warren!

WARREN: But I had nothing to do with it!

RAY: Warren...?

WARREN: Except for listening to her... that's all I did, she talked, I listened.

RAY: Well, that was a mistake, okay!

WARREN: See, you are mad!

RAY: No, I mean, listening to women is how you seduce women is to listen and pretend to be interested in what is not too interesting you know that.

WARREN: I was interested because she talked about you.

RAY: Well, you shouldn't have listened.

WARREN: You're my brother, I thought I was helping.

RAY: Oh Warren!

WARREN: Sure, okay, I always had... you know...

RAY: A BIG FAT FUCKING THING for her...!

WARREN: Right.

RAY: All I'm saying is that it was stupid. It was stupid of you and that's all. Okay?

WARREN: Oh shit, why do we always...

RAY: You bring it up because you feel bad, that's why! Look, it's over. You've been married a long time and...

WARREN: But you hate me... you hold a grudge.

RAY: What was I saying before we started talking about this?

WARREN: You were telling me how you met Denise.

RAY: Okay. She was working at this bar, by the office... Why am I telling you this story?

WARREN: I love this story!

RAY: Okay... it's late afternoon and I'm downtown at the Red Room and it's one of those days I'm getting drunk as shit and she's working there and she tells me, she has a thing for me.

WARREN: That's not how she said it.

RAY: You want to tell this story?

WARREN: She said, she had a crush on you.

RAY: Oh right, right, she told me she had a crush on me.

WARREN: *(Smiles.)* That's cute.

RAY: I didn't really feel the same way but I was so out of it and I felt like there was this hole in my life I had to constantly maneuver around to keep from falling into. You know how people lose people and start over, but I couldn't see my way into that until Denise showed up that night with a casserole, she was wearing a baby doll nightgown under her coat and she just sort of moved in, you know? Girl moved in. Took over.

WARREN: Baby doll nightgown.

RAY: Actually it embarrassed me at the time.

WARREN: I know.

RAY: Because you could see her... everything through it, and it shocked me actually... made me draw back and I had a hard time uh...

WARREN: Performing.

RAY: I had to get used to her... body, was different, smelled different.

WARREN: Baby doll nightgown.

RAY: She served dinner in that outfit. Moving around the kitchen, serving dinner with her everything just... you know, seeing everything, Sharky'd never do that.

WARREN: No, I know, she's a prude.

RAY: She has a lot of class, Warren. She always carried herself just so. You know? Very particular... her clothes, just right.

WARREN: Till she lost her figure.

RAY: She let herself go.

WARREN: That's a bit of an understatement.

RAY: She's still the same person. Look, women get heavy when they're happy.

WARREN: And when they're miserable.

RAY: I always thought she was happy.

WARREN: No, you didn't.

RAY: No, I know.

WARREN: *(Beat.)* Let's talk about Denise.

RAY: Denise is more of a...

WARREN: Down home girl... like the song by the Stones. Remember that?

RAY: I don't like the images of women the Stones have used in a lot of their music.

WARREN: God, you know...! An action like that, casserole, baby doll, that would change my life! You know, someone would care about MY needs for a change, I'd be a different man.

RAY: Warren?

WARREN: I never had somebody love me like that! I mean, that's what I envied about you and Sharky is how much Sharky loved you!

RAY: How can you say that to me?!

WARREN: Sharky doesn't love me like that! She never has.

RAY: Look, I'm over this, I am, absolutely, that was then and this is now and I'm happily married to Denise and it's fine, it really is, I'm content!

WARREN: Even when it's bad it's better than dating.

RAY: I dated a lot after the split. That was horrible. Picking up some poor woman, going out to dinner, getting stinking drunk and having to call her a cab so I could continue to drink on into the night till I blacked out. I had dates like that with women in the building where I worked, I see them now, we don't speak. They avert their eyes when they see me.

WARREN: I answered an ad in the newspaper.

RAY: An ad?

WARREN: For a date.

RAY: What, a personal ad? When?

WARREN: Just recently.

RAY: You did?

WARREN: But she scared me. I went and looked her over and got scared... she looked hungry, like she was gonna eat me. Big teeth. Big eyes. Red dress, Ray, have you ever dated a woman in a red dress?

RAY: Could you see her hands?

WARREN: *(Remembering.)* Yes. Yes. They were big.

RAY: Maybe it was a man?

WARREN: Oh shit, I never thought about that... wow. Hmmm. That's weird. A man. I've never had sex with a man. I mean not in a dating situation... just, you know, on the job... workin' vice, but hey, couldn't be worse than no sex... right?

RAY: Are you dating strangers when you're married?

WARREN: Dating, no. Answering an ad, yes, I did that.

RAY: That's creepy.

WARREN: Right, considering I broke up your marriage, right?

RAY: I don't like to think of it like that, Warren! I just don't... don't really like to think of it like that, I don't think of it like that, it's not like that, it's, it's something that happened a long time ago to people that no longer exist and nobody can know how these things occur, except sometimes in retrospect, but really, I don't want to know, you know? I just prefer to think it's history and it's nobody's fault.

WARREN: It's my fault.

RAY: Shut up!

WARREN: NO it is and I felt bad BUT then you met Denise and I thought, whoa. Jackpot. You know, with the figure and the baby doll… but you don't love her!

RAY: Warren… Denise is great. She is the best.

WARREN: But you don't love her.

RAY: No, no, it's just, she has a few annoying habits that… look, it's not a problem, I mean, after six years you get used to the way people are, I mean, you endure. Like everything in the house is perfect, not a speck of dust. But look at this place, it's furnished like a cheap motel. And the house stinks, she can't cook a meal without burning something and she won't open a window, so everything I own… Smell my shirt.

(He puts his arm under Warren's nose.)

WARREN: I can't smell anything.

RAY: It reeks of cigarette smoke, burnt food, this perfume she wears and the woman herself! I can't stand to come home sometimes, Warren. The thought of it makes me physically ill. That's why I made the garden, a place to go, a refuge of sorts if you don't have one, if you've lost your place in nature by losing the love of your life you make a habitat where you fantasize day in and day out that maybe someday your Jane will return to her Tarzan.

WARREN: Oh God, Ray.

RAY: It's a joke, Warren, lighten up… I'm teasing.

WARREN: No you're not.

RAY: *(Weak laugh.)* No, I know.

WARREN: Shit.

RAY: Odor is ninety percent of sex, you ever hear that?

WARREN: Just from you.

RAY: When I met Sharky she was a dancer at the Kahala Hilton and we were right up front and she dances by me and the smell of her body was like a sweeter version of my own musk… I took a deep breath of that and the orchids and the Plumeria and I was a lost man.

WARREN: I was sitting right there.

RAY: I felt like the floor was sliding out from under me and I turned and told you I was going to marry her.

WARREN: You were ready. Anyone could have had you. And don't forget, the magic of the islands… I bet if you went back to the Kahala Hilton today, you'd fall in love all over again.

RAY: No, because I took Denise there on our honeymoon and it wasn't the same. It was overrun with show business people and the hotel had put in this aquarium with a dolphin that swam back and forth in this shallow trough where kids or anybody could reach in and touch him and people kept touching him and the animal seemed half mad from all the touching. God! And Denise being fair burned easily and spent all day indoors complaining about how much I was drinking. Maybe we'd been together too long to expect a sense of celebration about our marriage, or maybe it was me, but I can trace the decline of my life from that trip, the sense of futility, the dolphin trapped in that tank. I got sick off a piece of fish I paid twenty-seven dollars for. Bad fish, in Hawaii, what are the chances of that? *(Pause.)* What did you two fight about?

WARREN: When?

RAY: Tonight.

WARREN: Oh. You know. Stupid shit.

RAY: Uh huh.

WARREN: *(Sadly.)* Yeah.

RAY: What was it?

WARREN: Coming home early, she came home early.

RAY: Home early is the problem?

WARREN: I don't always like being around other people. You know? Just the sound of people moving around the house, scraping chairs, the refrigerator opening and closing a million times, I guess I was just in that kind of mood.

RAY: Well, shit, Warren, she lives there.

WARREN: Well, shit, Ray, if you're gonna be on her side.

RAY: I'm just saying that she is living there, she is paying half of everything, right?

WARREN: More than half since I got demoted and I work regular hours, no overtime.

RAY: It was not a demotion, the evidence room is a very big responsibility.

WARREN: I was a detective, Ray, I was in line for a promotion.

RAY: What difference does it make… you'll still get your pension.

WARREN: I don't look at retirement the same way you do. I liked my job. I was a good cop, that's all I ever wanted to be.

RAY: But you blew it.

WARREN: What would you do if you were disappointed in love?

RAY: Get a divorce!

WARREN: I couldn't do that to you! Break up your home and then just bail. I had an obligation to stick it out.

RAY: You didn't do this for me…!

WARREN: Yes, of course for you, but man, I was so miserable… that's when I started using.

RAY: Look, the material point is, Sharky helps with the bills, she has the right to come home when she likes.

WARREN: I know but what about my rights, I had things I needed to do… I ASKED HER, what are you gonna do today? And she says, I'll be gone all day. And then cool as a breeze she blows back in early, surprises the hell out of me and then she gets mad and I get mad because I think, frankly, she was checkin' up on me to make sure everything was… you know…

RAY: You were being good.

WARREN: If I WANTED to get high I don't even know where I'd go anymore.

RAY: So what were you doing when she got mad?

WARREN: Well, you know, whatnot.

RAY: What's whatnot?

WARREN: This and that, this and that.

RAY: Warren?

WARREN: Well, art projects. Okay?

RAY: Art projects?

WARREN: Yes and she came in on me while I was doing them and started screaming and…

RAY: What were you doing that would make her scream?

WARREN: I told you, art projects.

RAY: What do you mean by art projects?

WARREN: Why do you say it like that, I have a college education.

RAY: Just tell me what that means.

WARREN: I take photographs.

RAY: I NEVER knew that.

WARREN: Now you do, big deal…

RAY: When did you start doing this?

WARREN: I don't know… awhile ago.

RAY: So Sharky was screaming at you for taking art photos.

WARREN: She got hysterical and was gonna call the cops.

RAY: The cops?

WARREN: Hysterical, you know how she gets.

RAY: What were you taking a picture of exactly?

WARREN: Nothing.

RAY: Warren?

WARREN: What difference does it make? It was an artistic statement.

RAY: I want to know what she saw that made her scream?

WARREN: It was a still life.

RAY: Like... fruit, flowers, dead birds?

WARREN: My neighbor's daughter, she wants to be a model and so I took some pictures of her as a favor to help her get started.

RAY: Pictures of your neighbor's daughter.

WARREN: Polaroids. That's how you do it, before you waste the film you take a few Polaroids. Because for one thing I don't actually have a good camera yet but these Polaroids are not cheap, the film's like twenty bucks.

RAY: How old is the girl, Warren?

WARREN: I don't know.

RAY: Yes you do too.

WARREN: Fourteen.

RAY: Shit!

WARREN: I was trying to help her out, help her get started. Where do you think Marilyn Monroe would be if that calendar guy hadn't taken her picture?

RAY: What was she wearing?

WARREN: Have you ever seen the painting of Venus on the half shell?

RAY: Warren...?

WARREN: What?

RAY: She was naked?

WARREN: Naked with a very LONG wig!

RAY: And where did you take these pictures?

WARREN: In my studio.

RAY: You mean the basement?

WARREN: If you don't stop sounding like a wife you're gonna have to fuck me and take care of me when I'm old.

RAY: That may happen anyway. So, you're taking nude photos of a fourteen year old girl in your basement, Warren, and Sharky came in on you and you're mad at HER?

WARREN: Art is a process, you know... it's personal, she didn't understand, she just got mad...

RAY: Can you blame her?

WARREN: I was doing a favor for a friend.

RAY: Warren, I'm looking right at you, I can see you, I can see inside you, I can see you had a thing for this girl.

WARREN: She's like a ripe fruit.

RAY: She's fourteen.

WARREN: This kid is very mature for her age, she has womanly ways.

RAY: Warren, she's a baby.

WARREN: You don't know these girls nowadays, man, they grow up fast what with MTV and all kinds of sexy talk in the school yard and these movies, all kinds of movies about sex and longing and the unfulfilled promise of love, and they can't say NO, they don't have language, the schools don't encourage debate so you can do what you like as long as YOU keep talking and it doesn't hurt them and you know they all want to be models so they can be wanted by millions of lonely men humping their mattresses in the middle of the night, jerking off to these images in their heads while their wives make up stories about how THEY can't have sex tonight. Bleeding, gas, imaginary pains, and if YOU complain it's always about what's wrong with YOU, I'm selfish because I wake her up when the bed starts shaking because I have to relieve myself manually, and she is disgusted and starts screaming and it makes you want to kill these women when they lose their love for you and all they want to do is use you for a paycheck and complain to their friends about what kind of animal in heat you've turned out to be and how it's all gotten worse as you've gotten older and uglier and all the time they're keeping this precious thing you need so deep inside themselves, so hidden, they keep it deep inside where you need to be, but they won't let you back in there, they can't let you in because of something that happened, you don't know what it is, it's a mystery, they won't talk to you about it and you ask them what's wrong and they say nothing, nothing, nothing and meanwhile you're dying of loneliness because it's lonely out here.

RAY: Take it easy.

WARREN: It's a lonely planet, Ray, and everybody is just walking around like it's all okay and it's not, it's not... it's fucked up.

RAY: (Beat.) So how's it stand with Sharky?

WARREN: Pretty raw.

RAY: Right.

WARREN: It's not... it's not good, Ray.

RAY: Why didn't you say something?

WARREN: What am I supposed to say? OUCH?

RAY: I don't know but they say talking helps.

WARREN: Women say it 'cause they like to talk you into things but you wouldn't know that because you're not married.

RAY: Yes I am.

WARREN: No. Not really. I found that out tonight. You're not. Not like I am, I'm married, even now, there is a shred of something akin to passion that runs like a golden thread through the tapestry of my hatred.

RAY: You should get a divorce, Warren.

WARREN: Easy for you to say.

RAY: I'm telling you as a brother who loves you, you are too miserable. Your misery is eating you up and spitting out an entirely different person.

WARREN: Don't you miss being married...?

RAY: I am married!

WARREN: The arguing, the sex, the food, the bathroom smells, the inconvenience of emotion...?

RAY: Warren, there are other ways to be married...

WARREN: What do you think the five senses are for?

RAY: To keep you from bumping into things.

WARREN: They are to hear, to see, to touch, to smell and to taste the flesh of another human being!

RAY: You didn't eat today, did you?

WARREN: Are you listening to me?

RAY: You didn't eat...

WARREN: These senses locate you, Ray, they put you in the world, they place you on the earth, in all its glory and horror, right here! Feeling, inhaling and touching yourself alive in this flesh and blood lifetime...

RAY: And you're drinking!

WARREN: *(Pulls off his shirt.)* Animal in the dirt, rolling in the dirt...! Groveling at the feet of the goddess!

RAY: *(Crossing.)* I'm making you something to eat...

WARREN: You can't even hear what I'm saying, you think it's the booze but I'm throwing you a life line!

RAY: *(Exiting.)* I'm opening a tin of sardines.

WARREN: *(Urgently.)* You think it's chemistry talking, but it's more than that... I am talking about what makes it real with another human being is sex and emotion and intimacy, Ray. Intimacy, is what we need, knowledge of the other, deep heartfelt knowledge of yourself, of another person, of several people... you ever go to a swap party, Ray?

RAY: *(Off.)* It's not my thing.

(Ray comes back with a tin of sardines, crackers and a glass of orange juice. He hands the juice to Warren who drinks it. Ray opens the tin and fixes Warren a cracker with fish on it.)

WARREN: *(Calming.)* Sex is what the senses are for... if you don't have that, what have you got?

RAY: Well, for one thing, control. Okay? I'm not like you, I'm not out of control... that's what I couldn't stand about being married to Sharky... that feeling of being out of control, after awhile, it's too much... and look at you, you're outta control...

WARREN: But that's what marriage is for, it's to keep us from getting lost in our animal, letting our animal run us around this lonely planet, Ray. Women are supposed to be the watchdogs and the saviors. I know that now. Now that I am cast adrift in this wasteland. Sharky saved you but she couldn't save me.

(Larry appears in the garden. Ray stands, Warren turns.)

RAY: Oh shit.

WARREN: Who is it?

(The men watch as Larry lets himself in the sliding glass door.)

LARRY: Hi, Ray. What're you doin'? Havin' a party? A boy party?

(Warren puts on his shirt.)

RAY: This is my brother Warren.

LARRY: Warren, Larry... glad to meet you. So you're Ray's brother. *(Beat, looks around, to Ray.)* That's nice. To have a brother. How you doin', Ray?

RAY: I'm good.

LARRY: That's not what I hear. I hear you suck.

WARREN: *(To Ray.)* Should I leave...?

RAY: No.

LARRY: No, stay here. You stay where you are, *(To Ray)* don't you love that, the respect of men for other men's privacy, that is so important, women never understand that, do they? They are too curious. Not that I'm not a curious person. But mostly about real things. Three dimensional objects as opposed to feelings. I don't really have feelings but I do have hobbies.

WARREN: I have a hobby.

LARRY: What is your hobby?

WARREN: Photography. Artistic photography.

LARRY: I study anatomy. It's a most useful science in my line of work. To know exactly how to separate a joint, pop, where to apply the pressure, crack, where to make an incision. *(Sound.)* The mess you can avoid with a little education.

WARREN: *(With intention.)* Ray loved school, he's a lawyer, I hated school, I'm a cop.

LARRY: Not anymore. Now you're a clerk.

WARREN: *(To Ray.)* How does he know that?

RAY: I don't know.

LARRY: It's because I'm in the know. I bet I know more about you two than each of you knows about each other.

WARREN: That would surprise me.

LARRY: Why?

WARREN: Because I am a student of human nature and my brother is one of my favorite subjects.

LARRY: Because you love him.

WARREN: I guess that's right.

LARRY: Emotional attraction. I don't feel that. In here, where feelings are supposed to live there is a void. Calm and cold.

(Larry pulls a collarbone out of his pocket.)

Ever see one of these?

WARREN: It's a bone.

LARRY: It's a clavicle or collar-bone of a sixty-four year old used car salesman in Vegas, washed up on his luck. The trick is to take the bone while the guy is awake. They scream like babies these old men, you wouldn't believe it. Then they pass out and wake up, this area around the chest is all caved in... it's just impossible to imagine the pain and you can't move without screaming in agony and then they put this prosthetic piece in there that never sits right. There's a clicking sound every time you take a breath just so you never forget what a loser you are.

(Larry moves to the door.)

However. This is not your fate. Clavicle. No sir. Our mutual acquaintances have instructed me to prepare a very special treat for you. So. I'll be seein' you Ray. Not now, but soon. By the light of the moon. *(Howls.)*

(Larry exits.)

WARREN: Eeeeyuck. *(Grimacing.)* Who is that guy?

RAY: Who do you think he is, he's a collector, he collects bones... you've never heard of Bone Daddy?

WARREN: Bone Daddy... THE Bone Daddy?

RAY: Exactly.

WARREN: How did you meet him?

RAY: How do you think? I made a bad loan.

WARREN: Ray… from maniacs you borrowed money?

RAY: I met him through my bookie.

WARREN: What bookie?

RAY: My bookie!

WARREN: You have a bookie?

RAY: It's just for football games, fights.

WARREN: You bet on fights and football games with a bookie?

RAY: And the dogs.

WARREN: You bet the dog races with a bookie?

RAY: Why do you say it like that, it's no big deal.

WARREN: How much are you in for?

RAY: Twenty.

WARREN: Oh man! Have you told Denise?

RAY: Of course not.

WARREN: She's got savings.

RAY: I know that.

WARREN: Maybe if you tell her about Bone Daddy?

RAY: Are you nuts? If I get the money from Denise I'll never hear the end of it. If I tell her why I need it I'll become a prisoner, I'll never be able to go anywhere or make a phone call. *(Mocking voice.)* Where ya' goin'? Who ya' callin'? Your bookie?

WARREN: How were you planning on handling it?

RAY: I was planning on ignoring the problem and hoping it would go away.

(Ray pours more drinks.)

WARREN: Yeah… that works just often enough to make it a viable option for guys like us, guys like us on the outside of the action.

RAY: I don't know if I'd put it that way, Warren.

WARREN: Oh, but that's how it is. We took a wrong turn and we end up here, sitting here, talking about the past, about what's happening now, each fresh disaster, pretending they don't have a thing in the world to do with each other.

RAY: They don't.

WARREN: Sure they do, because you and me, brother, we got off the train.

RAY: What train?

WARREN: THE train.

RAY: What is that?

WARREN: It's the path you were born to follow but you got off because you couldn't see into the tunnel, because you had no faith that there was a light up ahead and in the darkness you panicked and jumped off and started running and you've been running ever since.

RAY: Okay, look, I CAN... get... the money... from Denise, I didn't want to do it but I CAN do it.

WARREN: It's not about the money, Ray. You should never have split with Sharky.

RAY: *(Beat, incredulous.)* Warren?

WARREN: That was your mistake.

RAY: She left me for you! SHE left ME!

WARREN: She would have come back eventually. They always do. A woman loves like that once a lifetime. You shoulda followed your heart.

RAY: You're a sick man, Warren, you are disturbed!

WARREN: If you had, you wouldn't be in trouble with these maniacs. You gamble because you got off the train.

RAY: Look, I used to go to Vegas and win, asshole.

WARREN: When you were married to Sharky.

RAY: I'm gonna have to kill you now...!

(Ray starts for Warren, Warren ducks him, outmaneuvers him.)

WARREN: You had phenomenal luck.

RAY: If you come here and let me get a grip on your neck, I swear it'll be quick.

WARREN: Well, it's true.

(Ray lunges at Warren, Warren ducks, Ray trips, gets up, keeps coming.)

RAY: One good twist.

WARREN: Don't you remember?

RAY: Come here I said!

WARREN: Wait, what's that...?

(The sound of a key in the lock, Ray and Warren freeze, then Warren grabs his jacket and runs out the garden door. Ray hides the food, straightens up, sits. Denise enters. She stands watching him a moment.)

DENISE: What's the matter with you?

RAY: When?

DENISE: Now.

RAY: I'm fine.

DENISE: You look weird.

RAY: No. I'm fine, I'm just... well... okay, sit down.

DENISE: No.

RAY: I need to talk to you.

DENISE: Can't it wait, it's close to midnight.

RAY: I'd prefer to discuss this with you now, otherwise, I won't be able to sleep.

DENISE: What about my sleep? What if what you're going to discuss with me is going to sicken me and cause me to be unable to sleep.

RAY: Has that ever happened…?

DENISE: Yes.

RAY: When?

DENISE: The time you slept with my sister and you were drunk and decided full disclosure was…

RAY: Okay, fine, we'll talk in the morning. Jesus!

DENISE: What, you sleep with somebody?

RAY: God… No!

DENISE: You sure, because you look very similar…

RAY: No, it's nothing like that.

DENISE: Oh, well, now I'm all curiosity. Let's talk.

RAY: It's not that big a deal. Well, actually I guess it is. I'm in some trouble, financial trouble.

DENISE: Shit. *(Beat.)* How much?

RAY: About… thirty thousand dollars.

DENISE: Jesus, fuck you… What happened?

RAY: I been playing cards.

DENISE: And you lost thirty thousand dollars?

RAY: I had a bad year.

DENISE: How could you keep a secret like this?

RAY: I didn't want to worry you.

DENISE: *(Beat.)* You go to that card joint like once a week. Right?

RAY: More than that.

DENISE: Talk to me.

RAY: Other times, I go other times.

DENISE: When?

RAY: I can't remember.

DENISE: Like when I work?

RAY: I guess.

DENISE: Every night when I work?!

RAY: Possibly.

DENISE: And when else, like when my mom was dying and I had to go stay with her?

RAY: You know from that incident with your sister that I don't do that well when I'm left alone too much, Denise. You know that. I eat out every night, greasy food, indigestion, can't sleep, TV sucks, and I don't want to screw up again so I go out and...

DENISE: Just tell me about gambling.

RAY: I'm telling you how it happens.

DENISE: Like when you say you're going to see so and so and you come home late and make an excuse, are you really sitting someplace gambling?

RAY: I don't know.

DENISE: Tell me if you lied in order to gamble.

RAY: I DON'T REMEMBER I WENT A LOT, THAT'S ALL!

DENISE: Don't scream at me.

RAY: Sorry. Okay. Anyway. I now have this collector, who works for these maniacs from whom I borrowed money to pay my bookie...

DENISE: Your bookie!?

RAY: And he's talking very seriously about repayment. Or else.

DENISE: When you say he's talking seriously what does that mean?

RAY: That he's serious... It's a business with him.

DENISE: And this translates to what?

RAY: You know. Bad stuff.

DENISE: I don't know what you're talking about and you won't be explicit and it makes me think you're lying again...

RAY: I'm not lying! Okay? Christ!

DENISE: Then what does it mean when you say he's serious?

RAY: That he'll like, hurt me.

DENISE: How?

RAY: He takes bones from people's bodies, okay?

DENISE: Do the police know about this guy?

RAY: I don't know!

DENISE: 'Cause that is illegal. I'm no expert, but that sounds like it might be illegal.

RAY: *(Ironic.)* Really?

DENISE: Yes. So is loan sharking. Being an officer of the court I'm surprised you don't know that. You can call the police, Ray, you could call your brother.

RAY: Oh god... Denise?! No. Okay? That's not what's going to happen here, alright... this guy, is like... he's like, a force of nature, nobody deals with him because he's what he is… he's outside the law… there's a law for people like you and me but not for me anymore because I've gone outside the law, okay? Now I'm on the outside of the law, something that most people won't even admit exists, and I'm out here with a psychopath named Bone Daddy.

DENISE: *(Beat.)* Bone Daddy.

RAY: Yes.

DENISE: You want me to take my savings out of the bank and give it to a man named Bone Daddy?

RAY: I know it sounds nutty.

DENISE: The secret world of men and their games, that's all this is, scary talk about monsters… you boys, when will you grow up?!

RAY: Denise, this is not a joke! I gotta get some Goddamned money! Now, I know you got money when your mom died, and I need that money.

DENISE: That money is for our old age.

RAY: I won't have an old age if you don't help me out.

DENISE: It's not just my mom's money, it's mine. I worked for that money at jobs I don't particularly like and now I'm supposed to just give that money up because you like to gamble. You don't get it, thirty grand will clean me out, I won't have anything left. I'll have worked and worked and have nothing to show for it.

RAY: And what would you have otherwise… a condo in Florida? You hate Florida!

DENISE: I know that, but that's not the point, is it? The point is to have a dream. Something that gets you through the day. That gets you through the yes ma'am and no sir and can I get you another drink and the car breaks down and you're tired all the time and you don't have sex any-more…

RAY: What about my dream?

DENISE: This is why we haven't been making love, isn't it?

RAY: What are you talking about?

DENISE: You're losing your juice in these joints?

RAY: *(Distasteful.)* Denise…?

DENISE: That's why you can't get it up!

RAY: I hate that kind of talk. You're a beautiful woman but sometimes you open your mouth and it just… it shatters the illusion.

DENISE: Oh, I suppose you want me to act very genteel and feminine and all fluttering concern and consolation, that's not me, money means something to me because I have a work ethic, I come from a blue-collar family, a working class family, I didn't grow up in Rolling fucking Hills, I didn't go to a prep school…

RAY: Oh no, can't we please not do this lecture, I have heard this lecture, I have heard it, I don't need to hear it now, I really don't…!

DENISE: NO! We can't! We can't do anything you want.

RAY: Look, I'm gonna go back to work for the city and I'll have regular money again. My private practice would be okay if could get it started but I can't so…

DENISE: Why don't you try going to the office once in awhile?

RAY: Oh God, screw off… I do go…

DENISE: You're never there.

RAY: How do you know, are you spying on me?

DENISE: I drive by sometimes to see if you want to have lunch before I go to work and you're never there and then I call you up and it's always the machine. What are you, screening?

RAY: Sometimes I'm at the courthouse trying to get clients.

DENISE: Ray?

RAY: What?

DENISE: You're not at the courthouse.

RAY: If I say I am, then I am.

DENISE: No, you're not, you're gambling.

RAY: Not every day, I didn't go every day, some days I went to the court house, some days, I was there trying to get clients.

DENISE: Ray?

RAY: I was!

DENISE: Look. I know you didn't try and get clients at the courthouse. That's not you.

RAY: You don't trust me.

DENISE: How can I trust you when you lie.

RAY: Of course I lie, if I told you the truth I'd have no freedom.

DENISE: Freedom for what? For gambling?

(He wants to hit her, he growls in frustration.)

RAY: Do you understand that I was gambling so WE could have a better life, something YOU want…

DENISE: I want?

RAY: Yes!

DENISE: Everyone wants a better life.

RAY: I don't want it.

DENISE: You don't want a better life?

RAY: I don't even know what that is!

DENISE: How can you say that?

RAY: Because if you really stop and think about it, what is a better life? It's stuff. It's fake Monet "Water Lillies" and ugly furniture and cars and houses and vacations and insurance premiums and working yourself into an early grave for a big empty pile of shit.

DENISE: Cars, houses and vacations are regular life, not a better life.

RAY: So what's a better life?

DENISE: Time and money. If you have a better life you have time and money.

RAY: I was still following your lead.

DENISE: My lead?

RAY: Yes! Because you have unrealistic expectations of success!

DENISE: I do? I'm a waitress!

RAY: You have unrealistic expectations of *my* success, *mine!*

DENISE: Well, okay… I did expect that you'd do better than you have.

RAY: SEE?

DENISE: But so did you.

RAY: At first I did but then I didn't! How could I? I was working as a public defender. Okay!? I might have thought I was going to build some kind of reputation for myself. Bringing rich man's justice to the poor. But I was overwhelmed the first week. My clients were either stupid, evil, greedy or weak, usually all four. My case load was enormous. The paperwork, the plea bargains, the last minute deals, the investigating, the postponements, the bail jumpers, the very bad people calling me at home, calling me by my first name. Hi, Ray, did we get us a good judge, Ray?! I think I fixed those witnesses, Ray! I got a cut that won't heal, Ray! I think my old lady wants to fuck you, Ray!

DENISE: But that's why, Ray, you went out on your own, you were sick of your job, and you wanted a change so you made a change.

RAY: For us!

DENISE: No, that was a decision you made for yourself.

RAY: I was doing it for us.

DENISE: No.

RAY: Yes, the job was making me nuts and I thought if I started my own practice I'd be easier to live with, that is something I did for us, we discussed it!

DENISE: You told me you were quitting after you'd already quit. You told me on our honeymoon that you'd resigned.

RAY: Okay, but even my mistakes I made for the sake of our life together.

DENISE: Our life together.

RAY: Denise, you have to think of marriage like a business, we each put something into the business and we take out whatever we need, new shoes and uniform for you, a new desk and chair for me, a car for you, gambling for me... If you got sick, who'd pay the car payment? The partners. So, who's responsible for my debts?

DENISE: You are because you put YOUR money...

RAY: My money is OUR money...

DENISE: Without asking me, into gambling.

RAY: Oh, now I need your consent.

DENISE: If you're treating it like a joint venture.

RAY: Okay, see! THIS is what I hate about talking to you!

DENISE: You've been gambling and hoping to win so that you could continue to gamble, it had nothing to do with me.

RAY: I didn't want you to know how bad things were.

DENISE: You think I didn't know?

RAY: You didn't know that I was having problems with work.

DENISE: Of course I did... I'm paying the bills.

RAY: Oh great, another version of "I told you so."

DENISE: Well, it was stupid to go out on your own.

RAY: SEE?

DENISE: I said so at the time... that's not you, you're not a leader, you're a sheep.

RAY: OH GOD! DENISE??? *(A moment.)* This is... damnit, this is, you know... I just... this is what's wrong with the whole bloody system of marriage.

DENISE: What? All I said is you're not an ambulance chaser.

RAY: That's not what you said!!!

DENISE: What did I say?

RAY: You said I was a Goddamned sheep!

DENISE: That was just my way of saying you're not an alpha wolf.

RAY: But don't you see that your having this idea about me, about my abilities is part of the problem?

DENISE: Why are you always trying to put it off on somebody else?

RAY: It's a no confidence vote!

DENISE: If you were in your right mind you'd know what I was talking about.

RAY: No I wouldn't.

DENISE: Yes you would.

RAY: You're my mate!

DENISE: Your mate? Like Tarzan and Jane...?

RAY: Yes. It's a primal relationship and your approval has everything to do with my success.

DENISE: We're not talking about success, we're talking about getting by. Barely making it.

RAY: In the beginning when I first went out on my own and I was getting a few cases, not a lot, it would have been nice for you to encourage me...

DENISE: I did.

RAY: Instead of tearing me down...

DENISE: I didn't.

RAY: And making jokes.

DENISE: What jokes?

RAY: Like the one about that Mrs. what's her name with the bad nose job being able to play it like an ocarina.

DENISE: You didn't even know what an ocarina was.

RAY: What is it?

DENISE: A sweet potato pipe, made out of terra cotta, it's like a flute... *(She laughs.)*

RAY: I don't know what's so funny about it?

DENISE: She had three nostrils, it was funny.

RAY: It wasn't funny to her.

DENISE: That's the last joke I ever made with you because you don't get my jokes, you don't understand my sense of humor.

RAY: What about the fat lady that slipped on the lettuce?

DENISE: I don't remember saying anything about her.

RAY: You said that kind of litigation clogs the courts and the taxpayers are footing the bill. Footing the bill was a joke.

DENISE: No, it wasn't.

RAY: I didn't see the humor.

DENISE: I wasn't making a joke.

RAY: I laughed to be polite.

DENISE: You didn't need to.

RAY: I was trying to be a good sport.

DENISE: That's because you're full of shit.

RAY: I was keeping the peace. That's what a good husband does, he keeps the peace. He lets many things go by, he doesn't take issue.

DENISE: He lies, in other words.

RAY: It's not lying, it's keeping the peace.

DENISE: You're not being honest, you're not being forthcoming.

RAY: What's wrong with having private thoughts?

DENISE: Because that's not intimacy, that's not an intimate relationship. I know I'm not the world's greatest cook or decorator, and maybe I forget to open a window but all you have to do is say something, that's all, I'm not going to get mad. Living together is hard even for people who... people who really love each other, but that's not us, is it?

RAY: Well, we may not be as close as we should be.

DENISE: Yeah, but that's important because you want to trade on an intimate relationship that doesn't exist.

RAY: Trade? What are you saying, we're married!

DENISE: If we were married, really married, you couldn't have lied to me.

RAY: I didn't lie.

DENISE: You weren't honest.

RAY: You're not honest.

DENISE: How am I not honest?

RAY: You don't report all your tips?

DENISE: Do you know why you're doing this?

RAY: Well, if we're being honest, let's be honest.

DENISE: Because you're in a hole and since I'm the only one who seems dumb enough for you to con, you've come to me. You've come to me with all this crap about how I left you alone, I'm not supportive...

RAY: I think we should look at some of these other issues, and see how they contribute to the breakdown in communication.

DENISE: If you were so concerned why didn't you say something before?

RAY: I don't like to make waves but if I'm already at sea...

DENISE: Oh, so this is funny?

RAY: No.

DENISE: That was a joke, you're making a joke.

RAY: Okay, forget it. You don't want to help me, fine! We're strangers who live together, that's all. We don't need each other, we can't rely on each other... SHIT! This is just... (*Punching the air.*) fuckin' unbelievable!

DENISE: (*A long beat.*) So if I give you the money you're just gonna pay these guys and that's the end of it?

RAY: (*Beat, calming.*) That's one possibility. But here's what I was thinking. I could pay off as little as I could, as little as I can get away with, and then invest the rest and use the interest to retire the loan.

DENISE: Invest the rest.

RAY: Yes. Because we're in a recession, it's stupid not to ride the market, we're at the beginning of a bull market and you're keeping it in a savings account and it's stupid, it's a stupid thing to do with money.

DENISE: I'm stupid about money.

RAY: Maybe not stupid just ignorant.

DENISE: Right.

RAY: Okay, I know this sounds like a bad idea because what do I know about investing but I was talkin' to Tank and he was telling me about this investment club that he and Freddy were gonna put together with this bartender that used to work as a broker at Smith Barney and…

DENISE: Tank was the one that got you into that pyramid scheme.

RAY: We've all grown up a lot since then.

DENISE: It's just more gambling you unlucky son of a bitch.

RAY: *(Beat.)* Wait. Don't call me that. Don't… take it back.

DENISE: No.

RAY: You take it back or I swear to God…

DENISE: What are you gonna do, hit me?

RAY: No, see, if you say stuff like "I'm unlucky," it'll wreck my luck, that's the first law of gambling, you watch what you say.

DENISE: You're about to lose a piece of your skeleton over nonpayment of gambling debts and you're worried I'M going to queer your LUCK? All you have to do is wake up in the morning and your luck is in the toilet.

RAY: Okay, fine. However you want to run it, Denise. But I'm serious. I need the money. I'm on my knees…

DENISE: No, you're not. You're waiting to be bailed out. You think I'm going to cave in because I love you and because if our places were reversed you'd help me out.

RAY: That's right, there's another reason, I WOULD help you…!

DENISE: Yeah, but you never have two bucks in your kit, so if our situations were reversed you couldn't help me out. I'd have to let Lothar pull the bones from my body.

RAY: You know, you love to do this, you love this, you love to get me in a corner and beat the shit out of me, well, okay… okay!! Here… here I am!
(Ray gets down on his knees.)
Look at me!

DENISE: No.

RAY: Look at me! I'm on my knees, for the time being, while I still have knees, but Denny, if I screw up with these monsters, I won't have knees, okay?

No knees! Please, I'm scared. I want to keep my body intact. I need you to help me.

DENISE: Oh my God.

RAY: What?

DENISE: *(Pause.)* It's not enough.

RAY: What? What isn't enough, what... I'm on my fuckin' knees!

DENISE: I don't love you enough.

RAY: Excuse me?

DENISE: If you'd asked me as a friend it would make more sense. But you asked me as an obligation of marriage and I realized, just this minute... I don't feel that anymore.

RAY: Okay, maybe we should talk in the morning.

DENISE: No, there's no point.

RAY: You're upset, this has been a shock.

DENISE: I don't feel married to you anymore.

RAY: But we're married...

DENISE: Yes, but I don't FEEL it.

RAY: Denise, marriage is a legal commitment, you fuck feelings because feelings come and go like the tides, but a legal obligation remains valid, that is what is meant by "for better or for worse."

DENISE: But it's never gotten better it's only gotten worse and I don't know if it's ever been that great between us, it's been more like a friendship, except you don't really like me...

RAY: That's not true!

DENISE: You don't like to come home.

RAY: Of course I do, it's my home, I come here...

DENISE: No, you don't, you don't like it here, you come in and you sniff the air and you go outside, out to the garden... I can tell you're not happy.

RAY: Where are you getting this stuff?

DENISE: From you. I can tell, you don't like the house, the way I've fixed it up, in fact... I know you're going to get mad about this... because you do every time I bring it up, but... I don't think you ever got over your first wife, I think you're still in love with Sharky.

RAY: Oh STOP IT!! Just, I am so SICK of your raging insecurity, how can you keep on like this? It's demented, you know, it's psychotic! I have an enormous amount of feeling for you.

DENISE: Gratitude maybe, but not love... never love.

RAY: Denise...

DENISE: I can't blame you, I forced this, marriage. You didn't want to get married. You didn't even want a relationship. You told me that the night I came over in that… trashy lingerie with that stupid casserole. God, I've never been so embarrassed in my life.

RAY: There's no reason, it was great.

DENISE: I scared you to death.

RAY: That's not true.

DENISE: I couldn't help it. I knew we weren't really connecting and I wanted you. I wanted to quit working.

RAY: You did?

DENISE: Yes, I thought maybe we could have a baby…?

RAY: Oh, yeah but…

DENISE: No, I know… but I thought marrying a lawyer…

RAY: Right.

DENISE: But that's not the only reason I married you.

RAY: Well, if it was…?

DENISE: No, it wasn't. I loved you. I loved everything about you. I loved to listen to you talk about your shitty job. I loved how miserable you were. I loved how much you seemed to care about your marriage coming apart, how you felt when your wife left…? I thought if I could make you love me like that… I'd really have something… great. That's where my unrealistic expectations came into it. I just thought we could make each other happy.

RAY: We are happy.

DENISE: No, we're not.

RAY: I am.

DENISE: Ray, it's never been a good fit.

RAY: I've been very happy with you.

DENISE: Ray? Don't you think I can hear it when you lie?

RAY: I'm not lying.

DENISE: Do you really think I'm that stupid?

RAY: Denise, I don't think you're stupid, I think you're very bright.

DENISE: Oh my God.

RAY: What now?

DENISE: You really do think I'm stupid.

RAY: I don't!!

DENISE: You were patronizing me.

RAY: No I wasn't. *(Beat.)* Maybe just a little but I do think you're intelligent.

DENISE: See, the problem is I loved you unconditionally. That's why I've let a lot of your lies go by.

RAY: Everybody lies a little.

DENISE: You don't. You lie a lot. But think about this, Ray. Think about all that lying. Don't you ever wonder who really knows you? Who really knows your heart? When you die, who will mourn for you. Who will know you well enough to mourn your loss.

RAY: I'm close to my brother. Sort of.

DENISE: You haven't spoken to your brother since he sold your car to buy crack.

RAY: All I'm saying is he knows me.

DENISE: He knows all about your gambling?

RAY: *(Beat.)* Yes.

DENISE: So he knew and I didn't?

RAY: It's the kind of thing you tell a brother.

DENISE: I see.

RAY: Look, Denise this is not the time, I'm just, I can't, I will, but not now, okay because you've got to help me out here, I mean, this is a very, very extra serious problem, you know? It's not like a joke, it's like a big deal, a very big, extra big fat deal. I'm in a lot of trouble and I need your help. Do you understand, are you getting that?

DENISE: Yes, I understand that.

RAY: You do?

DENISE: Yes.

RAY: *(Relieved.)* Good. Great. So... okay. You're going to have to go to the bank tomorrow morning, get the cash, has to be cash, and okay, new thing, honesty, it's not thirty thousand, I only need twenty, twenty grand, so okay, we'll go get it and you're right, I'm just gonna pay off this guy, forget the investment scheme, we'll do that some other time, when we're back on our feet financially. You know? So you'll go, or... hey, we'll both go, we'll go early, we'll have a nice breakfast, you know, out somewhere, maybe by the beach and we'll go to the bank and then we'll spend the day together, just the two of us, then I'll get the money, take the money, you can come if you want, we'll go find this guy and pay this debt and we'll be free, we'll make a fresh start. I think this has been good, this talking like this, we should do more of this, you know? *(Beat.)* So, you feel like spending the day together, just the two of us?

(She crosses to her bedroom, goes in and comes out with her nightgown and toothbrush.)

DENISE: I'm going to a hotel. It was your place when I moved in and I'll move out.

RAY: I thought it was all settled.

DENISE: Goodbye, Ray. *(She exits.)*

(Pause. Warren comes in from the garden, stands looking at the front door.)

WARREN: *(Beat.)* Wow. That was like watching a big boat sink.

(Warren makes drinks.)

You think maybe she has somebody…? Just my observation with women is they walk out very easily when they've got somebody in their head, you know? Like when Sharky left so easily it was because I was in her head. You know? She had a sure thing, somebody she was sure of, so she was able to let you go, just like that…

(Ray groans loudly and comes at Warren in a rage, Warren ducks, eludes him, Ray is out of control, he screams incoherently.)

RAY: AHHHHHAHHAHHHHHHHAHHAHAHHGHHGHHGHG-GHGHHGHAH…

(Warren catches him from behind and takes him down expertly, he holds him.)

WARREN: Breathe, breathe deeply and relax… relax! Come on! Give it up, big boy! Okay! Breathe, now! Come on!

(Warren is stronger and Ray relaxes and lies limply in his brother's arms.)

RAY: How do you fuck if you don't have a penis?

WARREN: I don't think you do.

RAY: I've heard of guys thinking they had their legs when their legs had been amputated, swearing they could feel their legs, but what about your dick, what happens?

WARREN: *(Thoughtfully.)* Well, it depends, I suppose on if they just take the dick.

RAY: Right. They could take the balls. I'd have no fluids… what do you think would happen… would my voice get higher…?

WARREN: Stop it.

RAY: Seriously.

WARREN: It's not productive.

RAY: Will I be able to stop shaving?

WARREN: What are you doing?

RAY: Trying to look on the bright side.

WARREN: You know what you need? You need a job.

RAY: Maybe if they cut off my dick I could become a woman... get married. I wouldn't be able to have kids, the guy would have to love me for myself.

WARREN: Are you listening?

RAY: Did you ever see *Some Like it Hot?* Jack Lemmon dresses as a woman and by the end of the movie it looks like he's going to make a very good marriage to a millionaire played by Joe E. Brown.

WARREN: Look, all you need is one good case and you'd be clear of debt. What about this guy tonight... why don't you just take his case... this guy that was here with that...

RAY: Psychotic Gumdrop.

(Warren finds the check underneath some magazines on the table.)

WARREN: Look, here's this guy's check... for fifty thousand dollars.

(Warren keeps the check away.)

RAY: Gimme that... Warren?

WARREN: This is a large amount of money, it's more than you need.

RAY: Warren?!

WARREN: Rich people and their justice, Ray. It's all for sale. What's the case?

RAY: I'm not taking it.

WARREN: This girl killed somebody, right?

RAY: I don't remember.

WARREN: What have they got?

RAY: Plenty.

WARREN: Like what?

RAY: They have a signed confession, they have the knife.

WARREN: Okay, okay... well, you can get the confession bumped. *(Realizing.)* And I work in the evidence room.

RAY: Yeah, so?

WARREN: It doesn't take a genius to figure out why they chose you, Ray. This guy Larry knows about me, knows about you... why is that?

RAY: I don't know.

WARREN: It's a set up. Losing the knife. I can lose the knife.

RAY: No!

WARREN: Why not?

RAY: No, Warren! An act like this would change everything. It would change our lives in ways we can't even anticipate.

WARREN: Then what difference does it make? We're already off the train, we're already running in the dark...

RAY: You're talking about cooperating with human evil. That guy is evil, his daughter is damaged.

WARREN: Ray?

RAY: What?

WARREN: Who do we kill when we take a life?

RAY: Did you hear what I said?

WARREN: This is the argument you made against the death penalty and it worked, you got that guy life.

RAY: It doesn't apply here.

WARREN: Come on. Who's life do we take when we take a life?

RAY: *(Sigh.)* We take our own life.

WARREN: That's right. We take a piece of ourselves we've come to hate, we place it out there, on the face of an innocent person, and we murder that person, right? So, who dies?

RAY: Warren, I refuse to become involved in this.

WARREN: Ray, the girl was operating at her highest level of good, she was trying to the best of her ability to heal the war within herself by committing a murder, can't you understand that?

RAY: Yes, but it's still murder, Warren.

WARREN: She's a young girl. She made a mistake.

RAY: This is not the first person she's killed. *(Beat.)*

WARREN: It's not?

RAY: No.

WARREN: Oh.

RAY: For God's sake, Warren, she needs to go away. I know you know this.

WARREN: No, I know.

RAY: I know the one thing we have in common is our love of justice.

WARREN: Okay, so there needs to be some kind of net in place is what you're saying.

RAY: Net?

WARREN: No, okay, I hear you. How about this? What if when she gets out, instead of just walking away she comes to us.

RAY: Us?

WARREN: Or me.

RAY: If she gets off, she'll be free. It's kind of not our problem at that point.

WARREN: But where is the justice in that?

RAY: That's what I'm saying…!

WARREN: But what if when she gets out, we keep her.

RAY: Keep her...?

WARREN: I could keep her.

RAY: You mean, like kidnap her?

WARREN: Incarcerate.

RAY: That's insane.

WARREN: Everyday people slip through the holes in the world because they have failed to learn the lessons of life. Failed to refine their sensibilities. Common courtesy is so uncommon as to be a joke. We are neck deep in human excrement wondering where to take our next crap. What is so insane about sequestering a rebellious and murdering girl?

RAY: Well, Warren, it's illegal for one thing.

WARREN: So is murder.

RAY: Warren, what is going on with you?

WARREN: I'll tell you, Ray. Sharky has driven me mad. She has tried to fix what is not broken in me and changed the way I look at myself and now I'm permanently screwed up. What's the little girl's name?

RAY: Vicky.

WARREN: I want to heal my relationship with women through my incarceration of Vicky.

RAY: How did we get here?

WARREN: It's become a two-fold plan. I'll lock her up for murder but I'll rehabilitate her for me.

RAY: Will you take pictures of her?

WARREN: If I deem it part of the therapeutic process.

RAY: And for how long will you sequester this rebellious and murdering girl?

WARREN: Seven years, a cycle of time, but maybe, if she's amenable, forever.

RAY: Who's going to take care of her again?

WARREN: We will. Or I will. That will be my job. You will have to get some kind of a job and support us. Because I'll be fired, and I'll just stay home. Like a housewife taking care of the kids. She'll be like a daughter to us, you and me.

RAY: Yes, I'm married to my brother, we have one child.

WARREN: Think about it. Wouldn't it be great to have a kid?

RAY: I am thinking about it. Why am I thinking about this? It's crazy...

WARREN: Because crazier things happen all the time.

RAY: It's because I'm afraid.

WARREN: Sure. You're afraid of these evil men that have pulled you into a world of darkness...

RAY: Stop talking for a minute, okay?

WARREN: I am trying to save your life.

RAY: Losing evidence can't be that easy. You will be found out, you will be punished. Right?

WARREN: Right... So, I have to have an excuse. For instance, you can be on drugs. Drugs are the obvious choice, especially with a cop like me who has a history of abuse. So, I'll get high and lose the knife.

RAY: And it's just a coincidence you lose the evidence on my case?

WARREN: You don't take the case.

RAY: I don't?

WARREN: Anybody could take the case.

RAY: But I keep the money...?

WARREN: You fixed it.

RAY: And you'd do this for me?

WARREN: Yes.

RAY: Why? Why would you do such a thing for me? Give up a job you love, I mean, eventually you would get your old job back.

WARREN: I know that.

RAY: So why would you give that up?

WARREN: You're my brother.

RAY: No. Why really?

WARREN: That's it.

RAY: No, really.

WARREN: I want you to forgive me. For Sharky.

RAY: I have forgiven you, Warren, I couldn't do anything else but forgive you... I love you.

WARREN: No, you don't understand.

RAY: Tell me.

WARREN: When Sharky came home and started to scream I struck her not in anger so much as surprise. And she fell into the glass door and thrashing to keep from falling ended up cutting herself even worse, in fact, she punctured an artery.
(Ray sits down.)

RAY: Jesus.

WARREN: She was asking me to help but I couldn't... I saw what was happening, but I couldn't seem to consider it an emergency. How could I? It was a triumph. I was finally on level ground. She was so weak and pathetic that all my hatred came out and I remained absolutely motionless and

watched her dying. Her screaming turned to begging and the begging turned to crying till finally... and this is how I found out she still loved you... when she realized she was going to die, she asked me to tell you that she had always loved you, that there was never anyone else in her heart. And then, she apologized to me, she did... *(Smiles.)* She apologized which I must admit, felt good. That broke the spell, the apology. When she did that I tried to help her, but by then it was too late. She was gone. *(Ray looks around, at loose ends.)*
She told me she wasn't trying to fix me, she was trying to make me more like you. Isn't that sweet?

RAY: Where is she?

WARREN: *(Moves to the garden.)* I put her out there. Out there under the Plumeria and the gardenia, where the jasmine is in bloom, where the garden smells the sweetest. I put her out there for you. Deep in the rich fragrant earth. She'll be mother to your garden, nurturing it for years to come, if you leave her alone. Can you do that, Ray? Can you let her rest in peace?

RAY: *(Pause.)* Just like that? No funeral?

WARREN: We can have a funeral, we just can't invite anybody.

RAY: *(Beat.)* No.

WARREN: Think about it.

RAY: I thought of her everyday, Warren, woke up thinking about her everyday. Last thing on my mind at night. First thing in the morning. I still carry her picture in my wallet so when someone I don't know and never expect to see again asks to see a picture of my wife I show them Sharky and pretend we're still married, and that she's at home, waiting for me at home... the love of my life waiting for me to come home but I can never go home to her now, can I...?

WARREN: Ray, you could have gone home to her anytime. You knew she was unhappy. Why didn't you call her up? One little phone call from you and I'll bet the drugs, the gambling, the human misery, all this, could have been avoided.

RAY: *(Beat.)* Are you... blaming me?

WARREN: In part.

RAY: *(Beat.)* Right. Okay. I can see your point. I do see it. *(Beat.)* But I'm still calling the police on you...you amoral shithead.
(Ray goes toward the phone, Warren gets there first, takes the phone and moves away.)

WARREN: Can I say one more thing?

RAY: Give me the phone.

WARREN: If you leave her there in the garden, she'll always be there to come home to.

RAY: Warren?

(Warren hands him the phone.)

WARREN: I know, it's not the happiest ending... but at least you're together, Ray. It's a way of looking at it, I don't know if you can appreciate the symmetry, but it's there. You have what many people long for with their ex's. Closure.

RAY: How can you ask me to do this?

WARREN: Because we're lost men, Ray. And all we have is each other.

(The two men watch each other for a long beat.)

BLACKOUT

END OF PLAY

Finer Noble Gases
by Adam Rapp

BIOGRAPHY

Adam Rapp's plays have been produced by American Repertory Theatre, New York Theatre Workshop, the Bush Theatre in London, Berkeley Repertory, Victory Gardens Theater, the 24th Street Theatre in L.A., the Arcola Theatre in London, and The Juilliard School. A graduate of Clarke College in Dubuque, Iowa, he also completed a two-year Playwriting Fellowship at Juilliard. Awards: 1997 Herbert & Patricia Brodkin Scholarship, two Lincoln Center Le Comte du Nouy Awards, 1999 Princess Grace Award, 2000 Mabou Mines Suite Residency, 2000 Roger L. Stevens Award, 2001 Helen Merrill Award. Past productions: *Nocturne* (A.R.T. [Elliot Norton Award— Outstanding New Script, Best New Play by the Independent Reviewers of New England], New York Theatre Workshop, Berkeley Repertory); *Animals and Plants* (A.R.T.); *Ghosts in the Cottonwoods* (Victory Gardens, 24th Street Theatre—L.A., Arcola Theatre—London); *Blackbird* (Bush Theatre—London, Pittsburgh's City Theatre); *Stone Cold Dead Serious* (A.R.T.); *Dreams of the Salthorse* (Encore Theatre, San Francisco); *Faster* (Rattlestick, New York City).

HUMANA FESTIVAL PRODUCTION

Finer Noble Gases premiered at the Humana Festival of New American Plays in March 2002. It was directed by Michael John Garcés with the following cast:

Staples	Robert Beitzel
Chase	Dallas Roberts
Lynch	Michael Shannon
Speed	Ray Rizzo
Gray	Jeffrey Bean
Dot	Alaina Mills

and the following production cast:

Scenic Designer	Paul Owen
Costume Designer	Christal Weatherly
Lighting Designer	Tony Penna
Sound Designer	Vincent Olivieri
Properties Designer	Doc Manning
Stage Manager	Charles M. Turner III
Production Assistants	Justin McDaniel, Erin Tatge
Dramaturg	Amy Wegener
Assistant Dramaturg	Carrie Nutt
Casting	Orpheus Group Casting

CHARACTERS
STAPLES
CHASE
LYNCH
SPEED
GRAY
DOT

TIME AND PLACE
An East Village apartment near Tomkins Square Park in New York. Winter.

"You take a really sleepy man, Esmé,
And he *always* stands a chance of again
becoming a man with all of his fac—with
all of his f-a-c-u-l-t-i-e-s intact."
> From J.D. Salinger's
> *For Esmé—With Love and Squalor*

Robert Beitzel, Alaina Mills and Dallas Roberts
in *Finer Noble Gases*

26th Annual Humana Festival of New American Plays
Actors Theatre of Louisville, 2002
photo by Fred Furrow III

Finer Noble Gases

A filthy East Village apartment near Tomkins Square Park. A typical pre-war Skinner box. A naked window leading to a fire escape. A neon beer sign, turned off. A half-collapsed, stained and bucket-seated sofa, duct tape over the cushions. A coffee table with three glass bowls of pills: a bowl of blue pills; a bowl of pink pills; a bowl of yellow pills. The bowls are neatly arranged, perfectly spaced. A random, street-plucked chair. An equally random ottoman. A full drum set, a microphone stand and mic next to the drum set. An electric and a bass guitar propped on guitar stands. A bass amp. A guitar amp. A keyboard set up on a stand, an amp next to it. A few microphone stands set up with mics. Some random cords and wires snaking indecipherably. Sweat socks, junk mail, crumpled beer cans, old set lists, pizza boxes, indecipherable pools of things here and there. Drifts of debris. A wall of McDonald's Happy Meal boxes. A hallway leading to unseen bedrooms. A front door. A small TV surveillance monitor housed in the wall next to the door. Underneath the monitor, someone has scrawled "MIKE" in black indelible ink. There are several shoulder-height holes in the wall. A kitchen sink choked with dirty dishes. A filthy table with scattered chairs. A trash can painted like R2D2.

Chase and Staples, 30-ish, are sitting on the sofa, watching TV. They wear wrinkled thrift-store clothes. They are fully bearded and they smell. There is the feeling that the two of them have been living on the sofa since the previous spring. Staples sits very still. Chase fidgets a bit, his feet never touching the floor.

Next to the chair, Another Man lies on the floor. He is neither sleeping nor thinking. He is 30-ish, bearded, and lives in his underwear.

The only source of light is the blue throb of the TV and a yellowish glow from the back of the apartment where lights have been left on. The noise of the TV should play throughout, but barely audible; an animal being tortured.

STAPLES: I had this dream last night that I was a robot. Big metal robot. I was crying but nothing was coming out. I could feel the crying. In my throat.

But no tears. And I didn't have any balls. Instead I had a light switch. I kept trying to turn it on but all it did was make this buzzing noise.

(Chase puts his hand down his pants.)

CHASE: Wow.

STAPLES: I know, right?

(They watch.)

CHASE: You do the blues or the pinks?

STAPLES: The blues.

CHASE: The pinks are good. You shouldn't do more than two. Never do more than two. I think some guy did four once.

STAPLES: Whoa.

CHASE: I know, right?

STAPLES: Halfs or fulls?

CHASE: Fulls.

STAPLES: What happened to him?

CHASE: He got on a bus. The M-Fifteen, I think. Tied the driver to a pole and drove through yellow lights all the way to the Upper East Side, got out, ran to the Ninety-Second Street Y, ripped off all his clothes, jumped in the pool.

STAPLES: He did four?

CHASE: Four pinks, yep.

STAPLES: ...Did he have a gun or something?

CHASE: Gunless.

STAPLES: Wow.

CHASE: I know, right?

STAPLES: Could he like *swim?*

CHASE: Good question.

(They watch. Chase removes his hand from his pants.)

STAPLES: I took two once.

CHASE: Pinks?

STAPLES: Uh-huh.

CHASE: Halfs or fulls?

STAPLES: Fulls.

CHASE: Two full pinks?

STAPLES: One right after the other.

CHASE: When?

STAPLES: Coupla days ago.

CHASE: Was I around?

STAPLES: Yeah, you were around.

CHASE: Do you remember where?

STAPLES: You were in your room with that plastic thing.

CHASE: Oh. Right on.

(They watch.)

CHASE: Anything weird happen?

STAPLES: Tried to steal a Christmas tree.

CHASE: Whoa.

STAPLES: I know, right?

CHASE: Like *steal* steal?

STAPLES: Like theft, dude.

CHASE: Where?

STAPLES: New K-Mart by the Six Train.

CHASE: They serve breakfast there. Eggs and stuff.

(They watch.)

CHASE: You get caught?

STAPLES: Yeah. Two undercover security guards. They were cool.

(They watch.)

CHASE: What kinda tree was it?

STAPLES: It was a blue tree, Chase. Smelled like chewing gum.

(They watch.)

CHASE: Blue like what kinda blue?

STAPLES: Blue like when the tape pops out of the VCR blue. Kinda violety.

CHASE: Nice imagery, Staples.

STAPLES: Thanks, Chase.

(They watch.)

STAPLES: I thought it would look good next to the keyboard. Some lights. A wreath maybe.

CHASE: They got wreaths over at the hardware store on Seventh.

STAPLES: The one with all the paint.

CHASE: Little Green wreaths.

STAPLES: We coulda got one and painted it blue.

CHASE: To match the tree.

STAPLES: And the pills.

(They watch.)

CHASE: It's cool that it was scented.

STAPLES: I know, right?

(They watch.)

STAPLES: Sometimes you look at something. You weigh it in your mind. Like a rock. Or a gallon of paint. French coins are like that.

CHASE: Francs.

STAPLES: Yeah, stuff in your pocket feels better when it's heavy... But the really weird thing...

CHASE: Yeah?

STAPLES: The really weird thing is that I like *wanted* to get caught.

CHASE: You wanted it.

STAPLES: I did, Chase, I did. I thought maybe they'd yell at me. Stuff like *(As if invaded.) Stand up Straight!* Or *Look at me when I'm talking to you!*

CHASE: Did they?

STAPLES: Nu-uh.

CHASE: What'd they do?

STAPLES: They put me in a room. There was this big mirror. A few metal chairs. This woman came in and gave me a glass of water. Then she put the tree up and left me alone with it. I think they were studying me on the other side of the mirror.

CHASE: Like *studying* studying?

STAPLES: Uh-huh.

CHASE: What do you think they were studying?

STAPLES: Probably my mind. The like waves and stuff.

CHASE: Huh.

(They watch.)

CHASE: Did the woman like *do* anything to the tree after she put it up?

(Staples thinks.)

STAPLES: Um. I don't think I understand your question, dude.

CHASE: I don't know. I guess I'm asking about ornaments and stuff. Popcorn. Like did she *decorate* it.

STAPLES: Nu-uh.

CHASE: Huh.

(They watch.)

STAPLES: It was pretty weird. Lonely.

CHASE: Did like *you* do anything?

STAPLES: Um. Uh-uh. I *felt* like doing something, though. Like getting up and whirling my arms. Or just jumping up and down a few times.

CHASE: Did you get busted?

STAPLES: Busted and disgusted. I called Frank the Father. He called his lawyers. They took care of it.

CHASE: Frank the Father's a lawyer, too, isn't he?

STAPLES: Lawyer. Banker. CFO. UFO.

CHASE: Unidentified Flying... Financial Officer.

> (*Staples imitates a UFO flying through the air. He follows it with an invisible ray gun and then mimes shooting it out of the air. They both follow its descent to the earth and watch it crash. They laugh sadly.*)
>
> (*One of them farts like a French horn.*)

CHASE: Was that you or me?

STAPLES: I think it was you.

CHASE: Oh.

> (*They watch.*)

STAPLES: I think about doing stuff but I get tired. Like more stealing. Canned fish. Little plastic things. Gum.

> Or breaking a window with my *fist!* Wrapping it with the newspaper first and then *punching!* Or kicking a garbage can!
>
> (*Chase starts to twitch uncontrollably.*)

STAPLES: (*Calm now.*) Dude, you're like twitching all over the place.

> (*Chase twitches.*)

STAPLES: That's so cool. I wish I could twitch... Sometimes I'll look at my hand. Like at a finger. And I'll say to it, I'll say *Move.* And it will.

CHASE: Motor skills.

STAPLES: That's how aliens must do stuff. I mean if they're in a human body. 'Cause they don't have the muscle memories. So they have to tell themselves what to do. Hands and feet. Arms. They'll say *Walk legs.* Like in their language. They'll command themselves to do it. And they'll just start walking places. So there's more lag time with aliens. 'Cause they don't have the memories.

> (*Chase's twitching punctuates into an explosive bicep muscle.*)

CHASE: Feel my muscle.

STAPLES: Feel your muscle?

CHASE: Yeah.

STAPLES: Like *feel* feel it?

CHASE: Sure.

STAPLES: No way, dude.

CHASE: Come on, Staples, covet my power source! Feel the way my calories burn with whitehot fire!

STAPLES: That's way too close, Chase!

CHASE: Whitehot, blistering foxfire!!!

STAPLES: All I ask for is two feet!

CHASE: The truth of my muscle would crush thee!!!

> *(Chase releases his muscle.)*

CHASE: *(Catching his breath.)* You feel so much on the pinks. So much feeling.

STAPLES: The blues are cool, too.

CHASE: The blues give you the blues. Like someone's inside you playing a harmonica.

STAPLES: Someone really really small.

> *(They watch.)*

CHASE: Yeah. And then there's the pissers.

STAPLES: The pissers give you the runs.

CHASE: But they make you feel stuff.

STAPLES: Oh, they're total feelwhores.

CHASE: Like the pinks but quicker.

STAPLES: A little hotter, too. Like plants.

CHASE: Like plants?

STAPLES: Yeah, plants. Like in a greenhouse. How they do that thing to the Sun. Trap it or something.

CHASE: …Photosynthesis.

> *(The front door opens. Lynch enters, closes the door. He is 30, big, heavily bearded. He wears layers and layers of old sweats, batting gloves, a scarf, a dockworker's skullcap, construction boots, a weight belt. He is exhausted, hunched, slow-moving. There is the sense that he has to search for every step. While crossing, he stops behind the sofa and is lured by the TV. He watches. Only the sound of the shrieking animal.)*
>
> *(After a moment, Lynch takes a few long strides toward the TV and then kicks it in.)*
>
> *(The Man On The Floor rises and crosses upstage. He takes his underwear down and begins urinating thoroughly into a broken tom-tom drum.)*
>
> *(Lynch turns, stares at Chase and Staples for a moment and exits to the back of the apartment, closes a door.)*
>
> *(Chase and Staples stare at the kicked-in TV, while the Man On The Floor continues to urinate.)*

STAPLES: Chase?

CHASE: Yeah, Staples?

STAPLES: I don't know what to like um *do*.

CHASE: Either do I.

> *(Staples turns to Chase.)*

STAPLES: I'm getting up!

CHASE: Yeah?

STAPLES: Yeah, I'm getting up!

   (He doesn't move.)

CHASE: Maybe count to three or something.

STAPLES: Good idea.

CHASE: I'll count for you.

STAPLES: Okay.

CHASE: Ready?

STAPLES: Yeah, I'm ready. Go 'head.

CHASE: One. Two. Three.

   (Staples rocks himself forward and off the sofa. He lurches slightly, rights himself.)

   (The Man On The Floor finishes urinating, pulls his underwear up, crosses to a spot near the chair, lies down.)

CHASE: You okay?

STAPLES: Yeah, yeah, I'm good.

   (Staples turns and crosses to the front door like some kind of lost and forlorn spaceman. He stares at the surveillance monitor and then lifts his arm and turns it on. It issues a vague, bluish-white screen, a few obscure lines. Staples attempts to wave the light from the monitor toward the TV, as if it will some-how cause it to work again. Chase joins him and they wave with great fervor. They stop and watch the TV for a moment.)

CHASE: It's not working.

STAPLES: Not really, right?

CHASE: Nu-uh.

   (Staples crosses back to the sofa, sits.)

STAPLES: We could like watch Mike the Monitor.

CHASE: We could.

STAPLES: Maybe we should move the davenport. Make it easier to see.

CHASE: Good idea.

   (They stare at each other a moment.)

STAPLES: One. Two. Three.

   (Staples rolls over his arm of the sofa and begins budging it toward the moni-tor. Chase never actually gets off the sofa and attempts to move it by using whatever force he can generate by charging and ramming into one of its arms. They surf-scoot-pivot the sofa so that it faces the surveillance monitor. Chase sits back down, exhausted. They watch the monitor.)

CHASE: It's not bad.

STAPLES: Not too bad.

CHASE: I like how it's kinda blank.

STAPLES: Yeah. The blankness.

CHASE: It's like snow.

STAPLES: It is kinda.

CHASE: Like a little box of snow.

STAPLES: A little box fulla snowballs.

(They watch.)

CHASE: But it's not the same!

STAPLES: I know, right?!

CHASE: I keep expecting things!

STAPLES: Yeah, Chase, me too!

CHASE: Like a little caribou to appear!

STAPLES: I know, I know!

CHASE: And the rhino!!

STAPLES: How those birds were just sitting on his back like someone put 'em there!!

(They stare at each other.)

CHASE: One. Two. Three.

(Staples rises off the sofa, and returns it to its original position. Again, Chase never actually touches the floor and uses the same charging-ramming method. After the sofa is re-positioned, they sit, exhausted.)

(Chase suddenly charges to Staples' end of the sofa, violently pukes over the side, smothering Staples with his body. After a moment, he thaws from the hurling, wipes his mouth, returns to his side.)

CHASE: Should I call Doug the Dad?

STAPLES: Call Doug the Dad. If it doesn't work I'll call Frank the Father.

(Chase starts to burrow in the cracks of the sofa, searching for his cell phone. After a moment, he realizes that it is on the chair. Staples reaches into his pocket, lends him his cell phone. Chase attempts to dial the number, but can't remember it. He hands the cell phone back to Staples and then lunges for the coffee table rather Olympically, and then, without ever touching the ground, manages to traverse the space between the sofa and the chair, using whatever means necessary: the coffee table, the ottoman, etc. It should be an enormous feat. He winds up securing his cell phone rather miraculously, sits on the ottoman, speed dials, waits.)

CHASE: Hey, Daddy? It's Chase... Hey Daddy. How's it going? How's business?... Good, good...

What do I want? Well, nothing, Daddy. Just calling to say Hey. Hey and how's it going and how's Mary the Mom and all that... Oh, things are great. Really great.

Yeah, it's getting cold out, I think. Pretty cold. Scarves and mittens, you know?...

Oh the band is *so* good. It's been a real productive period. We're writing songs like crazy... Oh, everything. Vocals. Rhythm guitar. Some very clever leads now and then. Keyboards. A little drums here and there, rat-a-tat-tat, percussion, you know? I'll send you a tape... Sure, sure... Yeah, I got the check. I totally got it. Yeah, thanks, Daddy...

Well, there was one thing, Daddy. One small thing... Yeah... Yeah, I know... Well, it's pretty small, small as a kittycat, but it's important. Really really kinda huge and important... Well, our TV got messed up somehow... Yeah, the old Trinitron... Well, I don't know. It's like there's a big hole in it... In the screen... Well not a *hole* hole, more like a black um *void*. Yeah, a black void in the middle...

Could I maybe like use the credit card?... I know, I know...Well, we *do* need it, Daddy. Cause we're thinking about shooting a video... Yeah... And we need something to watch it on. I could just buzz over to the Wiz, you know? They got great deals over there. They might even deliver. *(He nods to Staples, smiles.)*

No?... Oh... You sure, dude? Okay. Okay, Daddy...

Yeah, I'm working. Working on the music, you know? Art's a full-time job. No compensation yet, but there will be. Big things ahead. Nothing but the sky...

Yeah, sure I'll come home for a few days... Maybe next month... I'll just jump on the Metro North. A little Northbound train action.

Okay, Daddy... Me, too... Tell Mom I say Hey... I know, I know... Sure... I'll send that tape off.

(He turns the phone off, slips it back into his pocket.)

CHASE: Your turn, dude. Frank the Father.

(Staples dials his cell phone, waits. After a moment he starts to make pig sounds into the phone. Pigs, monkeys, and sheep. He stops, turns the phone off, puts it back in his pocket, looks at Chase.)

CHASE: Voicemail?

(Staples nods.)

(The sound of a door closing. Moments later, Lynch appears from the back of the apartment. He is dressed in an enormous snowmobile suit. He steps slowly into the room as though he isn't sure where he is heading, stands very still.)

CHASE: Alaska man.

STAPLES: Glacier guy.

CHASE: What's with the snowsuit?

LYNCH: It's gettin cold.

CHASE: Yeah?

LYNCH: Sposed to get in the teens tonight.

STAPLES: Whoa.

CHASE: Better turn the heat up.

LYNCH: Things aren't workin out so well. It's better if there's snow when that happens.

(Chase and Lynch stare at each other. An awkward pause.)

CHASE: Where you goin, dude?

LYNCH: Get somethin for my toe.

CHASE: What's wrong with your toe?

LYNCH: It's numb.

CHASE: Like *numb* numb?

LYNCH: Uh-huh.

STAPLES: It's prolly from the TV.

LYNCH: Meaning?

STAPLES: Oh, nothing. It's just that you like totally kicked it in and such.

LYNCH: Felt like the right thing to do. The perfect time, you know? *(As if invaded.)* IT'S MONSTER MADNESS AT THE KIEL AUDITORIUM BIG TRUCKS *BIG BIG* TRUCKS TRUCKS SO BIG OTHER TRUCKS CAN RIDE AROUND INSIDE OF THEM!!!

(The explosion sends Lynch across the room, somewhere near the keyboard. He is oddly joined to a microphone, stares at it confused for a second, re-sets it on the stand.)

(Chase and Staples stare at each other. Lynch crosses to the neon beer sign, turns it on, then touches the keyboard for a moment.)

LYNCH: *(A reaching out.)* I feel really far away from things. Like everything's gettin smaller.

(Nobody moves.)

CHASE: Um. How was like work, dude?

LYNCH: Okay.

CHASE: What kinda stuff you move?

LYNCH: Sofas. Bookcases. Beds. Some statues.

CHASE: Like *statue* statues?

LYNCH: Men, Women. Men mostly.

STAPLES: Were they like nude?

LYNCH: Yeah.

STAPLES: Any hot bods?

(Lynch reaches into one of his pockets and removes a marble breast.)

STAPLES: *Dude.*

CHASE: *Dude!* Gettin a little on the *side!*

(Lynch starts to slowly move the breast through the air, almost dancing with it. He hums a melodious tune. Chase and Staples collaborate a bit. Lynch blows into the breast as if it is a conch shell, making his way toward Chase. He places the breast on Chase's head, his face, his beard. What seems like fun starts to get a little scary as he uses the marble breast to force Chase's head into the cushion of the chair.)

LYNCH: *(Releasing Chase's head.)* Can't have it!

CHASE: Cool.

LYNCH: *(To Staples.)* You either!

STAPLES: Hey, that's totally cool.

(Lynch puts the marble breast back in his pocket, crosses to the TV, sits on it.)

LYNCH: I used to know a lot more stuff. *(To Chase.)* When we were in school, you know?

CHASE: Sure.

LYNCH: Facts mostly. I was good with facts.

CHASE: Facts are good.

STAPLES: Yeah, dude. Facts are totally good.

(Lynch crosses to the window.)

LYNCH: I've been keeping a brick in my pocket. Left pocket.

CHASE: A brick and a tit.

LYNCH: Found it in the basement.

CHASE: The basement?

STAPLES: Like the *basement* basement?

LYNCH: Uh-huh.

CHASE: What were you like doing down in the basement?

LYNCH: Lookin for things. Gettin stuff together.

CHASE: Things?

STAPLES: Stuff?

LYNCH: Things and stuff. Lookin and gettin. Pretty much in that order. *(To Chase.)* There's all these robots everywhere.

(Staples tries to make himself invisible.)

CHASE: Robots?

LYNCH: Uh-huh. Millions of em. A hundred million.

CHASE: Cool.

LYNCH: *(To Staples.)* They're just layin there like they're sleepin. A hundred million robots.

(Chase and Staples stare at each other. Lynch turns, crosses to the Man On The Floor. From his mouth he drops a slow gob of spit on him. The Man On The Floor doesn't stir. Lynch watches him for a moment and then crosses to the front door. Before he exits, he removes a brick from his left pocket and smashes through the front of the surveillance monitor.)

LYNCH: *(Another reaching out.)* Bye.

CHASE: Bye.

STAPLES: Bye, dude.

LYNCH: Washington was a good president. But Lincoln was better. You can tell cause of the pictures. His beard and stuff.

(Lynch exits. His footfalls can be heard descending the stairs. Chase and Staples sit very still.)

CHASE: I have an idea.

STAPLES: Yeah?

CHASE: Heldinwell.

STAPLES: *Heldinwell?*

CHASE: The guy who lives downstairs. The weird guy in number three.

STAPLES: What about him?

CHASE: *He's* got a TV.

STAPLES: You're saying?

CHASE: We should totally take it.

STAPLES: Like rob him?

CHASE: Sure. I'll invite him up and while he's under my narrative spell you can use the fire escape and bust into his apartment and snag his TV.

STAPLES: Good idea.

CHASE: I know, right?

STAPLES: Sneaky.

CHASE: It's totally sneaky.

(Chase makes his way back to the sofa via the ottoman, the coffee table, as before.)

STAPLES: ...So, um, can I like ask a question?

CHASE: *(Transitioning from ottoman to coffee table.)* Sure.

STAPLES: Why do you get to be the narrative spell guy?

CHASE: Cause, dude, I'm a good conversationalist.

STAPLES: You are?

CHASE: Dude, I'm such a good conversationalist. My words and images. My use of metaphor and freakish nouns.

STAPLES: Are you trying to say that I'm like *not good* at images and freakish nouns?

CHASE: No.

STAPLES: Cause I can totally paint pictures with words, Chase. You know I'm so good at that.

CHASE: You are, you are.

STAPLES: I'm like a metaphor *factory*.

CHASE: *(Secure on the coffee table now.)* That's true, Staples. That's totally true. But where you're the factory I'm like the quality control division. I make the metaphor a little more slippery. I add the salt and pepper. The spicy spices. I'm like the quality control *chef* who takes on the metaphor as soon as it comes off the assembly line.

STAPLES: But, dude, I—

CHASE: *Plus*, you're on the blues. I'm on the pinks!

STAPLES: I'm such a good conversationalist, Chase. I have a large assortment of words and ideas.

CHASE: Why do you think I like hanging with you so much? Besides, you're the one who's always getting locked out and coming in through the window.

STAPLES: What's that supposed to mean?

CHASE: Nothing. Just that you're more familiar with the ways and means of the fire escape. It's one of the things you're really really good at.

STAPLES: ...Maybe.

CHASE: I'll call him.

(Chase leaps from the coffee table, lands on his side of the sofa rather impressively, pulls his cell phone out of his pocket, dials, waits.)

CHASE: Yes. I'd like the number of a *Heldinwell* on East Tenth Street in Manhattan... Cool. *(He winks at Staples.)* Hello. Is this Mister Heldinwell?... It is?... Oh, hey. This is Chase. Chase Fitzsimmons, your upstairs neighbor in apartment five...

Hey! How's it going?... Good, good.

Well, anyway, the reason I'm calling is cause I sorta hurt my back real bad today... Yeah, I slipped on the ice and landed on the old sacro*ster*num... Yeah, slipped and fell like an old person. *Whooop!*... Oh, the sacro*ster*num, that thing under the spinal canal... Yeah, in the lumber division... Anyway, I'm on these killer pain pills. These big pharmaceutical hockey pucks. And the thing is, I'm feeling a little fuzzed-out and insecure and both my roommates are away for the weekend. You see, I keep thinking someone's *behind me*. It's pretty bad...

(*Staples slowly turns around and checks behind the sofa.*)

CHASE: Well, I know it sounds silly, but I was wondering if you wouldn't mind coming upstairs and entertaining me for awhile. I keep wanting to turn around real fast but I know I'm not supposed to cause of my discs and stuff. The lumber division of the spinal canal is quite neurologically and anatomically sensitive... You would? Cool, cool. I'd really appreciate that... Yeah, I just thought we could talk for a while. Shoot the breeze, you know? Get to know each other neighbor to neighbor. Upstairs to downstairs. Man to man...

God, I *so* appreciate that... It's these pills, you know? I think I took too many. I almost broke down and called a film festival—

STAPLES: Dude!

CHASE: I mean *hospital!*... Oh, come up as soon as you can. ASAP. The door's open. Yeah, I keep wanting to turn around. Thanks, guy. I so appreciate it. See you in a few.

(*He hangs up.*)

STAPLES: Nice?

CHASE: Oh, totally nice. Kinda shy.

STAPLES: Huh.

(*A pause.*)

CHASE: Um. He's probably like on his way up the stairs right now.

STAPLES: You think it's gonna snow?

CHASE: I don't know, Staples.

STAPLES: I used to make snowmen. Big ones. With hats and stuff. Scarves. I'd sit next to them and we'd memorize baseball cards. Height. Weight. Hometown. We'd do state capitals, too. Albany. Tallahassee. Jefferson City... Do you know the state capital of Illinois?!

CHASE: Sure, Staples.

STAPLES: What is it?!

CHASE: It's Springfield, isn't it?

(*Staples stares off.*)

CHASE: You okay, buddy?

STAPLES: I keep thinking about the caribou. How it reminds me of all this stuff I can't remember. Like being on a school bus. The way the seats smelled. Stuff like that. And Magilla Gorilla!

CHASE: What about him?

STAPLES: I can't remember if he was a walrus or an Alaskan snow pony!!!

CHASE: Um. I think he was a gorilla, Staples.

STAPLES: Yeah?

CHASE: I'm pretty sure about that one.

STAPLES: I was thinking about getting a job today. Doing something with my hands. Catching fish. Making things. Little wooden toys.

CHASE: Toys are cool.

STAPLES: *(A little terrified.)* I had this dream last night that I was a robot. Big metal robot—

CHASE: Yeah, you were crying—

STAPLES: I was crying but nothing was coming out. I could feel the crying in my throat but no tears—

CHASE: And you didn't have any balls—

STAPLES: I didn't have any balls. Instead I had a light switch! I kept trying to turn it on—

CHASE: But all it did was make this buzzing noise.

STAPLES: I was going to this graveyard. Where all the other robots were buried. And I found this flower. It was pink. A tulip, I think. I ate it. It made me feel better.

CHASE: Look, if all goes well, I bet we'll get to see what happens to the caribou.

STAPLES: You think so?

CHASE: I *totally* think so.

STAPLES: I'd like that.

CHASE: Me too, Staples. Me too. You want me to count to three?

STAPLES: Would you?

CHASE: Sure, buddy.

(He squares his body to Staples.)

CHASE: One. Two. Three.

(Staples rocks forward and off the sofa, lurches a bit, rights himself, and then stares at the bowls of pills. He goes for a pink.)

STAPLES: Maybe I should take a pink.

CHASE: *(Standing on the sofa.)* I don't know, Staples! Maybe another blue. Keep the colors together.

STAPLES: Right.

(Staples reaches down, grabs a blue pill, puts it in his mouth, swallows. Then he turns and crosses to the back of the apartment.)

(Chase stretches out on the sofa, his head opposite the front door. He puts a pillow under his knees, affects the posture of a back injury victim. Moments

later, Staples appears wearing a snowmobile suit, similar to Lynch's, but a different color. He crosses to the stage left window, attempts to lift it. It doesn't budge. He tries again. No luck.)

STAPLES: It's frozen shut.

(A knock at the door.)

(Chase and Staples stare at each other, stare at the door, back at each other. Staples tries to lift the window again, screaming now. It still won't budge. Chase shouts at him to hide in the back of the apartment. He uses strange, guttural noises and a kind of primitive gibberish.)

(Staples moves as quickly as he can down the hall to the back of the apartment, like an astronaut in need of a toilet.)

(Another knock.)

CHASE: Come in.

(The door opens very slowly. A nondescript man enters. He is 30-ish, clean-shaven. He wears a plain gray suit and a vague tie. He wears black, thick-rimmed glasses. He carries a half-dozen tulips arranged in a glass vase. He leaves the door open. He is painfully shy, but can get into the occasional groove just like anybody else.)

GRAY: Are you Chase?

CHASE: I am. You must be...

GRAY: Um. Gray. Gray Heldinwell. From apartment three.

CHASE: Well, hey there, neighbor.

GRAY: Hey.

CHASE: How's it going?

GRAY: Pretty good.

CHASE: Well, come in, come in.

GRAY: Thanks.

(Gray closes the door and steps carefully into the room.)

GRAY: I brought you these.

(He crosses to Chase, hands him the tulips.)

CHASE: *(Amazed at their vividness.)* Flowers!

GRAY: Tulips.

CHASE: Wow. Um. Thanks... *Gray?*

GRAY: Yeah, Gray.

CHASE: ...Hey, Gray!

GRAY: Hey!

(Gray stands there awkwardly. Chase stares at the tulips, is strangely transfixed. Perhaps he licks one. Gray takes them away.)

GRAY: *(Setting them on the coffee table.)* When I was in the hospital Nurse H would always bring me tulips.

CHASE: Nice.

GRAY: Nurse H and I had similar tastes in things. We both like travel literature. And slanted rain. And knives.

CHASE: Knives?

GRAY: Yeah, we both have knife collections.

CHASE: What kinda knives?

GRAY: Nurse H has two dozen Willie Stonetooth Redpoints. I have a set of Captain Diablo Throwing Blades.

CHASE: Wow.

GRAY: You can only get Captain Diablos south of the border. They come in sets of ten. Varying weights and flight speeds.

CHASE: Cool.

(Gray continues to stand.)

CHASE: Be seated earthling.

(Gray stares at the empty stage left chair for a moment, then at the Man On The Floor.)

GRAY: I thought you said your roommates were out of town.

CHASE: They are.

GRAY: *(Pointing to the Man On The Floor.)* Who's that?

CHASE: Oh, that's Speed.

GRAY: Speed?

CHASE: Yeah, Speed. He just got here. Surprise visit.

GRAY: Oh. What's he doing?

CHASE: He's just sorta hanging out.

(Gray turns toward the door.)

CHASE: Take a seat!

(Gray stops, considers the chair again, turns toward the drum set, indicates that perhaps that would be a better choice, sits on a crate, accidentally steps on the kick drum pedal, jumps like a jackrabbit, practically annihilates the drum set, an explosion of sound. After a moment, he regains his composure, sits on the crate again.)

GRAY: So how'd you hurt your back?

CHASE: Well, I slipped and… Well, you know— *(A vague gesture.)* Whooop!

GRAY: *(Feebly imitating the gesture.)* Whooop.

(Pause.)

GRAY: That's what I was in the hospital for.

CHASE: What.

GRAY: My back.

CHASE: Really.

GRAY: They almost had to do invasive surgery. Pinched nerve.

CHASE: Ouch.

GRAY: Sciatic node between L-five and S-one. The pain was pretty excruciating. Two days of traction and a few months of physical therapy. I'm okay now.

CHASE: Wow.

GRAY: Yeah, I had to lay on the floor a lot... Did they medicate in triplicate?

CHASE: Um...

GRAY: Anti-inflammatory, muscle relaxer, painkiller?

CHASE: Oh. Well, um, yeah, actually. All of the above.

GRAY: The Carisprodol is pretty good. They give you that?

CHASE: They did. Yes. They *did* give me that.

GRAY: It's great right before bed. Especially coupled with the Hydrocodone. They probably gave you that, too, right?

CHASE: How'd you know?

GRAY: It's good for nerve pain. Hydrocodone's a synthetic narcotic. Generic spin-off of codeine. Well, they *say* codeine but it's actually closer to morphine.

CHASE: Wow, Gray, you're like pharmacologically blessed.

GRAY: The Naproxin's nothing to write home about, but an anti-inflammatory's an anti-inflammatory. Seen one you've seen them all.

CHASE: You're so right.

GRAY: *(Rising off the crate, crossing toward the sofa.)* I still have a pretty good relationship with my orthopedic guy. Doctor P, NYU Medical Center.

CHASE: Yeah, Doctor P, NYU Medical. Over there at...

GRAY: Thirty-first and First.

CHASE: Thirty-first and First. Right, right.

GRAY: You should be okay in forty-eight to seventy-two hours. As long as it's not a hot disc. You don't have a hot disc do you?

CHASE: Oh, no way. My discs are totally cool and non-hot.

GRAY: Then you're probably in pretty good shape.

CHASE: God I hope so.

(While Gray sits, someone farts like a French horn. Awkward pause.)

CHASE: So, how long have you been in the building, Gray?

GRAY: Awhile. I just signed another lease.

CHASE: You like the neighborhood?

GRAY: Of course.

CHASE: We got the park. The Russian Bath House. That funny hat shop across the street.

GRAY: That hat shop's not funny.

CHASE: Oh. I was just saying—

GRAY: I don't think it's funny at all.

CHASE: Okay.

(Pause.)

(Someone farts again.)

CHASE: Was that you or me?

GRAY: I think it was you.

CHASE: Oh.

GRAY: *(Collaboratively.)* Maybe it was Speed?

CHASE: Right on.

(They share forced laughter.)

CHASE: Care for a pill? We have blues, pinks, and yellows. We call the yellows pissers.

(Gray rises, considers the pills for a moment, backs away.)

GRAY: No thanks.

(Suddenly, Staples appears from the back of the apartment. He is still wearing the snowmobile suit. He is also wearing a hood now and snow goggles. He walks up to the window very quickly, somehow trying to make himself invisible. He tries to lift it again. He is successful this time. He crawls through the window, closes it behind him, and disappears down the fire escape. Gray is quite startled.)

GRAY: Who was that?

CHASE: Huh?

GRAY: That man.

CHASE: What man?

GRAY: The one in the snowsuit.

CHASE: I didn't see anyone.

GRAY: Oh. Well, a man in a snowsuit just walked through your living room, opened the window and exited down the fire escape.

CHASE: Really?

GRAY: Yeah.

CHASE: Are you sure, dude?

GRAY: Sure I'm sure.

(Gray rises, crosses toward the window, creeps up on it very slowly, seizes one

of the dinette chairs, then looks out quickly. After a moment, he re-sets the chair, crosses to Chase.)

GRAY: He's not there any more.

(Gray crosses toward the door.)

CHASE: *Sit, sit, sit!*

(Gray crosses to the living room chair, confused, regards Speed for a moment, sits. Chase shifts to the other side of the sofa. He feigns pain. Gray rises and attempts to help him, awkwardly reaching toward him, but never actually touching him. Chase settles with his head against the stage right side of the sofa, still feigning pain. Gray accidentally falls into Chase's lap face-first. Gray stands very quickly. An awkward moment. Gray attempts to regain his composure, makes his way back to the chair, sits.)

CHASE: What do you do, Gray?

GRAY: …Excuse me?

CHASE: What.

GRAY: I'm not gay.

CHASE: Huh?

GRAY: You think I'm gay?

CHASE: Dude, what are you talking ab—

GRAY: *(Standing.)* Didn't you just ask me if I was gay?

CHASE: Um, no. I asked you—

GRAY: Are you trying to take advantage of me?!

CHASE: All I said was—

GRAY: Cause I won't let that happen! I know Karate!

(Gray explodes with an exhibition of karate, approaching Chase rather aggressively. Chase stands on the sofa suddenly, somehow defusing the onslaught.)

CHASE: I *said* WHAT-DO-YOU-DO, *GRAY!*

GRAY: Oh.

CHASE: WHOA!

GRAY: …Sorry.

CHASE: NO ONE IS TAKING ADVANTAGE OF ANYONE!

GRAY: Oh. I'm so sorry.

(Chase, suddenly realizing that he is standing with little effort, begins feigning pain again, crumples down to the sofa. Gray attempts to help him again, but Chase wards him off.)

(Gray turns to the chair, where Speed has managed to drape his arm over the cushion.)

GRAY: *(Crossing back to the chair.)* I work for a prominent financial institution.

CHASE: Like a bank?

GRAY: It's a little more complicated than that.

CHASE: Okay.

GRAY: *(Removing Speed's arm.)* I'm involved with the information side of things. Sorting and processing. I deal with data.

CHASE: You crunch numbers.

GRAY: I do. I do crunch numbers. But I do so much more than just crunch them.

CHASE: Like what?

GRAY: Well, I soften them too. I soften *and* crunch. And there's a fair amount of spreading as well.

CHASE: Spreading?

GRAY: Sure.

CHASE: Like spreadsheets?

GRAY: Just spreading.

CHASE: Huh.

(Suddenly, Gray whirls around in the chair really fast, desperately looks over both shoulders, stops, turns to Chase.)

GRAY: You sure you didn't see that guy in the snowsuit?

CHASE: Pretty sure, Gray.

(Speed suddenly pulls a deflated blowup doll from underneath the cushion of the chair, screams, bounds apelike toward the hallway, punches a hole in the Sheetrock. Gray seizes the ottoman, raises it over his head as if to strike, but doesn't. Speed stares at him for a moment.)

SPEED: Magilla Gorilla.

(Speed crosses to the back of the apartment singing the first few verses of the "Magilla Gorilla" theme song, disappears. Gray regains his composure, sets the ottoman down, a little invigorated, sits.)

GRAY: *(Referring to Speed.)* You're in a band.

CHASE: I am.

GRAY: I'll bet you didn't think I knew that.

CHASE: Well—

GRAY: When you've lived in the building as long as I have you pick up on certain things. The walls are filled with information, trust me on that one. You just have to know how to listen.

CHASE: Huh.

GRAY: What are you guys called again?

CHASE: Well, we were called Lester's Surprise, but then we changed it to Lester's Sister. And then it was just Lester. I can't remember what we were after that.

GRAY: Less.

CHASE: Excuse me?

GRAY: I think you were called Less after that.

CHASE: Really.

GRAY: Uh-huh.

CHASE: Like *less* less?

GRAY: L-E-S-S. You guys used to put posters up all over the place. "Less is More."

CHASE: Huh.

(Gray rises, crosses to the vase of tulips, pulls it close.)

GRAY: Yeah, I used to get out some. People to see, places to go, you know?

CHASE: Sure.

GRAY: But not so much lately. Too much to do. Projects. Big plans. Lots of ideas.

(Gray sets the vase of tulips on top of the TV.)

CHASE: Huh.

GRAY: I have this lamp. White cut glass. It has a swan's neck. The head is shaped like tulips. Ten of them. A bouquet. Gives a real nice soft glow. An astral glow. I think they put argon gas in the bulbs. At least it says that on the little tag. I found it in that old thrift shop across the street. It hardly cost anything.

CHASE: ...Uh-huh?

GRAY: I'll just stare at it for hours. I'm not sure why. Sometimes I think I'm waiting for it to talk to me. Like the tulips will tell me what to do.

CHASE: Huh.

(Pause.)

GRAY: I was approached on the street today.

CHASE: Approached?

GRAY: Yeah, approached. Carefully approached.

CHASE: By who?

GRAY: Two men. Very important men.

CHASE: When you say "approached"—

GRAY: They just emerged. The way birds emerge.

CHASE: Birds.

GRAY: Large, dark birds. You mind if I turn the light off?

CHASE: Not at all.

(Gray vigilantly crosses to the neon beer sign, sets a chair to reach it, stands on the chair, turns the sign off.)

CHASE: So what did these "very important" men *do* after they um "emerged"?

GRAY: *(Still standing on the chair.)* Handed me some pamphlets. Took my information.

CHASE: What kinda information?

GRAY: Personal things. Height. Weight. Social Security Number. Stuff like that.

CHASE: Wow.

GRAY: They took a Polaroid, too.

CHASE: Friendly.

GRAY: Yeah, I was wearing my hat.

CHASE: Your hat?

GRAY: From Millie's Millinery.

CHASE: What's that?

GRAY: Um. That hat shop across the street.

CHASE: Right.

GRAY: *(Stepping down from chair.)* There's a meeting tomorrow. Big meeting.

CHASE: With those guys who "approached" you.

GRAY: I'm not supposed to talk about it!

CHASE: Okay.

GRAY: They gave me some money.

CHASE: To not talk about it.

GRAY: A lot of money. In a shoebox. It was heavier than if shoes were in it.

CHASE: Cool.

GRAY: I think a certain government official is in danger, let's just say that. And like they said, he deserves to be.

CHASE: Sure.

GRAY: I'm willing to go to certain lengths.

CHASE: Of course.

GRAY: Long Daniel's going to be speaking on Public Access in a few minutes.

CHASE: Who's that?

GRAY: Leader of the movement.

CHASE: One of the "money dudes"?

GRAY: Long Daniel's the visionary. They work for him. He's the guy in all the literature. *(Referring to the TV.)* Public Access. Channel Sixteen.

CHASE: I'd turn it on, Gray, but our TV's like totally cashed.

(Suddenly, Staples appears in the window with a large TV. Chase sees him.)
GRAY: Then I'll go get mine.
CHASE: Your TV?
GRAY: Sure.
CHASE: Oh, no, you don't have to do that!
GRAY: But I want to.
CHASE: But it's so inconvenient. And I wouldn't want you to hurt your back
    agai—
GRAY: You don't like me.
CHASE: Oh, that's so not true!
GRAY: You find me repellent.
    (Gray crumples down to the ottoman, almost prostrate on the floor now.)
CHASE: Gray. Hey. Hey now. I find you so totally *not* repellent.
    (Chase desperately signals to Staples to take Gray's TV back downstairs. Staples watches vaguely through the window for a moment, then nods, and disappears. Gray checks behind him for a moment.)
GRAY: *(Rising, regaining his composure.)* They don't talk to me at work.
CHASE: They *talk* to you.
GRAY: No they don't.
CHASE: Sure they do.
GRAY: You don't know.
CHASE: People just don't *not talk* to people.
GRAY: Just because I got caught with the rubber bands.
CHASE: Rubber bands?
GRAY: A big blob of rubber bands. I couldn't help it.
CHASE: Caught doing what exactly?
    (Gray sits on the sofa.)
GRAY: I was putting them down my pants.
CHASE: Whoa.
GRAY: Sometimes I'll grab a handful. When my boss isn't looking.
CHASE: Oh. What does that like um *do?*
GRAY: It takes the loneliness away.
CHASE: Huh.
GRAY: I think about the woods sometimes. Just getting away from it all. The
    smell of deer. Big timber. Blackbirds in the branches.
    (Pause.)
CHASE: Go get your TV, Gray.
GRAY: Okay.

(Gray rises, slowly crosses to the front door, turns back.)

GRAY: Maybe I could just leave it up here, you know? Then I could come up and visit whenever.

CHASE: Hey, it's definitely worth discussing.

GRAY: Okay.

(Gray turns to exit.)

CHASE: What kinda TV is it?

GRAY: Magnavox nineteen-inch stereo surroundsound with master remote.

CHASE: The kinda remote that's like heavy in your hand?

GRAY: Uh-huh.

CHASE: Totally go get it.

GRAY: Okay.

CHASE: But Gray?

GRAY: Yeah?

(Chase moves himself to an upright position, feigning great pain. As before, Gray reaches awkwardly, feebly, to help him, falls to his knees. Then suddenly, his hands find Chase's hair, his face, his beard. It's more about the relief of physical human connection than anything sexual. Nonetheless, another awkward moment.)

CHASE: Promise me you'll be careful.

GRAY: I will, Chase.

(Gray rises, crosses to the door, stops, and turns back one more time.)

GRAY: Um. I've never told anyone about that before.

CHASE: About what?

GRAY: The rubberband thing.

(Gray turns and exits.)

(A moment later the front door opens and a Girl enters on rollerblades. She is dressed in winter clothes and her face is covered with an enormous white foam-core elephant mask. She rollerblades smooth parabolas in the living room, in front of and behind the sofa. Chase watches her, somewhat stunned.)

(Moments later, Lynch enters. He is wearing his snowmobile suit and a large white foam-core bear mask over his face. He is walking with a cane, trying to move quickly but still having to find each step. He lurches after the Girl. She shrieks, eludes him, glides past him, down the hall and into one of the back bedrooms. Lynch follows her, still lurching. There is some playful shrieking and then moments later, the Girl appears again, still wearing the elephant mask. She glides to the sofa, sits.)

GIRL: Hi.

CHASE: Hey.

GIRL : Who are you?

CHASE: I'm Chase. Who are you?

GIRL : Dot.

CHASE: Where did you come from, Dot?

DOT: The park.

CHASE: Like the *park* park?

DOT: Uh-huh. That's where I discovered the Bear.

CHASE: The Bear?

DOT: Yep.

CHASE: You mean Lynch?

DOT: I prefer to call him the Bear. I'm the Elephant.

CHASE: I *see.*

DOT: He said he's gonna play me a song.

CHASE: Cool.

DOT: Tcwilliams at sugarnet dot com and bbwilliams-davis at sugarnet dot com headed back to Seattle today.

CHASE: Who are they?

DOT: My parents.

CHASE: They left you in the park?

DOT: Yep.

CHASE: How old are you?

DOT: Eleven. I'm small for my age. You guys need some life in this place. Smells like bad breath and farts.

(She rises off the sofa, starts to clean.)

DOT: You know there are hundreds of cleaning services advertised on the Web. With the right search engine I'm sure you could find something reasonable... Um, somebody puked next to the couch.

(She glides to the kitchen, grabs an old mop to clean the puke with, glides back to the sofa, mops.)

CHASE: Do you like have a *face?*

(She glides back to the kitchen, attempts to wash her hands, but the pipes are frozen. They knock and moan. She wipes her hand on a random dish towel or sweat sock, re-sets the mop.)

DOT: I prefer to keep my identity in constant flux. There are things crawling on your dishes.

CHASE: So Lynch just like *found you* in the park and brought you over?

DOT: I think it would be more accurate to say that I found him. He was limping across the dog run and had fallen down two or three times before I went over and helped him up. I was making masks on a bench and he said he needed to rest so he sat with me for a while and that's when we became the Elephant and the Bear.

CHASE: Wow.

DOT: His whole left leg is numb. I think it's nerve damage but he says it's something else. We bought the cane off the sidewalk for three bucks. Tcwilliams at sugarnet dot com and bbwilliams-davis at sugarnet dot com made sure to give me plenty of cash before they took off.

CHASE: Do you ever take the skates off?

DOT: I prefer to glide.

(She glides. She cleans the top of the kicked-in TV, grabs the vase of tulips.)

DOT: Before I found the Bear I was online at that little cyber café next to the park. I'm dot williams-davis at sugarnet dot com.

(She waves. He waves back.)

DOT: The local weather page said it's supposed to get really cold tonight.

CHASE: I heard.

DOT: Like close to zero. I'm glad the Bear let me come over.

(The door opens. Gray stands in the entrance holding his TV.)

GRAY: Hi.

DOT: Hi.

GRAY: I'm Gray.

DOT: I'm Dot.

GRAY: Nice to meet you Dot.

DOT: Nice to meet *you* Gray.

(He crosses the living room and places the TV on the floor in front of the other one. Dot bends down to clean it for a moment, which makes Gray feel very uncomfortable. He turns to Dot.)

GRAY: You're wearing an elephant mask.

DOT: I almost chose a rhinoceros, but elephants are more concerned with their dead. Do you like it?

GRAY: Sure.

DOT: I'm gonna take it off now.

GRAY: Okay.

(Dot glides to the kitchen table, removes the mask, sets it on a chair, turns around, poses rather dramatically.)

DOT: Are you perplexed by my true features?

GRAY: Um. No.

DOT: Perhaps you'd like to be put under the spell of my jewel-like eyes.

GRAY: No thanks.

(She glides toward Gray.)

DOT: How bout a hug? You look like you could use a hug. My hugs have special medicinal powers.

(Gray doesn't allow her to touch him.)

GRAY: Maybe later.

(Dot glides to the back of the sofa, sits with the vase of tulips.)

(Gray plugs in the TV, attaches the cable box, crosses to Dot, takes the vase of tulips from her, considers it for a moment, then hands her a single tulip. He then re-sets the vase of tulips on top of his TV, removes a large remote from his breast pocket, crosses to Chase, almost hands it to him, then starts for the door.)

CHASE: Where you goin, Gray?

(Gray looks at Dot, then back to Chase.)

GRAY: Um. They called me when I was downstairs.

CHASE: They.

GRAY: *Them.*

CHASE: The "money dudes"?

(Gray looks at Dot, and then Chase.)

GRAY: *(Careful.)* The call was in reference to that certain *government official* I was telling you about. They need me.

CHASE: They like *need you* need you?

GRAY: They sounded professionally desperate.

CHASE: For the "money job"?

GRAY: *(Finally handing Chase the remote.)* It's a Mission, yes. I have to go pack my knives. I shouldn't say anything else.

CHASE: Right.

GRAY: And I can't forget my hat. Gotta go.

(Gray is frozen.)

CHASE: Gray.

GRAY: Yes?

CHASE: Maybe you should take a pill.

(Gray crosses to the bowl of pills.)

GRAY: You think?

CHASE: Oh, absolutely.

GRAY: Which one?

CHASE: Take a pink.

(Gray takes a pink pill from the bowl, pops it in his mouth, then removes a nondescript mint green plastic bottle from his breast pocket, unscrews it, drinks, washing down the pill.)

278 ADAM RAPP

CHASE: Take two, dude.

(Gray takes another pink, washes it down.)

CHASE: Take a yellow, too.

(Gray takes a yellow, washes it down, returns the bottle to his breast pocket.)

CHASE: That should do it.

GRAY: If you don't see me anymore I want you to have the TV.

CHASE: Okay.

GRAY: It's good to feel like you're a part of something.

(Gray exits, closes the door.)

(The window is opened. Staples climbs through with a large McDonald's bag in his mouth. He no longer wears his hat and his snowsuit has been partly blown off. He is bare-chested. There is ice in his hair and beard. He closes the window, barricades the window with the kitchen table, turns to Chase and Dot.)

STAPLES: *(As if caught in a blizzard.)*

SNOW

SNOW AND ICE

SNOW AND ICE AND WIND

SLEET IN THE TREES

BIRDS FALLING TO THE PAVEMENT

FROZEN PIGEONS ALL ACROSS TENTH STREET

SO COLD THEY LOOK BLUE

FROST CRAWLING UP THE SIDES OF BUILDINGS

PEOPLE IN FRONT OF THEIR WINDOWS WEARING COATS

SCARVES

SKI MASKS

THE MOON LOOKS LIKE A HUGE ICEBALL

(Staples freezes. Dot touches his arm and he quickly snaps out of it, tossing Chase his Happy Meal box. Staples takes a seat on the stage left end of the sofa, removes his own Happy Meal box, emptying the contents onto his lap.)

(Speed enters from the back of the apartment wearing a welding mask, still in his underwear. Staples hands Speed his Happy Meal box. Chase hands his to Dot, who offers it to Speed. He retrieves the Happy Meal boxes.)

DOT: *(To Speed.)* I'm Dot.

(Speed thrusts the Happy Meal boxes into the air victoriously, then crosses to the Happy Meal wall, offers the new additions to the Happy Meal gods. Chase and Staples don't eat, but simply play with the toys contained inside.)

DOT: *(To Staples.)* I'm Dot.

STAPLES: Hey Spot.

DOT: You must be Staples. The Bear told me that you used to write songs with him but how now all you do is sit on the couch and watch TV. How you don't even eat anymore.

STAPLES: I eat. I just ate something the other day.

(Someone farts like a French horn. Chase turns to Dot, accusatorial.)

DOT: Don't look at me!

(Chase uses the remote, finds his channel on the TV. Once again, the sound of the animal being tortured. Chase and Staples are instantly mesmerized.)

DOT: In the library at my junior high they have these huge computer monitors. The size of small refrigerators. Three feet high some of them. The most beautiful screen savers you'll ever see. Mountains. Waterfalls. Pictures of magic cities. Colors that haven't even been invented yet. If you stand next to the hard drives and listen real close you can hear them singing. Like hummingbirds. A gazillion megahertz of ram just whirling away. *(Standing, gliding slowly toward the TV.)* Sometimes I go real early in the morning. When nobody's there. And I just listen. I listen for a while and then for some reason I hug each monitor. One by one. There's like fifty of them. *(Hugging Gray's TV now.)* I hug each one and I get a little part of that song inside me. It's the most beautiful way to start the day. *(Breaking from the hug.)* I think those birds on the rhinos are so cool.

STAPLES: It's like someone put em there.

(Dot glides to the ottoman, sits.)

DOT: In the library there's this one African Grassland screen saver with little birds. They ride around on this elephant and eat the bugs off its back. There's a lion, too, but he doesn't do anything. The elephant walks around and drinks water out of the wallows. That's where the rhinos play with their kids.

(Dot looks at Chase and Staples on the sofa and realizes that they have fallen asleep. Dot rises and glides to the coffee table. She reaches down, about to take a blue when Lynch enters from the back of the apartment. He has stripped down to his long underwear. He is no longer wearing the bear mask. He is limping absurdly, using his cane. There is a large knitting needle sticking out of his right foot. He is now barely able to find each step. Without speaking, he orders her to put the pill back in the bowl. She does so.)

DOT: Hey Bear.

(Lynch opens his mouth, attempts to say something. Nothing comes out. He tries again and is lured by Gray's TV. He watches it for a moment, limps over

to it, calls Dot over with his hand, hands her the vase with the tulips, signals to her to move away. Dot returns to the sofa, sits between Chase and Staples. Lynch then rears back and kicks in Gray's TV with his needled foot. Chase and Staples continue sleeping. Speed continues staring at the wall of Happy Meal boxes. Lynch crosses to the keyboard, taps on Speed's welding mask with his cane. After no response he bends down, attempts to turn on the amp under the keyboard, fails, removes an electric guitar that had been buried under a heap of debris, plays it unplugged while singing the following song to Dot.)

LYNCH: *(Singing.)*

**the element man
collecting noble gases
stratocaster plan
helium scam
for the masses**

**he's got a distance machine
powered by rocket fuel
he's got a color TV
and some microwave tea
to navigate his reprieve**

**distance, area and volume
space so hard to find**
(Lynch collapses. Dot crosses to him, helps him back to his feet. Lights fade to a rich blue out.)

(Slowneck's "40 Holes and 40 Goals" plays. During the song, Dot and Lynch start to slow dance, simply, childlike. The dance eventually leads to the back of the apartment.)
**there's a hole
in my head
there's a hole
in my pocket
there's a hole
in the floor
there's a hole
in the door**

i'm gonna find it
i'm gonna fill it
(*The light grows very dark and strange on the window. A door can be heard closing in the back of the apartment.*)
(*After Dot and Lynch exit to the back of the apartment, Staples wakes. He finds an old, discarded T-shirt, puts it on, crosses to the window, which is now completely covered with frost.*)
there's a hole
in my mattress
there's a hole
in my hand
there's a hole
in the afternoon
there's a hole
in the room
i'm gonna find it
i'm gonna fill it
there's a hole
(*Staples reaches out and touches the window. He withdraws his hand, and crosses to Gray's TV. He bends down and puts his hand through the hole, retracts it, stares at his hand, turns to the bowl of pills. He reaches in and takes a blue. Then another. Then another. Then several more. He swallows them all. He takes a pink. Swallows. And then a yellow. Staples swallows the pills, slowly and deliberately, staring out.*)
there's a hole
in the window
there's a hole
in the wall
there's a hole
in my shower
there's a hole
in the hour
i'm gonna find it
i'm gonna fill it
with a flower
(*Staples returns to the sofa, finds the tulip that Dot had handed him, still standing, grabs it, regards it for a moment and then starts to eat the petals one by one while turning a slow circle.*)

(After he has eaten all the petals, he sits in his spot on the sofa, leans back, staring out.)
huh-huh-huh
huh-huh-huh...
(Staples closes his eyes. The blue light slowly changes to a strange pink light on Staples. The song ends. Lights fade to black.)

(Lights up.)
(The apartment is still dark but a soft yellow light is starting to come through the window. Chase is holding an electric guitar, ready to play. Staples is at one of the microphone stands, upright, very much alive. Speed is seated at the drum set, no longer wearing the welding mask. Lynch is facing the drums, strapped with the bass.)
(Staples starts to sing "The Astronaut's Lament." It starts slowly and then builds into an upbeat pop song, then opens up into aggressive punk rock.)
STAPLES: *(Singing.)*
> **in the very tiny hours**
> **when the night turns into the day**
> **when your spaceships come**
> **and steal your plans**
> **and make your blue skies change to gray**
>
> **i sit alone in my room**
> **how can i be so lazy**
> **when the astronauts are giving it one more try**
> **why does the stratosphere look so hazy?**

(All the lights come on. It should be very bright in the theatre now.)

> **22 days ago**
> **i saw a number cruncher lookin at me**
> **he had a bowling ball tied to his bum left leg**
> **and he walked into the sea**
>
> **and he went down, down, down, down**
> **down to the end of the pier**

he jumped and drowned, drowned, drowned, drowned
but he couldn't get there from here

the junk dealer's getting his fix
the radio ain't playing songs
the kid downstairs is wearing my 3-piece suit
should I make my body strong?

the chief of police lost his gun
the subway map is missing a stop
the rifle dealer's taking a cigarette break
i wonder what he's got in stock?

my corduroy pants are too small
i think my dog is runnin away
if the eskimos can build a house outta snow
then maybe I can build one with hay

and he went down, down, down, down
down to the end of the pier

he jumped and drowned, drowned, drowned, drowned
but he couldn't get there from here

(The song slows down suddenly. A "freak-out.")
(Speed is excellent at the drums.)
(Chase is superior on the guitar.)
(Lynch grooves with the bass.)
(Staples turns on the keyboard during the instrumental break.)
(The whole of it turns into an extended jam session with inspired improvisa-
tion. After a minute or so, they find the bass line and return to the chorus of
"The Astronaut's Lament.")

and he went down, down, down, down
down to the end of the pier

he jumped and drowned, drowned, drowned, drowned
but he couldn't get there from here

and he went down, down, down, down
down to the end of the pier
he jumped and drowned, drowned, drowned, drowned
but he couldn't get there from here

(At the end of the song, Chase, Lynch, Speed and Staples look at each other with love and satisfaction, as though they perhaps just played their best few minutes of music ever. They stand very still and share the moment in silence. Then, slowly, one by one, they revert back to their previous states. Lynch sets the bass down, turns, and slowly exits down the hall, finding each step. He disappears to the back of the apartment.)

(Speed rises from the drums, crosses back to the wall of Happy Meal boxes, puts his welding mask back on, freezes.)

(Staples, suddenly disoriented, steps away from the microphone stand, returns to his spot on the sofa, grabs the stem of the eaten tulip, and sits in exactly the same position he was in at the end of the blue out.)

(Chase sets his guitar down and backs away to the sofa. He stares out for a moment as if lost. He sits. His mouth is open as if he has forgotten how to breathe.)

(Lights fade to blue and then to black.)

(Lights slowly fade up. The apartment is filled with yellow light.)

(It is now morning.)

(As before, Chase and Staples are asleep on the couch, Staples holding the stem of the eaten tulip.)

(Speed is back on the floor, now asleep, still wearing the welding mask.)

(A cell phone rings four times, then ceases.)

(Dot enters from the back of the apartment. She is still on her rollerblades. She is holding a bloody brick. She is in shock.)

(A cell phone rings again.)

(Dot stops, turns toward the sound of the cell phone. She glides over to Chase, grabs his cell phone, answers it.)

DOT: Hello?… Dot… Yeah, he's here, but he's sleeping… Oh, hi… Sure, I'll give him a message… Okay… Bye.

(Dot turns the phone off, places it next to Chase. She stares at him a moment, then shakes him. He stirs, wakes.)

CHASE: Hey Data.

DOT: Hey. It's Dot.

CHASE: Hey Dot.

DOT: There's a problem.

CHASE: What.

DOT: The Bear.

CHASE: Lynch?

DOT: He's not moving.

CHASE: He's probably like hibernating.

(She turns to face the hallway.)

DOT: I woke up in the middle of the night and he was hitting himself with a brick. His shins. Face. Feet. You could hear his bones breaking.

(The brick falls to the floor.)

DOT: He kept talking about the robots and how he couldn't feel anything. There's like six needles sticking out of his right foot. Blood all over the sheets. I think it's worse than hibernation. He pooped the bed... You should call someone.

CHASE: Okay.

DOT: Like the hospital maybe. I'd go online but they don't have that yet.

CHASE: What time is it?

DOT: It's morning. I have to go back to Seattle. School starts tomorrow.

CHASE: Have a good trip.

DOT: Oh, and you got a call while you were sleeping.

CHASE: Who was it?

DOT: Your dad.

CHASE: What did he want?

DOT: He said he'd heard about the storm.

CHASE: What storm.

DOT: The snowstorm. He just wanted to let you know he'd heard about it.

(Gray enters, crosses to the window, turns around. He is wearing the same gray suit and tie and an odd-shaped bowler hat. He is wet with snow. He is holding a bloody knife. There is blood and vomit on the front of his suit. He is shivering.)

GRAY: Hi.

CHASE: Hey Gray.

GRAY: Hi Dot.

DOT: Hi Gray.

GRAY: Hi.

(He stands very still.)

GRAY: It's really cold out. Lots of snow.

CHASE: You're holding a knife, dude.

GRAY: Yeah.

CHASE: And there's like blood on it.

GRAY: When it goes in it feels like nothing. It's so light. Even. Like nowhere. You think there will be screaming. Fighting. Music in the background. Like on TV. But it's not like that. Not if you put it in the way they show you. In the part where the voice makes a noise. It was so quiet. And he just sat down. He just sat down like he was old and tired. Like he'd walked for a long time and needed to rest...

It's so good to feel like you're a part of something.

(Dot grabs the vase of tulips, glides over to Gray, hands it to him. Gray drops the knife, accepts the vase of tulips.)

GRAY: My lamp broke. I knocked it over when I unplugged the TV. Broke into a thousand pieces. It's really cold down there.

(Dot hugs Gray. He lets her and starts to weep.)

GRAY: Can I stay up here with you? I'll be really still. Just a few days.

CHASE: Sure, Gray, sure.

GRAY: I won't move, hardly at all.

CHASE: No problem buddy.

GRAY: *(Breaking from the hug, to Dot.)* I heard the Sun's coming.

(Gray slowly crosses to the beer sign, steps onto the chair, turns it on. His movements are very slow, as though he is coming to some kind of expiration. He turns the sign on and starts to arrange the tulips in the light over the following.)

DOT: You should get up.

CHASE: Maybe.

DOT: Things will get better once you start moving.

CHASE: I had this dream last night.

I was a robot.

Big metal robot.

I was crying but nothing was coming out.

No tears.

And I didn't have any balls.

Instead I had a light switch.

I kept trying to turn it on but all it did was make this buzzing noise...

(Dot finds her elephant mask near the upturned kitchen table. She crosses to the sofa. Chase plants his feet on the floor for the first time, slowly stands, takes in the room for a moment.)

CHASE: I... I can't feel my feet.

(Dot drops her elephant mask on the sofa, then hugs Chase. She hugs him for a long time. She breaks from the hug, glides to the front door, exits, waves good-bye. Chase waves back.)

(After a moment Staples' cell phone starts to ring.)

(Chase thinks it's his.)

(He checks.)

(It's not.)

(He turns to Staples at the other end of the sofa.)

(The cell phone rings again. Chase reaches over, shakes him.)

(Staples doesn't stir.)

(Chase touches his cheek, draws his hand back, quickly retreats to his side of the sofa.)

(Gray continues to stare at the tulips arranged in the beer light.)

(Speed slowly begins to rise off the floor.)

(Chase starts to weep.)

(Blackout as the cell phone rings through the silence.)

END OF PLAY

Bake Off
by Sheri Wilner

BIOGRAPHY

Sheri Wilner was thrilled to return to Actors Theatre of Louisville, where her play *Labor Day* premiered at the 1999 Humana Festival and was a co-recipient of the 1998 Heideman Award. In 1999, Actors also produced her play *Joan of Arkansas* in the Apprentice Showcase. Her play *Hunger*, produced by the Contemporary American Theater Festival, was chosen for the Smith and Kraus anthology *The Best New Plays of 1999*. *Hunger* also received readings at the Williamstown Theatre Festival, The Women's Project, The Cherry Lane Alternative, and Ensemble Studio Theatre. Her other plays include *Relative Strangers* (published by Applause Books in *The Best New Plays of 2000*), *Little Death of a Salesman*, and her most recent, *Father Joy*. She is currently working on a full-length version of *Bake Off* for a commercial, Off-Broadway production. She received her M.F.A. in Playwriting from Columbia University and was a 2000-2001 Dramatists Guild Playwriting Fellow.

HUMANA FESTIVAL PRODUCTION

Bake Off premiered at the Humana Festival of New American Plays in April 2002. It was directed by Sullivan Canaday White with the following cast:

Paul	Jeffrey Bean
Rita	Kim Martin-Cotten
The Pillsbury Doughboy	Michael Shannon
Voice of the Announcer	Tom Teti

and the following production staff:

Scenic Designer	Paul Owen
Costume Designer	John White
Lighting Designer	Paul Werner
Sound Designer	Colbert Davis
Properties Designer	Doc Manning
Stage Manager	Heather Fields
Assistant Stage Manager	Debra A. Freeman
Dramaturg	Steve Moulds

CHARACTERS

RITA: Age 38-48.

PAUL: Age 33-40.

THE PILLSBURY DOUGHBOY: If not available, an actor in costume will do.

SETTING

The cooking floor of the Pillsbury Bake-Off.

TIME

1997; one year after the first man won the Grand Prize in the history of the Pillsbury Bake-Off.

"Men are making their mark at the Bake-Off Contest. The greatest number of men—14—competed in the 38th contest. *Perhaps, even more significantly, the first Bake-Off finalist to win the $1 million Grand Prize was a man.*"

—from the Pillsbury Bake-Off web site, www.bakeoff.com

Kim Martin-Cotten and Michael Shannon
in *Bake Off*

26th Annual Humana Festival of New American Plays
Actors Theatre of Louisville, 2002
photo by Larry Hunt

Bake Off

Paul is at his portion of the kitchen area unpacking ingredients and supplies from two white boxes. The boxes are marked with the numbers "15" and "16," but the numbers face the audience and are out of Paul's view. He is wearing the number "15" on his apron. Rita, wearing an apron marked "16," approaches the kitchen area. She sees Paul and is clearly annoyed. She steps into the kitchen area and Paul sees her.

PAUL: Hi there! I'm number Fifteen. You must be… number Sixteen.

RITA: How'd you guess? *(She looks at the equipment and supplies.)* Holy cripes, what did you do?!

PAUL: *(Alarmed.)* I don't know. What? What?

RITA: That's my box. Why the hell did you unpack my box?

PAUL: I didn't know.

RITA: What do you mean you didn't know?

PAUL: It was right here.

RITA: You expect me to believe that?

PAUL: I thought they were both mine.

RITA: Both yours? *(She turns the boxes around to show him the large numbers "15" and "16" printed on each.)*

PAUL: Oh god. Oh my god I'm sorry. Ma'am, I am so sorry.

RITA: You read it off my chest OK. How 'bout directing your eyes to flat surfaces from time to time?

PAUL: No, it's not like that. I'm sorry. I'm so nervous. I didn't even think to turn them around. I'm sorry.

RITA: Aw cripes, you mixed everything together. How much time do we have?

PAUL: Two minutes.

(While Rita speaks, she sorts through the items, placing her ingredients in her area, and Paul's ingredients in his. She could do this with her eyes closed.)

RITA: In 1949 Frances Jerzak from Topeka, Kansas almost got disqualified for bringing her own eggs. This… machination of yours would get you booted out of here for sure.

PAUL: Wait. Wait, please. There's got to be a more organized way to do this.

RITA: I'm doing it organized. This is organized.

PAUL: How?

RITA: Process of elimination. Whatever's not mine is yours. *(She picks up a bowl.)*

PAUL: Hold on. That's mine too. I need that. I think. I don't know.

RITA: You don't know?

PAUL: Everything's on paper. Just give me a second. Hold on. *(He takes a recipe card out of his pocket and studies it very carefully.)* Yes. Flour. Right here. See?

RITA: You weren't sure you needed *flour?* This is the Pillsbury Bake-Off.

PAUL: I like to check these things.

RITA: *(Snatching the recipe card from his hands.)* Your secretary type this for you?

PAUL: No. I typed it myself.

RITA: *(Reads.)* "Junior Mint Brownies." Gee, I wonder if you'll need those *Junior Mint*s over there?

PAUL: *(Grabbing the card back.)* I would greatly appreciate it if you would move all of the supplies back here to the center.

RITA: This is my stuff.

PAUL: I'm sure it is, but I think we should double-check. Just so there are no misunderstandings during the event. Perhaps I could find an official, someone who could oversee what we're doing. Mediate, if you will. *(While he looks around the cooking floor for an official, she begrudgingly moves all the equipment back to the center.)* Thank you.
(They begin to separate their ingredients. Paul is very tense and triple-checks everything. Rita finishes quickly and spends the rest of the time observing Paul. When she sees that he is unfamiliar with some of the utensils, her mood alternates between amusement and anger. Paul looks into the bowl of Junior Mints, picks one out and places it off to the side. He notices Rita watching him.)

PAUL: *(Indicating the mint.)* A souvenir. For my son.

RITA: There are four eggs here. How many do you need?

PAUL: Two. Wait. *(He checks his list.)* Yes. I need two.

RITA : So do I. No souvenirs left for Junior.

PAUL: Are you sure you need two? *(Rita glares at him.)* I'm just asking because now's the time, you know? Once this puppy starts, it starts. We can't yell "Time out." Can we? *(Beat.)* Maybe we should request another egg. Can we do that? 'Cause who knows, in the heat of the moment you—or I— may grab one too tightly, or drop it—by accident and then, "BLAM"— "All the king's horses and all the king's men…"

(A bell is heard over the loudspeaker.)

RITA: Too late. This "puppy" is starting.

VOICE OF ANNOUNCER: Ladies may I have your attention please. Ladies, may—. Excuse me. Ladies *and gentlemen* may I have your attention please.

RITA: Aw, cripes.

VOICE OF ANNOUNCER: Welcome to the 48th Annual Pillsbury Bake-Off. *(Loud cheers resound from the bleachers and cooking floor.)* Our finalists are at their ovens, with their fresh Pillsbury ingredients at the ready, about to prepare America's most scrumptious and creative recipes. But before we begin the competition, we would just like to take a moment to acknowledge a very special VIP in attendance. Seated next to Thomas Barnes, the illustrious CEO of Pillsbury Foods, is Mrs. Betty McBride. *(Rita's jaw drops and she scans the audience.)* At a hundred and two years young, the oldest living winner of the Bake-Off, Ms. McBride won in 1949 for her—

RITA AND ANNOUNCER: Betty's Apple Brown Betty.

VOICE OF ANNOUNCER: Please take a bow, Ms. McBride.

(Loud sounds of applause are heard. Rita cheers.)

PAUL: *(Holding up a bowl.)* Excuse me, is this flour or baking soda?

RITA: Cripes, have some respect. She's a baking legend.

PAUL: Oh. I…I didn't know.

RITA: For your information, there was no "Betty" before that Betty.

VOICE OF ANNOUNCER: OK, ladies. I mean ladies *and gentlemen* are you ready?

RITA: **YES!!**

VOICE OF ANNOUNCER: Then start your engines. On your marks… get set… BAKE!!!

(A loud bell sounds: ding-ding-ding-ding. Rita and Paul begin baking. Paul is as systematic and precise as a scientist. He preheats his oven, triple-checking the temperature. He then coats the bottom of a pan with margarine, painstakingly attempting to apply an even coat.

Rita is much looser in her technique, using her hands to scoop out ingredients instead of cups and spoons. She works from instinct, which allows her the ability to often look away from what she is doing to eye Paul.

At the same moment, they both reach for an egg. Paul smiles at Rita who glares back. They resume baking.)

PAUL: Junior Mints are my son's favorite candy. I figured there are worse things that could go into his brownies, right?

RITA: You know, even if your wife is sick or something, there's still no pinch-hitting allowed.

PAUL: Pinch-hitting?… Oh, I get it. No, it's not like that. *I* entered. I was selected. Not my wife. We're divorced. I make these for my son on the weekends. When he comes to visit. *(Rita begins mixing her eggs, aggressively.)* Hey, you're splattering—.

RITA: DON'T TALK TO ME!! *(She beats the eggs with increasing violence.)* I knew this would happen. I knew it!

PAUL: Knew what would happen?

RITA: I SAID DON'T TALK TO ME!! *(She adds ingredients to the eggs.)* Last year a man takes home a million dollars—the biggest prize in Bake-Off history and now men everywhere suddenly decide they like making cookies.

PAUL: I'm making brownies.

RITA: Yeah, well you know what I'm making?

PAUL: No.

RITA: "Rita's Unbeata… ble Applesauce Pecan Crumb Cake." You think you could make this, Mr. Brownie? Mr. Million Dollar Man?

PAUL: I'm not here for the money.

RITA: The Bake-Off's been around for years… there's never, *ever* been a prize so big and "miracle of miracles" it's the first year a man wins. What a random chain of events, huh? What an amazing fucking coincidence!

PAUL: That's not why I'm here.

RITA: You're not going to win. You hear me? You are not going to win.

PAUL: Ma'am, please… I can't cook and talk.

RITA: Yeah, and how much have you tried, Mr. Suddenly Single?

(An actor enters dressed in a Pillsbury Doughboy costume. He pushes his hands into his stomach and gives the Doughboy laugh.)

THE PILLSBURY DOUGHBOY: He-hee. Is everybody making friends?

RITA: This isn't right. He shouldn't be allowed here. I bet this is the only thing he's ever baked.

THE PILLSBURY DOUGHBOY: He-hee. Everyone can bake. Baking is fun.

RITA: Oh yeah, it's a real roll in the hay.

THE PILLSBURY DOUGHBOY: Nothin' says lovin' like somethin' from the oven. He-hee. Happy Baking! *(The Pillsbury Doughboy exits.)*

PAUL: Guess that's the final word. You can't go any higher up than him.

RITA: How many dinners for your family have you ever cooked?

PAUL: What does that have to do with this?

RITA: EVERYTHING! It has everything to do with this, Mr. Making-A-List-And-Checking-It-Twice. It must be nice to play in the kitchen only when you want to. Most of us were assigned kitchen duty without having any say in the matter.

PAUL: Look lady, I don't know how else to say this. You're bothering me.

RITA: Oh, you poor man. Is making forty percent more than the women who have the same job as you getting to be too much of a strain?

PAUL: Shit! One-quarter cup butter, not one-third! Don't talk to me anymore. OK? No talking.

RITA: *(With contempt.)* Brownies.

(They return to their preparations. Rita combines another set of ingredients. Paul stirs his melted mints. Having made one error, he is now even more cautious. His anxiety drives Rita crazy, and in their preparations a direct correlation develops between his level of nervousness and her level of violence until he finally explodes.)

PAUL: Please stop it! STOP IT!! You're scaring the shit out of me!!

RITA: Hey, if you can't take the heat…

PAUL: I can take the heat. It's you I can't take.

RITA: How old's your son?

PAUL: Thirteen. Why?

(Rita looks out into the audience.)

RITA: I want to know where he's sitting.

PAUL: That's none of your business.

RITA: How's he like having his dad in the Pillsbury Bake-Off? You his new hero?

PAUL: I'm trying to be. If you really must know, I am trying to be a hero. His kind of hero.

RITA: His kind of hero? What does what mean?

PAUL: What decade are you living in? This is not 1949. Times have changed. Men cook now. Some of the most famous chefs are men.

RITA: *All* of the most famous chefs are men. Women who cook well get to have Thanksgiving at their house every year. Men who cook well run five-star restaurants and get their pictures pasted on bottles of over-priced sauces.

PAUL: Please, he's watching us. I don't want him to think there's anything wrong with this—.

RITA: Yeah, well maybe there is something wrong with this and maybe I want him to know.

PAUL: Ma'am, please, I'm appealing to you as a parent. Do you have children?

RITA: Five.

PAUL: Well mine thinks there's something wrong with him. Mine is losing everything that's special and good about him because he's trying to squeeze through some ridiculous mold that he doesn't fit through. I'm here to show him that I'm proud of who he is. That all I'll ever want from him is that he be true to himself. That he accepts himself. So please, I beg you, let me do that.

RITA: Lucky for you your son didn't need his little ego boost a couple of years ago. Then you would have only won fifty thou.

PAUL: I'll tell you what, if you leave me alone, and I win, you can have the million dollars. That's not why I'm here—.

RITA: I don't want your million dollars. I am more capable than you will ever be of winning that million dollars. I have been baking my whole life, not just when my son developed a pre-pubescent crisis.

PAUL: It's more than a pre-pubescent—. Why am I arguing with you? I am not the only man in this contest. Why don't you start picking on the other guys and leave me alone?

RITA: There are no other men in this contest.

PAUL: Yes there are. There are five to be exact. *(He points across the cooking floor.)* Look right there, there's one, at Oven Fifty-Four.

(Rita scans the rows of contestants.)

RITA: Holy shit. You assholes are everywhere!! Hey you! Number Fifty-Four! Hey Fifty-Four, I'm talking to you! *(She reaches for an egg and goes to hurl it in the direction of Oven Fifty-Four.)*

PAUL: That's mine! *(Paul grabs the egg out of her hands.)* What is the matter with you?!

RITA: This is what they give us. *This. (She spreads open her arms to indicate the cooking floor.)* Why do you want it, huh? *(She stands up on the counter.)*

PAUL: Jeez, lady, get down.

RITA: Why do you want this? *(She looks all around the cooking floor.)* This is quite a kingdom, isn't it? This is quite the fucking kingdom. *(Shouting out to Oven Fifty-Four.)* What's the matter? You tired of running Fortune 500 companies? You tired of sitting in your Congressional seats and ruling countries? Now you'd rather have this? *This?!* Well you can't have it. You hear me? YOU CAN'T HAVE IT! They give this to us and as much as it reeks and stinks to high heaven this is what is ours and you're not going to get your fucking hands on it. *(To Paul.)* Tell that to your son.

Wherever the hell he is. *(She scans the audience.)* Where are you Junior? Where are you? Ah, there you are.

PAUL: Stop it!

RITA: This isn't yours. You hear me? Stay away!

PAUL: Please. Stop. He's only thirteen. Please. *(Paul calls out to his son.)* It's OK, Billy. Everything's OK.

RITA: Everything is not OK. Your being here is *NOT OK.* *(To the child.)* THIS IS NOT OK, BILLY!

(The Pillsbury Doughboy enters, running.)

THE PILLSBURY DOUGHBOY: Is there a problem here?

RITA: Is there a problem here? Yes. There is a big problem here.

THE PILLSBURY DOUGHBOY: He-hee. SECURITY!

RITA: You scared of me, Doughboy? Huh? You scared of me? What kinda boy are you? Show some dough balls, why dontcha? You got dough balls, Doughboy? Where are they? *(She pokes him in the stomach.)*

THE PILLSBURY DOUGHBOY: He-hee!

(She pokes him again, lower.)

RITA: Here?

THE PILLSBURY DOUGHBOY: He-hee! Help!

RITA: Here? Where are they? What part of this marshmallow body proves that you're a boy? If you got something, show it, Doughboy.

THE PILLSBURY DOUGHBOY: Security!

RITA: Are women supposed to be attracted to you? Are you supposed to be some kind of sex symbol? OK then. *(She grabs the Doughboy's head and begins kissing and fondling him. He makes Doughboy-sounding struggling noises and tries to push her away.)* Yum. You taste good, Doughboy. You taste good. Not quite done yet though. Ten more minutes at 350 I think. *(Paul pulls her away.)*

PAUL: Leave him alone.

THE PILLSBURY DOUGHBOY: *(Husky, masculine voice.)* Crazy bitch.

RITA: What?

(The Pillsbury Doughboy removes the head of his costume.)

THE PILLSBURY DOUGHBOY: You heard me, keep your paws to yourself you crazy bitch.

PAUL: *(To the Doughboy.)* Now wait a minute.

RITA: AGGHHH! *(She throws everything on the counter down onto the floor.)*

THE PILLSBURY DOUGHBOY: Holy shit!

PAUL: Lady—. Rita, please. It's OK Billy, just a little accident. Everything's fine.

THE PILLSBURY DOUGHBOY: Hey, we need a clean up here! Clean up at Fifteen and Sixteen.

RITA: Mrs. McBride, where are you? Where are you, Mrs. McBride?

THE PILLSBURY DOUGHBOY: *(While putting his head back on.)* It's gonna be a long fucking day. *(To Paul.)* Thanks for everything, pal. *(He shakes Paul's hand. Rita turns around and sees them shaking hands. Pointedly to Paul, in the Doughboy voice.)* I hope you win. He-hee!
(The Pillsbury Doughboy fraternally slaps Paul on the back and then exits. Paul looks at Rita.)

PAUL: I'm sorry. I—. *(Beat.)* What a putz, huh?

RITA: This is ours. *(Out to Mrs. McBride.)* Mrs. McBride, tell them this is ours. Mrs. McBride, Betty, tell them this is ours.

END OF PLAY

Snapshot
a dramatic anthology by
Tanya Barfield, Lee Blessing, Michael Bigelow Dixon, Julie Jensen, Honour Kane, Sunil Kuruvilla, David Lindsay-Abaire, Victor Lodato, Quincy Long, Deb Margolin, Allison Moore, Lynn Nottage, Dan O'Brien, Val Smith, Annie Weisman, Craig Wright and Chay Yew

Developing *Snapshot*

If it's true, as a famous Chinese proverb purportedly claims, that "One picture is worth a thousand words," then why not unleash the enormous artistic potential of that maxim? A brave new Humana Festival experiment was designed to do just that, by using a single image to inspire the creation of multiple dramatic texts. Actors Theatre of Louisville asked seventeen talented playwrights to respond to a remarkable photograph, and the resulting work—a collection of scenes and monologues titled *Snapshot*—turned out to be as diverse as the group of writers we'd asked to lend their considerable imaginations to this project.

A photograph seemed to us to be an evocative starting-point for this challenge—a catalyst that would spark many different reactions to a central question. Photographs capture and document a single moment in time and space; they are snapshots of history, of a reality bounded by the photo's frame. But what, we wondered, lies outside, beyond, behind the photograph? And what stories, memories, or associations does an image of *place* inspire? In this multi-writer venture, many minds encountered and transformed *Mount Rushmore, South Dakota, 1969*, a compelling image of the monument by renowned photographer Lee Friedlander.

There are several reasons why this particular image initially captured our attention. For one thing, it contains the reflection of a famed American monument, and we wondered what monuments mean to us at this point in our history, to the generations that have inherited them. Because we were commissioning these pieces in the late fall of 2001—in the wake of terrible events that radically altered Americans' perspectives in a number of ways—the idea of thinking about American icons and monuments had particular resonance. What is striking about Friedlander's image, also, is that Mount Rushmore is not captured head-on, but is instead reflected in the glass of the visitors' center—so that what the tourists are looking at seems to be looming behind them, facing *us*. Beyond the rich thematic territories suggested by the photograph, there were also wonderful possibilities for dramatic collisions between characters, because the photo depicts a public space where people from many walks of life are constantly arriving and departing.

We shared these thoughts with the playwrights, and then encouraged them to work from their own associations and obsessions—so the scenes and monologues *could* be set at Mount Rushmore, but they didn't have to be. As you'll see, the playwrights have envisioned a thought-provoking array of different scenarios and characters—some existing in relation to the monument, others more metaphorical or inspired by some other facet of the image. The pieces ended up ranging from delightful comedy to utterly serious meditations on recent real-life tragedy, but in their marvelous diversity of approaches, the playwrights seemed to be picking up on some of the same frequencies. What was remarkable about the way in which the project came together was that there were shared thematic threads which, in the hands of each playwright, found very different expression. Some of these threads include ideas about immortality or the inability to change (suggested by the stone visages and the fixedness of the image itself), characters' personal connections with the presidents, and a meditation on the United States' problematic history and global identity that emerges from the play as a whole. The photograph proved to be a great springboard for the creation of a play—for to borrow Craig Wright's description of the monument in *Bomb Squad*, "It's a conceptual land mine, left here to do its thing, and every time people see it, ideas go off in their heads. Boom!"

Snapshot, the collection of dramatic perspectives that resulted from this exploration, was performed by the twenty-two members of Actors Theatre's 2001-2002 Apprentice Acting Company, though all or some of the pieces could be produced with a smaller cast. The order here was carefully determined for our production, and was found via many lively dramaturgical discussions—so part of the challenge was to shape the experience by building a progression that would help bring the event together as a whole. This is the third year running that Actors Theatre has created such an event, commissioning pieces specifically for our young company of actors to perform in the Humana Festival, and we think it's a practice very much in the spirit of the festival's celebration of playwrights and new work. With *Snapshot*, we were able to explore a new set of questions with seventeen amazing writers, approaching an ever-evolving experiment through a new lens.

—*Amy Wegener*

BIOGRAPHIES

Tanya Barfield is currently in Juilliard's Playwriting Program. Her plays include: *The Quick, Dent, Pecan Tan, The Houdini Act* and *Wanting North*. She has been in residency at The Royal Court Theatre in London, New York Theatre Workshop, and Mabou Mines. Before becoming a playwright, Ms. Barfield was a performance artist. Her solo piece, *Without Skin or Breathlessness*, has received numerous fellowships and awards.

Lee Blessing's *A Walk in the Woods* was seen on Broadway and London's West End. Off-Broadway: *Eleemosynary, Cobb, Thief River, Chesapeake* and *Down the Road*—plus *Fortinbras, Lake Street Extension, Two Rooms*, and the world premiere of *Patient A*, all in the 1992-93 Signature Theatre Season. A new play, *Black Sheep*, premiered at Florida Stage last December. *The Winning Streak*, directed by the author, premiered at the Ensemble Theatre of Cincinnati. Other plays include *Going to St. Ives, Independence, Riches, Oldtimers Game* and *Nice People Dancing to Country Music*. Awards: The American Theatre Critics Association Award, the L.A. Drama Critics Award, the Great American Play Award, the Humanitas Award and the George and Elisabeth Marton Award, among others. His plays have been nominated for Tony and Olivier Awards, as well as for the Pulitzer Prize. Mr. Blessing is the author of over twenty plays and screenplays. He currently resides in New York City.

Michael Bigelow Dixon was Literary Manager and, in his last year, Associate Artistic Director at Actors Theatre of Louisville from 1985 to 2001. He is currently the Literary Manager at the Guthrie Theater in Minneapolis, and he recently directed the world premiere of Lee Blessing's *Black Sheep* at Florida Stage. Mr. Dixon has written more than 20 published and produced plays, most with Val Smith, and has edited 28 volumes of plays and criticism with Amy Wegener, Tanya Palmer, Liz Engelman and Michele Volansky. He directed the world premiere of Naomi Wallace's *Standard Time* in the 2000 Humana Festival, as well as Actors Theatre's productions of *Wit, Nixon's Nixon*, and *The Creditors*.

Julie Jensen's play *Last Lists of My Mad Mother* has had a dozen productions, including one in Edinburgh, Scotland, and another in New Jersey, directed by Olympia Dukakis. *Two-Headed*, commissioned by A.S.K. Theater Projects in Los Angeles, won the Mill Mountain Playwriting Competition and was produced in New York and Los Angeles, where it was named one of the best plays of the year by the *Los Angeles Times*. *The Lost Vegas Series* won the Joseph Jefferson Award for Best New Work and was produced in Chicago and London. *White Money* won the Award for New American Plays and has been produced coast-to-coast in this country. Ms. Jensen is a recent recipient of a NEA/TCG Residency Grant, and a major award from the Pew Charitable Trust. She is currently Resident Playwright at Salt Lake Acting Company in Salt Lake City, Utah.

Honour Kane's work has been produced by The Public Theater New Works, Sydney's annual Mardi Gras Arts Festival, and New Georges. Her plays have been developed by A.S.K. at Lincoln Center, PlayLabs, and A.S.K. at London's Royal Court Theatre. A resident of New Dramatists, she holds fellowships from the NEA, the New York Foundation for the Arts, a Pew Fellowship in the Arts, and a Bunting Fellowship at Radcliffe.

Sunil Kuruvilla's plays have been developed at various theatres including New York Theatre Workshop, the Williamstown Theatre Festival, and Portland Center Stage, and he has been commissioned by such theatres as The Joseph Papp Public Theater, The Wilma Theatre and South Coast Repertory to write new work. Recent awards include the Cole Porter ASCAP Award and the Truman Capote Literary Fellowship, and he has been commissioned by Showtime to write a screenplay adaptation of *Fighting Words*. That play recently had its world premiere at the Factory Theatre in Toronto, Canada, and will be produced this fall at the Yale Repertory Theatre. His play *Rice Boy* had its world premiere at the Yale Repertory Theatre and its West Coast premiere at the Mark Taper Forum. The play will be staged next season at Canadian Stage in Toronto. Mr. Kuruvilla's work has been generously supported by the Canada Council and the Ontario Arts Council. He graduated from the Yale School of Drama in 1999.

David Lindsay-Abaire's *Fuddy Meers* premiered at Manhattan Theatre Club in the fall of 1999, and later transferred to The Minetta Lane Theatre for a commercial run. It has since received over a hundred productions around the country and abroad. David's most recent play, *Kimberly Akimbo*, was commissioned by South Coast Repertory, premiered at that theatre in 2001, and received an L.A. Drama Critics Circle Award, a Garland Award, and the prestigious Kesselring Prize. *Kimberly* opens in New York in January 2003 at MTC. His *Wonder of the World* was produced this past season at MTC, after premiering at

Washington, D.C.'s Woolly Mammoth Theatre, where it was nominated for a 2001 Helen Hayes Award as Outstnading New Play of the Year. David's other plays include *A Devil Inside, Dotting & Dashing* and *A Show of Hands*, among others. He recently signed a two-picture deal with Miramax Films, is currently developing a television show with NBC and Conan O'Brien's production company, and is finishing up his screen adaptation of *Fuddy Meers*. He has received awards from the Berrilla Kerr Foundation, the LeComte du Nuoy Fund, Mixed Blood Theater, Primary Stages, the Tennessee Williams Literary Festival, and the South Carolina Playwrights Festival. David is a graduate of Sarah Lawrence College and the Juilliard School's Playwriting Program, as well as a proud member of New Dramatists, the Dramatists Guild, and the WGA.

Victor Lodato is a playwright and actor. A 2002 Guggenheim Fellow, he is also the recipient of a 2002 Helen Merrill Award. Other honors include fellowships from the National Endowment of the Arts, The Princess Grace Foundation, The Robert Chesley Foundation, Art Matters, and The Puffin Foundation, as well as a New Forms Grant (Rockefeller Foundation/NEA). Earlier this year, his play *The Eviction* received its world premiere at the Magic Theatre, and won a Roger L. Stevens Award from The Kennedy Center Fund for New American Plays. His play *The Woman Who Amuses Herself* was selected as the 2002 winner of the Mill Mountain Theatre New Play Competition, and will be staged in 2003. Other works have been produced at Ensemble Theatre of Cincinnati, a.k.a. Theatre (Tucson, Arizona), and Institute for Studies in the Arts. He has received workshops and readings at Manhattan Theatre Club, The Guthrie Theater, A.S.K. Theater Projects, MCC Theater, Primary Stages, The Play Company, The Playwrights' Center, and The Bay Area Playwrights Festival. For the past two summers, Mr. Lodato has developed work at the O'Neill Playwrights Conference (*The Bread of Winter* and *Motherhouse*). He has recently completed a new play (*Wildlife*), commissioned by South Coast Repertory. This fall (2002), he will be a playwright-in-residence at the Camargo Foundation in Cassis, France. His writing has been published in *North American Review, Virginia Quarterly Review, The Southern Review*, and *Northwest Review*. Mr. Lodato is a Phi Beta Kappa graduate of Rutgers University and a member of New Dramatists.

Quincy Long's play, *The Lively Lad*, was recently produced at the Powerhouse Theatre at Vassar by New York Stage and Film, and will be produced next season by Zoo District in Los Angeles. *The Joy of Going Somewhere Definite*, to be produced in Chicago in the fall by CollaborAction, was commissioned and produced by the Mark Taper Forum. It won a Fund for New American Plays Award and was also produced by the Atlantic Theater in New York, where it was directed by William H. Macy and starred Felicity Huffman. Mr. Long has adapted the play for film for Mel Gibson's company, Icon Productions, and has also adapted another play, *Shaker Heights*, for Atlantic Films. *The Year of the Baby*, produced by Soho Repertory, was a recent *Village Voice* Pick of the Week. Mr. Long's plays have been produced regionally by Berkeley Repertory Theatre, Magic Theatre, Undermain Theatre, Salt Lake Acting Company, Perishable Theatre and others. Mr. Long is a recipient of playwriting grants from the NEA and NYFA, and has been commissioned by South Coast Repertory Theatre, The Mark Taper Forum, Sundance Children's Theatre, Soho Repertory Theatre, A.S.K. Theater Projects, and most recently by Playwrights Horizons and the Ensemble Studio Theatre/Sloan Foundation Science and Technology Project. He was a finalist for the Outer Circle Drama Critics Award in 1994, a runner-up for the Kesselring Prize in 1993, and a winner of the ASCAP/Cole Porter prize for playwriting. Mr. Long is a graduate of the Yale School of Drama and a member of Ensemble Studio Theatre, New Dramatists and the HB Playwrights Unit. He is from Warren, Ohio and lives in New York City.

Deb Margolin is a playwright, performance artist and founding member of Split Britches Theatre Company. She is the author of six full-length solo performance pieces, which she has toured throughout the United States, and is the recipient of a 1999-2000 OBIE Award for Sustained Excellence of Performance. Her solo performance piece titled *O Wholly Night and Other Jewish Solecisms* was commissioned by the Jewish Museum of New York in 1996 and subsequently enjoyed a successful run at the Interart Theater in New York City. Ms. Margolin's play *Critical Mass* premiered at Performance Space 122 in New York in 1997, and her next play, *Bringing the Fishermen Home*, was workshopped at Dixon Place in New York City, was part of the New Work Now! Festival at the Joseph Papp Public Theater, and premiered in April of 1999 at the Cleveland Public Theater under the direction of Randy Rollison. In 2001, PS122 presented Ms. Margolin's play *Three Seconds in the Key*, a meditation in illness, love and basketball, which was given a workshop production at the Joseph Papp Public Theater. Her latest play, *Why Cleaning Fails*, ran in January 2002 at HERE Arts Center in New York. Ms. Margolin has lectured extensively at universities throughout the country, has been an artist in residence at Hampshire College and the University of Hawaii, and is currently a faculty lecturer in Playwriting and Performance in Yale

University's Theater Studies Program. She served in the fall of 2000 as artist in residence in New York University's Department of Undergraduate Drama, and served additionally as a theater panelist for the New York State Council on the Arts. A book of Ms. Margolin's performance pieces and plays, titled *Of All The Nerve: Deb Margolin SOLO*, edited by Lynda Hart, was published in 1999 by Cassell/Continuum Press.

Allison Moore is a displaced Texan currently living in Minneapolis. Her play *Eighteen* was developed at the 2001 O'Neill National Playwrights Conference and produced at Kitchen Dog Theater in Dallas. Another of her plays, *The Sad Misadventures of Patty, Patty's Dad, Patty's Friend Jen and a Bunch of Other People*, was co-produced by Cheap Theatre and the Playwrights' Center in Minneapolis. Her other plays have been developed and read at The Playwrights' Center, Williamstown Theatre Festival, The Cherry Lane Alternative, InterAct Theatre, Florida Repertory Theatre, and The Centenary Stage Company. Ms. Moore is the recipient of the Iowa Arts Fellowship in Playwriting, the Kemp and Felton Fellowships, the Rosenfield Playwriting Award, and is the recipient of the 2002-2003 Jerome Foundation Fellowship. She holds an M.F.A. from The Iowa Playwrights' Workshop.

Lynn Nottage is a playwright from Brooklyn. Her plays include *Crumbs From the Table of Joy, Mud, River, Stone, Por 'Knockers, Poof!* (Heideman Award), and *Las Meninas*, which premiered at San Jose Repertory in the spring of 2002. Her plays have been produced Off-Broadway and regionally by The Acting Company, Actors Theatre of Louisville, the Alliance Theatre, Buffalo Studio Arena, Crossroads Theatre, Freedom Theatre, Oregon Shakespeare Festival, Playwrights Horizons, Second Stage, South Coast Repertory, Steppenwolf Theatre Company, Yale Repertory, the Vineyard Theatre and many others. Ms. Nottage has received Playwriting Fellowships from Manhattan Theatre Club, New Dramatists and the New York Foundation for the Arts. She is also the recipient of a Playwrights Horizons' Amblin/Dreamworks Commission, AT&T Onstage Award and a NEA/TCG (1999-2000) grant for a year-long residency at Freedom Theatre. She is a member of New Dramatists and a graduate of Brown University and the Yale School of Drama.

Dan O'Brien's plays have been developed at The O'Neill National Playwrights Conference, Manhattan Theatre Club, Ensemble Studio Theatre, The New Harmony Project, Primary Stages, and the Magic Theatre, among other theatres, and produced at the Williamstown Theatre Festival, The Kennedy

Center, California Repertory Company, HERE, and Perishable Theatre, among others. His plays have won the Osborn Award (American Theatre Critics Association) and the Mark Twain Comedy Playwriting Award (Kennedy Center/ACTF). A former Thomas J. Watson Fellow, Mr. O'Brien was recently a playwright-in-residence at Manhattan Theatre Club. He has written commissioned plays for Manhattan Theatre Club and Ensemble Studio Theatre and is currently commissioned to write a play for The Kennedy Center. He is a graduate of Middlebury College and Brown University's M.F.A. playwriting program, and lives in New York City.

Val Smith is the author of numerous plays that have been published and produced nationally. Her first full-length drama, *The Gamblers*, won the Playhouse on the Square's Mid-South Playwright's Competition, and was produced at American Stage Theatre in New Jersey. Her second full-length, *Ain't We Got Fun*, was commissioned and produced by Actors Theatre of Louisville in the 1993 Classics in Context Festival—The Roaring Twenties. She is the recipient of awards from the Kentucky Women's Foundation and the Kentucky Arts Council. Her most recent full-length play, *Marguerite Bonet*, was published in *Best Plays by Women of 1998*. Her ten-minute play *Meow* premiered in the 1998 Humana Festival.

Annie Weisman's most recent play, *Totally Meaningful Ritual*, was commissioned by A.S.K. Theater Projects and will be read as part of the Mark Taper Forum's New Work Festival in August 2002. Her play, *Hold Please*, was commissioned by South Coast Repertory and premiered in their 2001-2002 season. Her play *Be Aggressive* premiered at La Jolla Playhouse in July 2001, and goes on to productions at TheatreWorks in Pala Alto and Dallas Theater Center in 2002. *Be Aggressive* will be published by Dramatists Play Service and in Smith and Kraus' *Best Plays of 2001*. Annie is collaborating on a new musical for Trinity Repertory and writing commissions for the Mark Taper Forum and South Coast Repertory. Her work has been developed by the Sundance Theatre Lab, Manhattan Theatre Club, SoHo Repertory, Geva Theatre, Austin Scriptworks, and A.S.K. Theater Projects. She is currently writing an original comedy pilot for HBO. A Southern California native, Annie is a proud member of The Dramatists Guild and a graduate of Williams College.

Craig Wright's plays include *The Pavilion*, *Orange Flower Water*, and *Molly's Delicious*. He has received several awards for his writing, including fellowships from the McKnight Foundation and the National Endowment for the Arts. In addition to being a playwright, Mr. Wright has worked as a fishmonger, advertising copywriter and hotel developer. He is currently a member of the rock band Kangaroo and lives in St. Paul with his wife, Lorraine LeBlanc, and their son, Louis.

Chay Yew's plays include *Porcelain*, *A Language of Their Own*, *Red*, *Wonderland*, *As if He Hears*, *Dirt and Desire* and *A Beautiful Country*. He also adapted Wei Jingsheng's *The Courage to Stand Alone* and Lorca's *The House of Bernarda Alba*; his performance text includes *Home: Places Between Asia and America*. His work has been produced by the New York Shakespeare Festival's Public Theater, Royal Court Theatre (London), Long Wharf Theatre, Manhattan Theatre Club, La Jolla Playhouse, Intiman Theatre, Portland Center Stage, East West Players, Dallas Theater Center, Cornerstone Theatre Company, The Group Theatre and TheatreWorks (Singapore), to name a few. He is the recipient of the London Fringe Award, George and Elisabeth Marton Playwriting Award, GLAAD Media Award, APGF Community Visibility Award, Drama-Logue Award and the Robert Chesley Award, among many other honors and grants. Mr. Yew has produced the Mark Taper Forum's Taper, Too season from 2000 to the present. A member of New Dramatists and The Dramatists Guild, he is concurrently the Director of the Asian Theatre Workshop at the Taper and the Artistic Director of Northwest Asian American Theatre/The Black Box in Seattle.

HUMANA FESTIVAL PRODUCTION

Snapshot was commissioned by Actors Theatre of Louisville and premiered at the Humana Festival of New American Plays in March 2002. It was directed by Russell Vandenbroucke with the following cast:

A Quick Tour of the Monument . . . . Joey Belmaggio (Guide) by Craig Wright	
Monument . . . . Jake Goodman, by Honour Kane	Ellie Clark
Scene at Mount Rushmore . . . . Christopher Illing (Bobby), by Quincy Long	Alan Malone (Did)
Tyler Poked Taylor . . . . Jake Goodman (Loyal) by Lee Blessing	
Rock Scissors Paper . . . . Melanie Rademaker by Deb Margolin	

Little Pezidents. . . . . Colin Sullivan (Dave),
by Michael Bigelow Dixon and Val Smith   Elisa Morrison (Karen)

Defacing Patriotic Property. . . . . Ryan Clardy
by Tanya Barfield

Her First Screen Test. . . . . Lindsey White
by Dan O'Brien

Thrift of the Magi . . . . Anthony Luciano (Trey),
by Annie Weisman   Kristi Funk (Tina)

Night Out . . . . Donovan Sherman,
by Sunil Kuruvilla   Ellie Clark

Here and Now . . . . Matt Bridges
by Chay Yew

The Great Father . . . . Tom Wooldridge,
by Victor Lodato   Camilla Busnovetsky

American Klepto . . . . Colette Beauvais
by Allison Moore

Becoming American. . . . . Barbara Lanciers
by Lynn Nottage

History Lesson. . . . . Stacy L. Mayer (Maggie)
by David Lindsay-Abaire

Bomb Squad . . . . Dave Secor (Man),
by Craig Wright   Camilla Busnovetsky (Ranger)

On Lincoln's Head. Amy Guillory (Babe),
by Julie Jensen   Kate Umstatter (Annette)

and the following production staff:
Scenic Designer . . . . Paul Owen
Costume Designer . . . . John White
Lighting Designer . . . . Tony Penna
Sound Designer . . . . Colbert Davis
Properties Designer . . . . Doc Manning
Stage Manager . . . . Sarah Hodges
Dramaturgs . . . . Amy Wegener
and Tanya Palmer

Mount Rushmore, South Dakota, 1969
by Lee Friedlander
Courtesy Fraenkel Gallery, San Francisco

A Quick Tour of The Monument
by Craig Wright

A tour guide, dressed as a park ranger, addresses the audience. Note: the same slightly perfunctory, slightly perplexed vocal tone should be used throughout without variation.

GUIDE: Welcome. My name is Victor Collins. Now, sit back and relax while I give you a quick tour of the monument. But before I begin, let me remind those of you with pets, no pets are allowed near the monument, with the exception of service dogs. Thank you.

Four U.S. presidents, each remarkable in their own remarkable way, are depicted in the heart of the monument. George Washington, the first U.S. President and commander of the Revolutionary Army. Thomas Jefferson, our third President, the author of the Declaration of Independence, and advocate of westward expansion! President Abraham Lincoln, our sixteenth President, whose leadership restored the Union and ended slavery on U.S. soil. And President Theodore Roosevelt, our twenty-sixth President, who promoted construction of the illustrious Panama Canal and ignited progressive causes such as conservation and business reform. Behind the busts of these four great men the monument extends infinitely in each of the four cardinal directions, and in three more, as well; an effort, no doubt, on the artist's part to communicate the scope of the ideals which inspired the monument's development. The so-called "Black Hills," which surround and envelop the mountain out of which the presidential portraits emerge, were formed over a period of billions of years at a cost of life which undoubtedly rivals the one million dollar price tag conventionally associated with the presidential portraits themselves. Below the presidential visages, the monument consists of thousands of miles of rock, magma, and mystery, and above, a matchless construction of vapor arises, upward and upward into starry depths, as unfathomable in their own way as the watery seas which mark the outer edges of the monument's innermost core. What is this monument, and what does it exist to commemorate? Questions like these have dogged humankind since the dawn of recorded time. And what is the meaning of the sparkling circuit of words that rims the ragged edges of the monument, the words that pour forth as though from the mouth of a guide? More precisely, what is the nature of the mind in which the monument is contained? Take your time; look around; draw conclusions; enjoy your stay, take only photographs, leave only footprints, and let me remind you, no pets are allowed near the monument, with the exception of service dogs. Thank you.

Monument
by Honour Kane

Setting: The dispatch room, Office of Emergency Management, New York City.
Characters: Two telephone operators.
Time: 08:47:23.

What do you think makes the loudest explosion? A car backfiring? A volcano erupting? A gun? An atomic bomb?

An explosion louder than you can imagine is how we begin our story.

Two OEM dispatch operators sit at computer terminals. They wear headsets that connect them to New York's emergency telephone line, 911.

It is their job to log incoming calls into their computerized system and verbally relay the information to emergency personnel dispatchers. They type very quickly.

OPERATOR ONE: Building explosion.
OPERATOR TWO: Explosion on top of World Trade.
OPERATOR ONE: Plane into top of building?
(Pause. They look at each other.)
(The calls begin again.)
OPERATOR ONE: From floor 47, anonymous female caller states building shaked and smells gas.
OPERATOR TWO: Male caller states he is on the 87th floor. States four persons with him. States there is fire.
OPERATOR ONE: People screaming in background… states cannot breathe… possible smoke coming through door… floor… 103… Call disconnected.
OPERATOR TWO: Male caller Caggiano. People trapped on the 104th floor. Check room. 35-40 people.
OPERATOR ONE: Female caller states her son and another male is trapped in room 8617.
OPERATOR TWO: Female caller states people are trapped on top of building. States need someone top of location.
OPERATOR ONE: Male caller wants to know how to get out of building.
OPERATOR TWO: Male caller states trapped on floor 22. Hole in hallway. Smoke coming in. Unable to breathe. Male caller states will break window.

(Our second operator receives a call from a New York City Police Department rescue helicopter.)

OPERATOR TWO: Go ahead Air Sea 14…

… people falling out of building…

(Pause. They look at each other.)

OPERATOR TWO: *(Continued.)* Air Sea 14 unable to land on roof.

(Pause.)

(The calls begin again.)

OPERATOR ONE: Second plane hit the building… Unknown extent of injury. Male caller states 2 World Trade Center, people are jumping out of a large hole. Possible no one is catching them.

OPERATOR TWO: On floor 104, male caller states his wife is on the 91st floor. States stairs are all blocked. States worried about his wife.

OPERATOR ONE: Female caller states possible female in wheelchair on 86th floor alone.

OPERATOR TWO:
Male caller states on 106th floor. About 100 people in room. Need directions on how to stay alive.

OPERATOR ONE:
Several jumpers from the window at 1 World Trade Center.

OPERATOR TWO:
Male caller states he's on 84th floor—number 2 tower. Can't breathe—caller disconnected.

OPERATOR ONE:
Female caller Diana states husband friend Tony is still alive on the 101st floor.

OPERATOR TWO:
Female caller states someone is waving a white flag first building that was hit, 10 floors down from the top.

OPERATOR ONE:
2 World Trade Center. 105th floor. People trapped. Open roof to gain access.

OPERATOR TWO:
Female caller Melissa. States floor very hot. No doors. States she's going to die on phone. Wants us to call mother.

OPERATOR ONE:
Female caller states 2 World Trade Center
floor 105. States floor underneath
her collapsed.

OPERATOR TWO:
... male waving jacket...

OPERATOR ONE:
1 World Trade Center.

People on the top waving...

... are alive...

... please send help.

OPERATOR TWO:
... male just jumped.

... people crying...

... no voice contact...

OPERATOR ONE: 2 World Trade Center. 106th Floor... 105th Floor... crum-
bling...
(Our second operator turns to the first.)
OPERATOR TWO: Pentagon in Washington has been struck by airplane.

OPERATOR ONE:
Male caller states son called... on
floor 93. States in the second
tower that was hit. States
smoke is getting worse...
... call disconnected.

OPERATOR TWO:
World Trade Center has collapsed.

(All the lines go dead.)
(After a moment, the calls begin again.)
OPERATOR ONE: EMT 4. Trapped. Building fell on them.
OPERATOR TWO: Police officers in building that just collapsed.
OPERATOR ONE: Numerous personnel... trapped... in basement... in the rubble...
OPERATOR TWO: Female caller states her brother is in the World Trade
Center... 104th floor. States no one has come for him yet.
OPERATOR ONE: Does appear that top of tower possible leaning at this time.
Air Sea 14. Is buckling. Leaning to southwest—
OPERATOR TWO: North tower is leaning.
OPERATOR ONE: North tower possible getting ready to fall—
North tower collapsing—
Entire tower down.
(All the lines go dead.)

Scene at Mount Rushmore
by Quincy Long

Cast: BOBBY
    DID, Bobby's older brother
Location: Mount Rushmore

Bobby and his brother Did gaze upwards.

BOBBY: That sure looks like her, don't it, Did?

DID: Looks like who, Bobby?

BOBBY: Like Momma.

DID: What?

BOBBY: Second from the left there. Looks like Momma with her hair down.

DID: Them is men, Bobby.

BOBBY: Who?

DID: All of them up there. They's Presidents. And Presidents is men. So far anyways.

BOBBY: Sure look like Momma to me.

DID: I ain't paying you no attention, Bobby. I am here to see my Presidents in stone; to contemplate my country how it used to be.

BOBBY: Maybe Momma was a man.

DID: I'm a pop you one you keep this up.

BOBBY: Oh, hey now.

DID: You ain't changed a bit, Bobby. Always making fun. Woman dead and in the ground and here you go making fun.

BOBBY: I ain't making fun, Did. I see her up there. I see her everywhere I look. Only reason you don't, you didn't grieve her when she died, which is why you can't see it.

DID: I grieved our momma.

BOBBY: Nah you didn't. You got up and read out of the Book. And you read good, real good. I'd be a liar I didn't own I was jealous the way you stuck out. But you did not grieve our momma, and I think you should, Did, because, my humble opinion, that's the trouble with Janney.

DID: Oh, now it's my wife now.

BOBBY: No, I admire your wife, Did. She's a good woman. A handsome woman. And a cook in the kitchen too. But how she come to get so fat? You ever ask yourself?

DID: That ain't fat, that's wholesome looking.

BOBBY: When the floor groans underneath of your weight, Did, that is fat. And Janney is fat because of she eats too much. I seen it. And she eats too much because of how you run her down. I hear it. And you run her down because you ain't grieved your momma. I know it.

DID: Oh boy oh boy oh boy. You is and always was the pure momma's boy wasn't you?

BOBBY: You can't hurt me with that.

DID: Always the little helper at the grocery. Picking up the basket. Toting it to the house. Wiping down the milk. Momma's regular little chore girl.

BOBBY: Can't nobody hurt me no more with that old slam. I come to peace with who I am. I traced it and faced it, brother.

DID: Well, goody for you.

BOBBY: Remember the time you and Daddy was back of the barn with that axle to lift, and I come to help you, and you shooed me out of there?

DID: Hell, I don't know.

BOBBY: Groaning and sweating in your undershirts. I remember it like tomorrow.

DID: Yesterday, Bobby.

BOBBY : What?

DID: You remember it like it was yesterday.

BOBBY: Yes I do, Did. The mortification of it. The shame. That I was not allowed, not invited to participate with the work of the farm. That I was not fit somehow to be a part of it.

DID: You wasn't but a little kid back then.

BOBBY: I was old enough, Did. But I come to terms with all that. Since I left the farm I come to realize that lifting axles up off the ground is not in my line. I been called to another portion. My talents is more toward lifting the heavy load of sorrow from off the shoulders of my fellow man, up to and including my big brother Diddie if it needs be.

DID: Well, I'm glad to see you found yourself, Bobby. And I appreciate the concern. And maybe I am just a disappointed sinner with a fat wife. But how that comes of not grieving a woman I never did love, that I cannot understand.

BOBBY: Oh, Did.

DID: No. No. You think because she took me to a bathing beach once I should grieve her? You think because she made me Pork Chop Sizzle for my birthday once I should grieve her? You think because I come out between of her particular legs instead of a million billion other women in the world I should grieve her? Well I don't. I reject that as the philosophy of an emotional person.

BOBBY: She was your one and only momma, Did.

DID: But I didn't know her, Bobby. You grieve the ones you know, and the woman was nothing but a mystery to me.

BOBBY: She was a mystery to herself what I come to understand.

DID: Well, I'm sorry for that. And I'm sorry she died before her time. And I'm sorry I didn't love her like I should of, but dang it all Bobby—

BOBBY: Did you know she died with your name in her mouth?

DID: What?

BOBBY: Died calling for Did. For her first born, yeah.

DID: Who told you that?

BOBBY: Daddy.

DID: No.

BOBBY: He called me drunk one night.

DID: Well, he's liable to say anything drunk.

BOBBY: No, he told me things. Other things. How she'd never wanted children. The farm. The dirt. The work. The worry. None of it.

DID: Oh, and that's what I'm supposed to grieve, huh? Some stoney woman never wanted me? Never calls me 'til she's dead? That's what I'm a supposed to cry big crockababy tears about?

BOBBY: That's it, Did. That's the job.

DID: Well I ain't up to it.

BOBBY: Yeah you are. Sure you are. Look at them Presidents all carved out of rock. You think whoever done that woke up every morning happy to climb a mountain? But he done it. And died doing it. And his son carried it on. That's what we do here. We got no choice in it.

DID: Ain't I glad I invited you along on my once-a-year vacation.

BOBBY: I was touched you asked me, Did.

DID: Well I may never again, but I grant you one thing, Bobby Lee.

BOBBY: What's that?

DID: Goddamn if that don't begin to look a bit like Momma now the light has shifted.

BOBBY: That's funny, brother.

DID: What?

BOBBY: Because I don't see it no more.

Tyler Poked Taylor
by Lee Blessing

Loyal, a young man about eighteen, stares up from the observation deck at Mount Rushmore. He's alone, muttering quietly, swiftly to himself—a kind of mantra.

LOYAL: Tyler poked Taylor Fillmore pierced Buchanan Tyler poked Taylor Fillmore pierced Buchanan Tyler poked Taylor Fillmore pierced Buchanan Tyler poked Taylor Fillmore pierced Buchanan Tyler poked Taylor Fillmore pierced Buchanan—
(With sudden aggressiveness to someone on his right, unseen.)
What are you looking at? Back off. *Now.* There's plenty of room out here.
(Watching as the unseen person retreats, returning to his mantra.)
Tyler poked Taylor Fillmore pierced Buchanan Tyler poked Taylor—
(Suddenly to someone unseen on his left.)
Mom, can I have a little privacy? You and Dad just... find somewhere else, okay?
(Watching them move off, returning to his mantra.)
Fillmore pierced Buchanan Tyler poked Taylor Fillmore pierced—
(The mantra is transferred to house speakers and continues, very soft. As Loyal speaks live, it's as though we now hear his thoughts under the chanting.)
God, I wish I didn't live in Rapid City. Dad makes us come up here every year. "Someday you'll be President, Loyal." That's what Dad says, every damn year. "You'll be one of them. You'll be up on that mountain."
(With a furtive look at his parents, then staring up again.)
Washington was first. First in war, first in peace and first in my bedroom late at night. I dreamed of him deep in the woods, holding the dying General Braddock in his arms. He knew from that moment he would be a leader of men. I followed him for years. Lived in his billet, shined his boots, his sword. Watched him write by candlelight. And when he blew out the candle— My father in spirit, my teacher, my lover. I dressed him every morning, kissed him and watched him ride out through the cherry trees into battle. Jefferson when I got older. So handsome, so wise. I sat in his study, watching him write his correspondence. Every hour I'd remove a piece of my clothing. Finally he'd close his notebook. We'd make love

all night. There were letters he wouldn't finish for days. I knew Lincoln before the beard—splitting rails with his shirt off. He'd gleam with sweat. So would I, just watching. I was a Rough Rider with Roosevelt on the Great Plains. All the men would sit outside in the frozen morning light, huddled over their coffee, while in the tent Teddy lay weeping in my arms, telling me about the asthma that stifled his childhood.

(Staring off to his left, toward his unseen parents.)

All right! I'm *coming!*

(The chanting stops. Loyal stares up again.)

I knew I was never going to be President. So instead I made love to them. Every year. Here. Staring up into their enormous, gentle eyes—wishing that one of them, any of them, all of them were my real father. Wishing I could whisper into their ears the words I've saved for tonight—when I'm finally eighteen, and here.

(A beat. He takes a deep breath.)

Tyler poked Taylor Fillmore pierced Buchanan Tyler poked Taylor Fillmore pierced Buchanan Tyler poked Taylor Fillmore pierced Buchanan Tyler poked...

(Slow fade to black.)

Rock Scissors Paper
by Deb Margolin

A girl of eighteen is sitting in a chair, facing an unseen therapist, whose back is to the audience. She speaks even the most revealing lines without a hint of self-consciousness.

GIRL: Whatever my mother's looking for is always *behind* her. I've noticed that. It never fucking fails. Whatever she can't find is always where her ass is. I'm upstairs, and she's screaming where the hell is *whatever it is*, and I'm just like, Mom, turn around! Just turn around, Mom! They say mothers have eyes in the back of their heads—well, yeah, right! My mom has trouble with the two in front! Once she was like, I smell fire, and she's looking around sniffing, and the garbage can was on fire right where her butt was but she just never turned around.

We took this family vacation recently to Rapid City, South Dakota, which even the name Rapid City is pretty funny, and we tried to act like a family, only we all just based it on shows on TV. Trouble was, we all used different shows. For my mom it was like, Bill Cosby show, where the wife is some dignified Doctor, for my dad it was *Home Improvement*, and for me it was like, *Roseanne.* So it was like three shows playing at once. Pretty bad. I wish my brother were still alive. I miss him bad. We fought like dogs but when he died it was like when a kid gets off the seesaw real fast without telling you and you're the one who's up in the air on the other side. I hate that he died, I just hate it. He once gave me this dirty picture, he said he got it from Joey diFlorio, this tough kid at school. It was really small, this picture, it was like, black and white and all, and my brother said it was a real picture of people doing it that Joey took himself, even though it was printed on like newspaper or something. Anyhow, I still have that picture, and it's like my brother whispering in my ear, laughing.

So there we are in Rapid City and my parents want to see Mount Rushmore, you know, that's that big rock or mountain or something with those men's heads carved into them. Movie stars, or whatnot. They had pictures of it all over the little dump we were staying in, and it just reminded me of those Siamese twins with one body and a whole bunch of different heads. Now that must be hell! But at least maybe one of them would have the sense to turn around and look at their collective ass if the garbage can was on fire! So my mother wants to go see this Siamese twin real bad, right, but I just wanted to be alone, I wanted to look at that picture, you know, maybe meet some like decent people my own age or something, right, so I said I just got my period and I wanted to stay in bed and maybe I'd meet them there later. They trooped off with their cameras and binoculars and Dad's Immodium pills and all that, and there I was by myself. It felt real good, but scary too, because I started remembering everything. Remembering stuff is like a burglar, you know what I mean? It just breaks in, even if you've got the door locked and you're like, sleeping or whatever. I got the picture out, and I remembered it like lying on my brother's desk where he used to cut his stuff. He had all these knives and like weird equipments he used to use to divide up the "fruits and vegetables," as he called it, and he bought all these sandwich bags and he had scales, and he weighed stuff on scales, and he "cut" it with different other stuff, like aspirin and just stuff around the house, and people used to come over all the time! And Mom just said, God, he has a lot of friends! This quickie-mart, right behind her back!

I put the picture back in my pocket, and I went downstairs. There was this cute guy with an earring in his nose, or I guess you're supposed to say a nose ring in his ear, or whatever, and he had a short shirt on and big cargo pants... kind of hot... and I was just not feeling normal because of thinking about my brother, so I put my finger across his stomach as I walked by him, and Jesus, was he shocked. I walked right out of that little dump and onto a trolley car of some kind to take me to the Siamese twin. Sure enough, there were my parents, standing in front of a glass wall, binoculars in hand, staring at those assholes carved into the mountain, and I thought of that game me and Kip used to play called Rock Scissors Paper, and I thought: if I could make that dirty picture bigger and put it over those assholes' heads, I'd win hands down, paper beats rock, paper always beats rock, it's just so endlessly cool, because in a way it makes no sense, but the rule still stands, it just stands, and you could tell my parents couldn't see the heads too well, they were squinting and adjusting their binoculars.

Funny thing was, the four heads, the idiots, were reflected perfectly well in the glass right behind them, and I just started laughing and crying, and I just started screaming, *Turn around Mom!* That's why they sent me here. *Turn around, Mom, just turn around!*

Little Pezidents
by Michael Bigelow Dixon and Val Smith

Somewhere near South Dakota, in a very remote gas station, Dave sits...stewing. Karen enters carrying something.

KAREN: Hey, you'll never guess what I found at the place next door. *(Dave glares.)* What? Here.

(She drops a Pez dispenser, which features Abe Lincoln's head, on the table in front of Dave, who glares.)

DAVE: Gee thanks.

KAREN: It's a Pez dispenser. That's Abraham Lincoln's little dome. Isn't he cute? Tilt him back and have a Pez. You'll feel much better about everything.

DAVE: *(To Abe.)* What do you think, Abe? *(As Abe, à la Pez puppet.)* "Pez makes me want to go see a play."

KAREN: Ooooh, that's not good. *(As George Washington, with George Washington Pez dispenser.)* "But, as father of our country, I cannot tell a lie, I think Pez is great. Mmmmm. And look at you! You're looking very Abe-alicious today."

DAVE: *(As Abe.)* "Fuck off, George. And as I meant to say in my Gettysburg address, fuck off Karen."

KAREN: *(She holds George Washington Pez dispenser out in front of her.)* Talk to the Pezident.

(Dave glares.)

DAVE: In case you haven't noticed, we got ourselves a little problem here. While you were out, I got the bill. That tow truck cost four hundred bucks, that was a hundred miles, each way, and the guy insisted on cash, so I'm completely broke, and on top of that I just called, I don't have collision insurance, 'cause I couldn't afford it, and now the car is totaled, which means I still owe money but I have to get a new one, and we definitely don't have the money for that. But it's nice to know we've got enough money for Pez dispensers. They'll be a real comfort.

KAREN: They're a collectible... and a comfort.

DAVE: If we actually got to see Mount Rushmore, maybe.

KAREN: You'da been disappointed. It's smaller than you think. And you'd take a picture, everybody does. They line up and add their face to the row so, hey look, there are five famous people on the mountain. They think it's clever, but it's really pretty stupid when you get back home.

DAVE: You mean we came all this way, you wrecked the car, we nearly died, we're in debt for life, and it wasn't even worth it? Whose idea was this roadtrip anyway? "Let's get out on the open road, see America…"

KAREN: Don't be a monumental asshole, Dave. Think about it, when did getting turned into stone become such a great thing?

DAVE: Ex-squeeze me?

KAREN: I mean, somebody looked at Medusa and turned into stone, right? All those snakes. Who was that? And who was it on TV… oh yeah, Carol Kane as Lot's wife in *Sodom and Gomorrah*… she turns around, wants one more look and blammo, she's a chunk of salt. Big chunk o' rock salt.

DAVE: *(As Abe.)* "Uh… George? Come in, George…"

KAREN: Then there's the ossified man in that old horror flick about freaks in a side show, at the circus, right, and he's all calcified and scaly and gross, and of course he loves the woman equestrian, but…

DAVE: What's your friggin' point?

KAREN: The ossified man and the female equestrian don't live happily ever after. *(As George.)* "Hey, I cannot tell a lie. I chopped down the cherry tree, but the people forgave me and elected me President." So how hard is it, Dave? I'm sorry I hit the deer. *(Dave's glare softens, but only momentarily.)* At least we didn't get hurt.

DAVE: *(As Abe.)* "Four score hundred and seven thousand more dollars ago, our fathers brought forth a Miata…"

KAREN: Brakes weren't very good.

DAVE: Not at that speed. Not at night. Not in a deer crossing zone. Not like twenty seconds after I told you to watch out for friggin' wildlife.

KAREN: Hey, shit happens, Dave. But you can't just stop in the middle of the road and stare. Headlights are a universal warning. Look out, life's coming at you. You gotta keep moving or blammo, don't look back, you'll turn into stone.

DAVE: Yeah, well, some people make better hunters than drivers. And now we're fucking stuck in the middle of nowhere. "See America…"

KAREN: *(As George.)* "I thought the same thing, but then my men at Valley Forge wrapped their feet in rags and we marched off to war."

DAVE: *(As Abe.)* "I don't think rags are gonna do it this time, George."

KAREN: I talked to a trucker when I was buying these. He's willing to take us to Pierre. From there, we'll catch a bus or something. My folks'll wire us money if we can get to a bank. We'll get home. It'll work out. What do you say?

DAVE: I'd say these Pez dispensers really cost us about ten thousand dollars each.

KAREN: It's less than that. I got all four, so they only cost five thousand each. Which might be a deal, 'cause some day who knows how much they could be worth on the *Antiques Roadshow*.

DAVE: Why don't I find that funny?

KAREN: See. Here's Thomas Jefferson.

(She pulls out a Thomas Jefferson Pez dispenser.)

Put it with the others. See. Three of a kind.

(She arranges it with the other two.)

And to complete Mount Rushmore, here's Mickey Mouse.

(She pulls out a Mickey Mouse Pez dispenser.)

DAVE: Isn't it supposed to be Theodore Roosevelt?

KAREN: I like Mickey better. And he should be up there. Mark my word, one day he will. Disney will see to that.

DAVE: Why do you have to make everything a fucking joke?

KAREN: Turning into stone at your age is no good, Dave. *(Beat.)* Blammo.

(Dave sits there. He slowly turns into stone as Karen watches.
Does she go to him and touch him? He's rock.
And the lights fade to black.)

Defacing Patriotic Property
by Tanya Barfield

A Man, alone. He wears a suit and tie. He is somewhat disheveled due to lack of sleep; he is somewhat hyper too. At first, it may appear as if he is speaking to a psychiatrist.

MAN: You know, death, dying, decomposition, decay, *decidedly* not subjects I take lightly. I just want to tell you that. Let you know. Make that clear from the start. I mean, even this, even this act you and I are about to engage in is a relationship of sorts, right?

Doc, I was thinking… death, well, that's something that could benefit from a certain rehearsal process, even in the best of circumstances. Just as even the most lively conversation is only a replica of communication. But it's all a precursor to, well, you know, the big D. That little hang-nail, little nagging, little voice, little miniature rat scratching apart my thoughts: someday it's gonna happen. To you.

But for you, it's not philosophical, right? You make a little cut, a tuck, an incision… vandalize eyes, ratify a new me.
  (The doctor doesn't understand.)
You *are* a surgeon, aren't you?
  (The Man becomes a little defensive but tries to explain things as clearly as possible.)
Look, I got the idea in South Dakota. Drove all the way to Beverly Hills. It took hours. You understand? Okay, maybe, I haven't been clear.
  (Suddenly serious.)
I'd like to replace my face.
To look more… immortal. More stately. That's what you do, right? Anti-death, stave off time and uncertainty. But I'm a different case. I'd like to look more like the past.
  (The doctor clearly still doesn't understand. The Man excitedly takes out a brochure.)
I brought the brochure. Mount Rushmore National Memorial. Which one do you think would be more appropriate?

(He looks at the brochure for a moment in awe.)
They're so big. You can't tell from this picture, but they are. Bigger than big. Herculean heads. Colossal chins. Mammoth mouths. Granite grandeur. There I was dwarfed, beholden, to fantastic faces, the facade of founding fathers.

Teddy or Tommy, what do you think? ...What? You don't?...
(Disconcerted.)
Well, what kind of plastic surgery do you do? Breast implants?! Oh, no, I don't think that's analogous at all.

You only deal with people that want to look younger?

All right, fine, fine, I'll find someone else. But let me ask you one thing, without choices: what's this country coming to?

Her First Screen Test
by Dan O'Brien

Character: GIRL, a young woman.
Time and Place: Dressing room, the Depression.

A Girl enters a dressing room, begins taking off her clothes.

GIRL: We don't have much time. I'm the next act on stage. I was the vixen librarian, and now I'll be something new.
You'll see.
Just for you, first.
And then for them out there.
Are you shooting me already?
Okay, here goes: *(She starts to undress.)*
Fuck!
—What?
Sorry, it's stuck!
I said, the God damned button—
—stuck on a God damned—
—See?
I've got this mouth on me. I'm sorry.
It's like a sewer, my father said. . . .
. . . .
Hmm?
Of course it's a silent film.
What other kind of film is there? I can say whatever I God damn please!
(Her button comes undone.)
—Praise Jesus! *(Taking off her blouse.)*
I'm really a funny girl at heart.
A funny, religious girl.
A funny religious girl who happens to be burdened with a splendid body.
It's not easy being splendid: *(Taking off her skirt.)*
You've got more to lose that way.
And no one wants a funny girl to be pretty, anyway, it's an obstacle to ambition.

—Hmm?

. . . . (She begins to unlace her corset.)

Oh: My ambition is to be a star, of course.

To become a star of the vode-veal stage, and then:

Go legit.

Hit the silver screen.

Which is where you come in, my new friend. . . . *(Her corset comes undone.)*

My shy new man friend . . . . *(In a shift now, stockings and petticoats.)*

Tell me something: Do you really think I stand a chance?

. . . .

Thanks.

. . . .

Thank you.

. . . .

Thanks so much for choosing me.

. . . .

—More?

Can I turn around at least? *(She does.)*

. . . . Don't the Injuns—?

I said, the Indians have a theory that a person's picture steals her soul. *(She removes the brassiere from underneath her shift.)*

But I don't think that's true.

It's when I step out on stage that I feel that I'm dead. . . .

It's crazy, I just know that I'm dead. . . .

I mean, it doesn't mean anything if no one remembers you, after. . . . *(She begins to take off her shift.)*

—Oh.

Sorry, yes, no I didn't mean—.

Of course not—!

You're an artist!

You're just doing your job!

—What do I look like to you?

. . . . *(She steps behind a screen.)*

. . . . *(Throws her petticoats over the screen.)*

. . . . *(Begins to put on a costume we can't see.)*

. . . .

. . . .

. . . .

Does it sound like I'm crying?
I'm changing, that's all.
—I've changed.
Let's see if you recognize me now.
(She's about to step out from behind the screen—
Maybe a foot and a leg steps out from behind the screen—
Black out!)

Thrift of the Magi
by Annie Weisman

Tina (mid-20's), in a snugly-fitting baseball cap, thumbing numbly through a rack of clothes at a thrift shop. Trey (mid-20's) thumbs through a rack, his back to her. At the same pace, they rhythmically, expertly, look at each t-shirt, then slide it to the back. They get to the end of their racks, then turn to new racks, this time facing each other. Looking, sliding. Tina stops, looks at a t-shirt, holds it up to Trey.

TREY: *(Considers it for a beat, then crisply, definitively.)* No.
    (She puts it back. They go back to looking, sliding. Tina stops, holds up another t-shirt, more confidently this time.)
TREY: *(Dismisses it totally.)* Uh, no!
TINA: *(She turns it around, shows him the back, points to the logo.)* But—
TREY: Trust me. No.
    (She puts it back. They go back to looking, sliding. Tina stops, very tentatively holds up another shirt.)
TREY: Yes! Oh my God, that's hilarious. Yes, yes.
TINA: *(Checking price.)* $24.99 for a used t-shirt! Oh my God! Honey, these are so expensive, maybe we should just go to Goodwill. I don't even care that much about our outfits for the stupid party, maybe we can just—
TREY: It's tonight! We don't have time to dig through Goodwill! They charge more here, because they buy everything at a premium, they shop on eBay and they get important stuff, quality shit. This isn't THRIFT, it's VIN-TAGE, there's a big... Oh my God, this is genius! *(Holds up a wind-breaker.)*
TINA: I don't get it.
TREY: What?
TINA: I'm sorry, but to me that just looks, GAP. Which isn't WRONG, it's just not, you know, particularly...,
TREY: GAP? Have you totally... See this pocket? This was a thing, in the seventies! You could stuff the whole windbreaker into its own pocket and put it in your travel bag. How fucking seventies is that? It's so, Arab Oil Embargo! It's so, "Is this trip necessary?" It's so genius! It's Middle Americana on a wire coat hanger. It couldn't be better.

TINA: I think my dad still wears that…

TREY: I can't explain this stuff to you… I can't just EXPLAIN to you what it is I see in a piece, you have to just trust that I have the eye.

TINA: I trust you, I just think, I don't see why that's the be-all… I mean, my dad wears that, that very thing for real, and I don't really feel comfortable making fun of it, just because some vintage clothing store deems it valuable.

TREY: If you don't want to go to this party, you can say so.

TINA: Of course I want to go! I'm the one who… you said you didn't like Leo, you called him "scurrilous" and I'm the one who said I really thought it was important for both of us to be there.

TREY: I said it was a good idea for a party, though. I said I didn't like him, but I liked his idea! I think a retro-tourist Americana party is kind of brilliant and I think we should go and if we do we should fucking look great!

TINA: You said we are our ideas! You said if I kept liking Woody Allen then I was condoning his behavior!

TREY: You make the world's least logical leaps, you know that? The worst. If we go, I at least want to give a full effort to the idea.

TINA: Then maybe we shouldn't go at all! I mean if I don't have the EYE! Then maybe you don't want to be SEEN with me!

TREY: Jesus, Tina, can you keep it down, this isn't the Salvation Army, for Christ's sake. Of course I want to be seen with you, who else would I want to be seen with?

TINA: Great, that's so sweet. You should print a line of greeting cards, really, with sentiments like that.

TREY: You know what I mean. You know! God. I really…

TINA: You really what?

TREY: You know what I mean.

TINA: Maybe I don't!

TREY: Jesus.

(They go back to flicking the clothes, this time, they are out of sequence, angrily flicking after one another, a flick fight. Suddenly, Tina stops. She slowly holds up a shirt.)

TINA: It can't be. This is exactly… this is the vintage Fat Albert t-shirt you have… and it's got the same damaged decal as yours, what are the odds? Oh my God, $49.99, for a t-shirt, you're right, this thing is valuable. Jesus. I thought you were crazy. I guess you do have the eye after all. Wait a minute, this has your initials in the tag, oh my God, you sold this on eBay? But it's your favorite!

TREY: Well, I've been waiting to tell you… I finally sold it so I could get you these—they're Farrah Fawcett's original hair combs from the pilot episode of *Charlie's Angels!* They even came with a certificate of authenticity. How brilliant is that! See, this is what I was trying to say, you know? It's how I, you know, feel. About you. You know what I mean?

(Tina takes off her cap. Her hair is cropped spiky and short.)

TREY: Oh my God, your Farrah 'do!

TINA: Preston dared me. He said he'd give me fifty bucks if I went Pat Benatar with it. And I thought, well, with fifty bucks I could go on-line, and get you that missing decal on eBay.

(She pulls a piece of paper out of her purse. A pause.)

TREY AND TINA: You did that, for me?

TREY: Tina I love you.

TINA: I love you too Trey.

TREY: Fuck the party. Let's order Chinese and watch a John Hughes movie.

TINA: I love you so much!

(To the sound of sliding wire hangers, they come together and kiss. Lights fade.)

Night Out
by Sunil Kuruvilla

Scene: 2 a.m. A small town in upstate New York. A Man, 24, and a Woman, 28, search in the snow beside her house, looking for his keys. She uses a flashlight while he struggles in the dark, bending low so he can see the ground.

WOMAN: They're gone.

MAN: Don't say that.

WOMAN: There's too much snow.

 (They continue searching.)

WOMAN: How many did you lose?

MAN: Thirty. I told you.

WOMAN: Why so many?

MAN: My school keys are on that ring.

WOMAN: It would leave a big mark.

MAN: I need your light.

WOMAN: Be nice.

 (The Woman comes close to share her flashlight.)

MAN: Stay there.

 (The Woman goes back to her area and continues looking.)

WOMAN: Stop moving around. We're not going to find your keys if you mess up the snow.

MAN: What time is it?

WOMAN: We still have a few hours.

MAN: More than that!

WOMAN: It's getting light out.

MAN: No it's not.

WOMAN: You want me to check the time?

MAN: What if he leaves work early?

WOMAN: He won't.

MAN: He could get sick and come home.

WOMAN: Don't say that.

MAN: Where are they?

WOMAN: My fingers are cold.

MAN: You didn't put them somewhere?

WOMAN: Why did you come outside?

MAN: To put my kleenex in the garbage.

WOMAN: You couldn't do it when you left?

MAN: I'm always afraid you'll forget and leave it under your bed. I hate having that smell in the room. You have Triple A?

WOMAN: No.

MAN: You're sure?

WOMAN: We don't.

MAN: Why not? Everyone does.

WOMAN: Do you?

MAN: You're sure you didn't hide them?

WOMAN: No I said.

(Man drops to his knees feeling the snow with his hands.)

MAN: I have to get my car out of your driveway.

WOMAN: We can call a tow truck.

MAN: You know how expensive that is?

WOMAN: Don't worry about the money.

MAN: Where do I tow it? Three hours back to the Catskills? You have no idea.

WOMAN: I can pay.

(The Man stands and walks around, searching.)

WOMAN: Stop moving around.

MAN: Look inside.

WOMAN: We did.

MAN: If they're inside and your husband finds them later on. Didn't think of that did you? What if my keys are inside?

WOMAN: You dropped by to see him. You wanted to say sorry.

MAN: A year later?

WOMAN: You could.

MAN: I drive all this way to apologize for kissing you last Christmas? I've avoided him all this time—suddenly I'm right here, middle of the night? You think he's an idiot?

(Man falls to his knees and runs his fingers in the snow.)

MAN: Give me your flashlight.

(The Woman keeps her flashlight, watching the Man search in the snow.)

MAN: You must have put them somewhere.

(Woman starts to go inside.)

MAN: Where are you going?

WOMAN: Inside.

MAN: No. Just stand there.

WOMAN: Why?

> (Silence.)

MAN: Where'd you put my keys?

> (They stare at each other.)
>
> (Silence.)
>
> (The Man goes back to searching in the snow.)

WOMAN: Stop moving around.

MAN: Go inside.

WOMAN: Look at the snow.

MAN: I don't care.

WOMAN: Look at the snow.

> (The Man looks at the snow, then at the Woman.)

WOMAN: Even if we find your keys—it's a mess. He'll see all the footprints.

> (Silence.)

MAN: Someone tried to break in.

WOMAN: In this town?

MAN: It could happen.

WOMAN: No it couldn't.

MAN: Maybe.

WOMAN: You don't live here.

MAN: Just say it.

WOMAN: He'll ask if I phoned the sheriff.

MAN: Say yes.

WOMAN: What if he checks?

MAN: You turned the light on then. You turned the light on and the person ran away. Say that. Sound upset. You don't know who it was but you scared him off.

> (The two stare at each other.)

MAN: You're pretty sure he won't come back ever again.

Here and Now
by Chay Yew

Middle-aged Man and Woman at the base of Mount Rushmore.

They stand apart, both looking into their binoculars ahead at the monument.

MAN:

> Here
> we are again,
> after all these years,
> through sun,
> through rain,
> you standing near,
> your hand in mine,
> armed with supersized Cokes,
> Double XL-sized Kmart matching shirts,
> two pairs of rented binoculars
> staring into our nation's past.

(Man puts his binoculars down.)

> Here
> we are again,
> like days of old,
> us,
> young;
> us,
> alone;
> us,
> lying idle on sweet grass,
> your head touching mine,
> a clearing of birch,
> off a lonely highway.

Us,
after making love,
drowning in the sky above,
filling our minds
with cumulous possibilities
and dreams infinite,
when we felt
infinite.

Did I ever tell you
my dreams,
dreams bursting with grandeur,
of flying high,
racing to ends of the earth?

Dreams
of being an explorer of countless stars countless worlds,
an astronaut;
an author
breathing words of heroic fire;
a builder
of buildings to kiss the endless skies;
a president
uniting disunited peoples of these united states.

Did I ever tell you
I still dream these dreams,
even now,
here,
standing next to you,
with a stony face so worn, so wan,
with a body too heavy, too cumbersome,
I can't believe I am me?

Me,
white shirt and tie,
bathed in a dull wash of office fluorescent,
making ends meet,
chasing Dream American.

Me,
pushing papers pushing campaigns,
pushing Americans to supersize
to double XL,
to Kmart,
to buy Dream American.

Me,
white shirt and tie,
at life's end,
made obsolete
by younger versions of me
in white shirts and ties.

Me,
made redundant
by machines invented
by younger versions of me,
their faces brown yellow black,
dreaming dreams of grandeur.

Did I ever tell you
you were my second love
second choice?

The first
was Alice,
the first,
whom I always compared you to,
the way her hair danced to slightest wind,
you;
the way the curve of her body pressed tight to dresses,
yours;
the way she baked peach cobbler,
you.

You,
my template Alice.

This Alice of my youth
swam but once
in the summer blue of my eyes.
This hot Alice now cool
swims in the circle of our friends,
married to our best friend,
lives a life of grandeur,
she laughing I laughing you laughing,
three lukewarm martinis in hand,
our eyes never swimming.

So
I settled,
made do
instead for someone else,
you.

Someone
plain and ordinary as day;
someone
who patiently listens to my dreams impatient;
someone
who loves me despite them.

Did I ever tell you
I came to an inch of leaving?
My white shirts and dreams
packed,
crammed in suitcases,
intent on flying
to the further reaches of the world,
one Wednesday afternoon,
while you were picking up the kids from school?

Did I ever tell you,
like statue stone,
I stood,
instead,

immovable,
in our hallway,
implacable,
plane ticket in hand,
for an hour
only to return to our bedroom and unpack,
in time to kiss you on the cheek when you came home?

Did I ever tell you
I learned,
late in life,
my unreasonable attachment to
the timbre of your voice;
the way your fingers
make journey across my forest chest;
your gentle breath on my neck,
arms around my flabby waist,
our bodies entwined in cotton sheets?

Did I ever tell you,
I have taken to staring at you,
moonlight brushing your face,
while you lie in deepest slumber,
dreaming dreams?

Did I ever tell you
I couldn't,
for fear
that you would leave,
for fear
that I
will be left alone?

Perhaps
there's nothing
to tell.

No words,
no vowels,
no sounds,
could ever replace,
ever describe,
the familiar warmth,
your hand slipping into mine.

(Man slips his hand into Woman's. Woman does not notice.)

So
here we are again,
two of us,
in our twilight years,
retired from the world and life,
traveling alone together
to far reaches of the earth,
for the rest of our days.

I peer into
the gigantic stone faces
of our fathers fore.

(Man removes his hand from Woman's. He resumes the original position as we first saw him at the top of the play.)

(Pause.)

I see
only
your face.

The Great Father
by Victor Lodato

Characters
WOMAN: *Nervous, a nervous smile; late twenties.*
MAN: *Precise; late twenties.*

A Man is staring out, into the sky. A Woman watches the Man from a distance, then approaches him.

WOMAN: Excuse me?

MAN: *(Not turning to look at the Woman.)* Yes.

WOMAN: Hi, I was... I'm sorry to bother you, I just—saw you looking. Up there.

MAN: Looking—yes. Oh yes.

WOMAN: *(Looking out, into the sky.)* At the...

MAN: Yes.

WOMAN: *(Relieved.)* Thank god. I was worried maybe I was... *(She turns toward the Man; short pause, then confidentially.)* I—see things sometimes.

MAN: Hard not to.

WOMAN: Why's that?

MAN: Unless you were blind.

WOMAN: *(A small laugh.)* No no no—when I said I *see* things, I meant...

MAN: Oh.

WOMAN: Things that—aren't there. *(Looking out again.)* Out of the blue, you know. Out of nowhere. *(Short pause.)* Disconcerting.

MAN: Would be.

(Beat. The Woman takes a pack of gum from her pocket.)

WOMAN: Piece of gum?

MAN: No thank you.

WOMAN: *(Unwrapping, then putting a piece of gum in her mouth.)* I find it very soothing to chew gum, I don't know why that is. I think it has something to do with the... *(Chews a bit loudly, demonstrating.)* With the rhythm.

(The Man turns to look at the Woman for the first time.)

MAN: Do I know you?

WOMAN: *(A few chews.)* Spearmint. No, I—I don't think so. *(Holding out gum.)* Please, have a stick.

(*The Man takes a piece.*)

MAN: You're very…what's the word?

WOMAN: Annoying?

MAN: *Attractive.*

WOMAN: *(Laughs.)* Oh. No.

MAN: No?

WOMAN: People often say that but it's not… I'm not…

MAN: You're not attractive?

WOMAN: Common mistake.

(*He stares at her; she smiles.*)

WOMAN: The whole thing's rather complicated.

MAN: Yes, well… I think I'll save this for later.

(*He puts the piece of gum in his pocket, and turns to look at the sky again.*)
(*The Woman looks out, in the same direction.*)

WOMAN: My father used to say I was pretty. But… he's dead now. And he was a drunk.

MAN: I didn't mean to offend you.

WOMAN: Not at all.

(*Beat. She chews loudly. He looks at her. She smiles nervously. He turns away. Both are looking out, into the sky.*)

MAN: *(Turning toward the Woman.)* What kind of medication are you on?

WOMAN: Excuse me?

MAN: Don't be shy. What?

WOMAN: *(Pause; takes the gum out of mouth.)* Avatar. You?

MAN: Primordial.

WOMAN: *(Wrapping the gum.)* Oh, they had me on that for a while. Made me feel like I was living under a wet blanket.

MAN: Avatar's no joy ride. Nasty side effects.

WOMAN: I've developed a twitch. Around the lips.

(*Beat. The Woman puts the gum in her pocket.*)

MAN: I don't remember ever seeing you before. Been here long?

WOMAN: A few months now.

MAN: Really. What ward?

WOMAN: Nineteen.

MAN: East wing?

WOMAN: *(Nodding.)* I used to be in the west wing—but I'm… *improving*, as they say. Now I'm an east wing girl. *(Short pause.)* Why are you looking at me like that?

MAN: You have a…nice-shaped head.

WOMAN: No—now what did I say? Because that's going to lead us right back to attractive—and we don't want to go there.

MAN: Sorry, it's just—

WOMAN: Listen, what I would really like is—I would really appreciate it if you would tell me—exactly what you see. Up there. Because that's what I need to know.

(The Man looks up.)

WOMAN: You do still see it?

MAN: Yes.

WOMAN: Good. Tell me what you see?

MAN: Okay. I see clouds.

WOMAN: *(A sudden desperation.)* Clouds—*no*. Is that what you were looking at, oh my god—*clouds?*

MAN: Wait, wait—calm down—clouds… and then behind the clouds—

WOMAN: Yes, behind the clouds, that's what I'm talking about. That's always the issue—*behind, what's behind, what's underneath*. Go on. Behind the clouds…

MAN: It almost looks like…

WOMAN: What?

MAN: Faces.

WOMAN: Yes. Oh, thank god. Faces, right? How many?

MAN: Four.

WOMAN: Huge, right?

MAN: And white.

WOMAN: Like tombstones.

MAN: Yes.

WOMAN: Awful.

MAN: Quite.

(Beat.)

WOMAN: One looks just like my father. The bastard.

MAN: Really? One looks like my father.

(They turn and look at each other, then back to the sky.)

WOMAN: What else?

MAN: Blood.

WOMAN: On their lips.

MAN: Vampires.

WOMAN: *Precisely. (Short pause.)* Do you dream of death sometimes?
(*They look at each other.*)
WOMAN: Since I was a child I've dreamed of these people with beautiful long hair running up a mountain and they're screaming and nearly naked and it's snowing and men in blue coats on horses are chasing them and shooting them and a lot of people, even children, are dying.
MAN: I've had that dream.
WOMAN: And the snow begins to turn dark. Because of the blood.
MAN: Yes.
WOMAN: But my father always used to crawl into my bed and he would get very close, and he'd whisper in my ear: it's just a dream, close your eyes, it's just a dream, baby—nobody's screaming and nobody's going to get hurt, nobody's going to die. And he'd press himself into me. Shhh. Nobody's going to get hurt.
MAN: Fathers lie.
WOMAN: *(Pause.)* Yes, they do. They break their promises.
MAN: And the people running up the mountain die.
(*The Woman looks out again, into the sky.*)
WOMAN: Why do they have such huge heads?
MAN: *(Looking out.)* I don't know. *(Short pause.)* Maybe to keep us little.
WOMAN: *(Rambling.)* And then these faces, where do they go at night? When you can't see them. Do they follow you in the dark? These are the questions I've been asking myself. And what country is this and how did I get here? And who are the men in the blue coats? And do they know where I live?
(*He looks at her. Beat.*)
MAN: You could come to my room. You could... *(He gently touches her arm.)*
WOMAN: *(Pulling back.)* No.
MAN: Because it'll be dark soon.
WOMAN: You can't just touch me like that. You can't just...who do you think you are?
MAN: You came up to me. I was only...I meant it as a friend.
WOMAN: *(Suspicious.)* As a friend?
MAN: That's all.
WOMAN: Who do you think you are?
MAN: *(Pause.)* I have bad dreams, too.
(*Beat; then they both look out again, into the sky.*)
MAN: I know a place. *(Short pause.)* A place where they can't find you.
WOMAN: *(Not looking at him.)* Where?

MAN: I could show you.

WOMAN: I don't believe you.

MAN: It's true.

WOMAN: But they always find you, the fathers—no matter what. They always find you.

MAN: Not where I'd take you.

WOMAN: *(Pause.)* It is going to be dark soon.

MAN: Let me take you there.

WOMAN: Where is it? Where is this place?

MAN: It's inside the—

WOMAN: *No.* Oh my god, don't say it out loud. *(Short pause; then out of the side of her mouth.)* They're listening. *(Short pause.)* Just think it. Just imagine it.

MAN: All right.

WOMAN: *(Pause.)* Are you thinking it?

MAN: Yes.

WOMAN: Now we just have to keep looking at them. As if we weren't afraid.

MAN: Right.

WOMAN: As if we could just lie down in our beds and close our eyes without a care in the world.

MAN: As if we weren't afraid.

WOMAN: As if we didn't have a past.

MAN: As if we were free.

WOMAN: As if that. Yes.

> *(They continue looking out, into the sky. They breathe. The Man reaches out for the Woman's hand. She lets him take it.)*

MAN: Breathe.

WOMAN: *(Pause.)* Breathe.

> *(Slowly, the lights fade to black.)*

· · ·

I did not know then how much was ended. When I look back now from this high hill of my old age, I can still see the butchered women and children lying heaped and scattered all along the crooked gulch as plain as when I saw them with eyes still young. And I can see that something else died there in the bloody mud, and was buried in the blizzard. A people's dream died there. It was a beautiful dream...the nation's hoop is broken and scattered. There is no center any longer and the sacred tree is dead.

—Black Elk

American Klepto
by Allison Moore

A young woman and a piece of petrified wood.

WOMAN: I don't know how it got here. It's just a piece of wood. Okay, petrified wood. Don't do that. This entire trip you've been judging me, seven hundred miles and now you judge my moisturizer, my hiking boots, my cell phone—which, I might add, you were very happy to use yesterday when the tire blew and you remembered you never replaced the freakin' spare. Who I am is suddenly wrong out here. I mean, why does it matter if I want to buy some moccasins or a leather hairclip? Why does it matter if the stitching isn't authentic to the tribes of the area? Why does it matter if I'll never wear them when we get home? Did it ever occur to you that I am trying to connect? That this might be a profound expression of engagement? But everything I touch, you say Don't touch that! Don't buy that! If you buy that hairclip, you're supporting the rape of a culture all so that white middle class tourists can go home with a souvenir—and yes I know "white" is a construct!

I am a good person. I am not an exploiter, or a thief, or. I mean, where did you get that pen? Do you know? When was the last time you actually went out and bought a shitty disposable pen? But there it is, in your pocket. How did it get there? I'll tell you: *You took it.* Junk drawers across the country are filled with pens like this because we take them. That's what Americans do. We take pens, from everywhere. From grocery stores, from gas stations, from work. If you took a computer that would be theft, but no one cares if you take a pen, or some paperclips, they order in bulk. But technically, you're stealing. You are a thief. You have stolen pens. That's what we're talking about here.

I know there was a sign, I know it's federally-protected land, but. When I was a kid I found a ton of fossils at Canyon Lake—I'm talking close to a hundred of them, little snails and water plants. No one ever said You're decontextualizing our geological history. They said Wow! These are heavy! And let me tell you something, if I hadn't found them, someone else would have. They'd be selling for five bucks a pop in a gift shop somewhere.

I know! We should put signs everywhere, not just in National Parks. "Take only pictures, leave only footprints" on banners like corporate mission statements in office buildings everywhere. Prosecute little girls picking flowers, jail time for arrogant asshole eco-motherfuckers with stolen pens!

(Beat.)

I swear to God I didn't mean to take it, I don't remember taking it. I remember standing in the middle of the desert thinking how it reminded me of Gettysburg in winter, how the petrified wood looked like corpses lying in the sand. And you said It really does look painted, like you're walking around inside one of those paintings we saw in Taos. And we couldn't stop touching that trunk because it looked like it was decaying, it had been decaying, but it had stopped, frozen by the sun and time. And I picked up a little piece and poured water on it to bring out the colors, and. I don't want to rape anyone, I just wanted the Goddamn hairclip.
(She examines the piece of petrified wood.)
It's not even a very pretty one.

Becoming American
by Lynn Nottage

Place: Accra, Ghana.

Dial tone.

TAPE RECORDED VOICE: *(Heavy Texas drawl.) Hello, this is John Barksdale. I'm down here on vacation in the Florida Keys, and listen buddy I'm in a bit of a spot. It seems the wife left her bag with my wallet and our personal items on the beach unattended. We took a dip and some joker wandered off with our things. It's all gone, damn it, credit cards, cash, everything. Gone. We've been saving for this trip for two years, all I know is it's ruined.*
(The Instructor clicks the off button. The tape stops.)
INSTRUCTOR: Why am I stopping? Anyone?
(A moment.)
The call comes in. It's John Barksdale from San Antonio. He needs your help people. You are his angel for the two-to-three minutes that it takes to guide him successfully through his problem. You are the 1-800 answer to his crisis. The operator.
(Clicks the on button. Tape resumes.)
TAPE RECORDED VOICE: *(Heavy Texas drawl.) I'm in trouble here, ain't a thing I can do unless I sort this little thing out.*
(Clicks button. Tape stops.)
INSTRUCTOR: What can I do? You ask. I know that you're a thousand miles away in this office space in downtown Accra...Ghana. But it doesn't matter to John Barksdale From San Antonio, Texas, not while he's standing on one leg leaning against a pay phone wondering what he's going to do about his vacation. He doesn't need to know, nor does he want to know that you live across the Atlantic Ocean in some small city with a two-syllable name. Or that your name is Kwame, Kakuna, Hamid or Saidiya. No, he wants Brad or Tom, Julia or Meg Anderson from Des Moines.
(Checks notes.)
He wants you to be American. That's what it comes down to. It's why I've been brought here, today, to give you folks a few pointers on becoming American for the two-to-three minutes that it takes to solve John's

problem. Don't get nervous, don't overthink, overthinking is uniquely un-American. You know everything you need to know already. That's right.

("America the Beautiful" plays.)

So John Barksdale from San Antonio calls, a touch of panic in his rum-tinged voice, his desperation palpable, his hard work, a knot in his throat, anger rising. He's shouting!

(Clicks button. Tape recording resumes.)

TAPE RECORDED VOICE: (Texas drawl.) I've lost my credit card, buddy, I'm on vacation in the Florida Keys, listen I'm in a bit of spot!

(Tape stops. A moment.)

INSTRUCTOR: Your moment has arrived. You speak.

"Hi John, I'm Meg don't worry we're going to take care of everything for you. Just a moment, while I check your account, John." Say his name. Americans like to hear their names spoken aloud, they like recognition, they respond to familiarity. "John, could I have your credit card numbers please." He'll give them to you, he'll give you anything as long as he believes you're sitting behind a desk at the corporate headquarters in Dallas. He'll give anything to Brad or Tom, Julia or Meg. Which brings us to your first step, selecting a name. Make it simple. I like movie stars, they've already put time and thought into their names. But don't be alarmed if John wants to know a little more about you, to put himself at ease, to feel connected to you, his savior.

TAPE RECORDED VOICE: (Texas drawl.) Where are you from Meg? I detect a little accent.

(Click. Tape stops.)

INSTRUCTOR: Don't panic. Do you say I'm from Accra, Ghana to John from San Antonio? John who thinks Africa is a country and India a small reservation in New Mexico that he drove through when he was a boy. He has the commemorative blanket to prove it. No, the outer world is a frightening proposition to a credit card-less consumer hovering in financial limbo. Ghana scares John, you scare John. He wants to be soothed and calmed and reassured that our company is on top of things. So.

TAPE RECORDED VOICE: (Texas drawl.) Where are you from Meg? I detect a little accent.

(Click. Tape stops.)

INSTRUCTOR: Step two. Choose a place, like say…South Dakota, a large sparsely-populated state in the North central part of the American Union. The "coyote state," it conjures images of prairies and low hills, the

Badlands and Black Hills. It is picture-perfect America, he won't even question your credibility. But I say, go further, pick a small town from the atlas, establish roots. A place where the neighbors all know you. I recommend that you learn a little something about your state, about your America, get comfortable with your sports teams, and why not know the names of the Presidents gracing the face of Mount Rushmore. These are talking points, things that John wants you to know as you sort through his personal financial history.

TAPE RECORDED VOICE: *(Texas drawl.) Where are you from Meg? I detect a little accent.*

INSTRUCTOR: You are from "the coyote state." You are from where he needs you to be. You are American for the two or three minutes that it takes to solve his problems.

History Lesson
by David Lindsay-Abaire

Lights up on Maggie, a park ranger. She's in the middle of giving a speech to a bunch of tourists (the audience).

MAGGIE: And what's interesting about George Washington, and most people don't know this about him, he wasn't just the father of our country, he was also the father of the first septuplets born in the United States. Martha gave birth to seven children on October 5th, 1762. Five of the children were very badly behaved, so they were sold into white slavery, while the two remaining, Maxwell and Hortense, drowned tragically in the Potomac while trying to retrieve their father's wooden teeth, which had fallen out of his mouth while he was beating a seagull with a canoe paddle.

(Beat.)

For those of you just joining the group, my name is Maggie, and today's my last day here at the Mount Rushmore National Memorial. There have been some cutbacks at the National Park Service, so I've been let go, which in my opinion is a huge loss to tourists like yourselves who are hungry for history, because I happen to be what we in the industry call "a font of knowledge."

(Back to the speech.)

Now if you look to the right, you'll notice that the next head belongs to Thomas Jefferson, who, and this may come as a surprise to you, was actually born without skin from the neck down. In fact, he spent most of his childhood in and out of hospitals because of his susceptibility to disease, what with the exposed muscle and sinew and whatnot. But in 1772, his good friend Benjamin Franklin fashioned a crude epidermis out of sheep bladders and carpenter's glue, held together by pewter hooks that Paul Revere forged in his silver shop. Paul Revere, you may have heard, was a smithy, which is one of my favorite words. He was also a eunuch, which was not very common in the 1700s, though there were a few. I believe Sam Adams was also a eunuch, and… Nathan Hale, who I've been told had a wonderful singing voice. So, that's probably something you haven't heard on any other tour today. It's interesting, isn't it?

(Suddenly.)

Oh, by the way, if any of you happen to have a question, feel free to raise your hand and stick it up your ass. That's just the kind of mood I'm in. I see I'm losing some of you. Well that's alright. It's more intimate this way, isn't it? And I happen to be very comfortable with intimacy, unlike a certain Victor Collins, my direct supervisor here at the National Park Service, and my former lover. He's the man responsible for my layoff, as well as my monthly herpes outbreak.

(Back to the speech.)

Moving on, we have the esteemed Theodore "Teddy" Roosevelt, our twenty-sixth president, and a well-documented pederast. He spent much of his presidency traipsing through Cuba and Panama in search of little boys to induct into his Rough Rider Club, whether they liked it or not. Bully, indeed. He appeared briefly in a burlesque-house comedy titled "Tally-Ho, Kathleen!" He enjoyed playing chess, and long walks on the beach.

(Off-topic.)

Coincidentally, so does my Ex-Lover-slash-Boss, Victor Collins. Any complaints about today's tour can be directed to him. His office is located just past the gift shop, behind the glass doors. He'll be the fat fuck in the stupid hat and chinos. He's hard of hearing, so I encourage you to yell whenever speaking to him, and use as much profanity as possible. He's more responsive when berated and under pressure.

(Back to the speech.)

Next up, we have Abraham Lincoln, our first Jewish president, and the inventor of dirt. He was, of course, our tallest president, standing ten feet, two inches tall; he spoke fluent Mandarin and walked with a peg leg. A thrice-convicted arson, Abraham Lincoln grew up in an adobe hut and had X-ray vision. He was one of our greatest presidents and his wife was mentally unhinged. Speaking of mentally unhinged, let's pretend I'm Victor and you're me.

(As Victor.)

"Aw gee, Maggie, it's nothing personal. I gotta fire *someone*, and heck I was gonna break up with you anyway. You're incredibly passive-aggressive, and that's not the kind of person I want to spend my life with. You were gonna be upset either way, so this is like two birds with one stone."

(Now herself.)

Hey anyone have a stone? Let's go throw it at Victor's head!

(Beat.)

I'm just kidding. Violence is never the answer, as was so wisely stated by our thirty-ninth president, Chita Rivera.

(They're leaving.)

Okay, well you two obviously have places to go.

(Calling after them.)

Have a great afternoon, and enjoy the rest of your stay here at Mount Rushmore, the only monument in America made entirely out of cheese.

(Blackout.)

Bomb Squad
By Craig Wright

The scene is a lookout balcony, facing Mount Rushmore. A serious Man enters with an official-looking case. He opens it, and then begins to undress, placing his clothes carefully into the case. As the Man is about half-undressed, a Ranger enters. Note: this could be the same Park Ranger from "A Quick Tour of the Monument."

RANGER: Sir, can I…may I ask what you're doing?

MAN: I'm with the Bomb Squad.

RANGER: But I wasn't notified—

MAN: I was called in to defuse a bomb, little lady, and it's a very delicate situation, so please step away.

RANGER: But my superiors—

MAN: Your superiors are the ones who called.

(The Man is still undressing.)

Now, please step away, unless you want to be…

(He removes his pants, revealing his colorful, Speedo-style briefs.)

….changed forever.

RANGER: *(Stepping back.)* So…are you saying…there's a bomb in the monument?

MAN: No. I'm saying the bomb *is* the monument.

(The Man pulls a small vial of fragrant oil from the case and begins anointing himself with it.)

RANGER: *(Nervously suspicious.)* That doesn't make any sense. This is…. You're undressed.

MAN: I'm not as undressed as I could be, little lady. I have a veritable arsenal of nudity at my disposal; and if you continue to be obstructive, I just might use it; and then what will you have on your hands? Hm?

RANGER: I'm… sorry…

MAN: It wouldn't be pretty, that's for sure.

(The Man hands her a boombox from the case.)

MAN: Here, hold this.

RANGER: I'm going to go get my manager.

MAN: *(Waving a finger hypnotically in the air.)* No, you're not. You know why?

Because you want to be a hero. And this, little lady, is the only chance you'll ever get. Okay?

RANGER: *(Cowed and convinced.)* Okay.

(The Man starts dancing, without music, in a style that's half-stripper, half-tribal ceremony. As he dances, he scatters flower petals around himself in a circle.)

MAN: This monument...this so-called monument was placed here years ago by who? Was he an artist? A criminal? Does it matter? It's a conceptual land mine, left here to do its thing, and every time people see it, ideas go off in their heads. Boom! Ideas like, preserving one specific way of life at any cost is more important than the global flow of values and lifestyles over the nearly infinite span of time? Boom! Ideas like, men? Boom! Ideas like, human progress equals divine progress and human ideals are God's ideals, excuse me? Boom! Now it's all very well and good—get ready to start the music—it's all very well and good to carve these things as little memorials because there isn't anything that happens that doesn't have a little glimmer of divinity about it, you know, it's nice to keep track of where the snake was last seen before it shed its skin, you know? But when they become so powerful that all people see when they look at them is their own poisonous vanity staring back, then that is an explosive situation, even though it might take hundreds of years for the slow-motion explosion to happen, it's massive and it does serious damage to the fabric of consciousness and something, you know, something has got to be done! Start the music!

(The Ranger starts the CD. The Man sings.)

MAN: **ALL THE LITTLE FLOWERS ON ALL THE LITTLE BRANCHES**
ALL THE LITTLE BIRDS UP IN THE SKY

THEY GOT A MESSAGE FOR YOU
THEY GOT A MESSAGE FOR YOU
AND IF YOU LISTEN, IF YOU LISTEN, IF YOU LISTEN GOOD,
IF YOU LISTEN, IF YOU LISTEN IN YOUR NEIGHBORHOOD,
IF YOU LISTEN, IF YOU LISTEN, IF YOU LISTEN
YOU'LL HEAR WHAT IT IS

(At this point, the Man pulls a small, live dog from the case and holds him in his arms as he dances to the music.)

RANGER: Sir, there are no pets allowed near the monument with the exception of service dogs!

MAN: What do you think this is? It's my service dog! He's good for my heart! He helps me see things more clearly! He's my little buddy!

RANGER: But my superiors—

MAN: Who are your superiors? Have you ever even met them? I haven't! In fact, I don't think you have any! I think you are the most superior being I've ever met and all this talk about you having superiors is a bunch of dissimulation and cabalistic self-limitation! This is America, man! Lighten up! The idols can take a hit! Come on, dance with me! Your nation is depending on you! You don't want the whole nation to drown in a miasma of its own antique ideals, do you?

RANGER: No…

MAN: Then dance!

(The Ranger, after some non-verbal or ad-libbed coaxing, joins the Man in the song and dance. Perhaps a crowd starts to gather.)

BOTH: **ALL THE CONSTELLATIONS, THE FAMILY OF NATIONS AND ALL THE SWIRLING SYMBOLS IN YOUR MIND**

THEY GOT A MESSAGE FOR YOU
THEY GOT A MESSAGE FOR YOU
AND IF YOU LISTEN, IF YOU LISTEN, IF YOU LISTEN GOOD,
IF YOU LISTEN, IF YOU LISTEN IN YOUR NEIGHBORHOOD,
IF YOU LISTEN, IF YOU LISTEN, IF YOU LISTEN
YOU'LL HEAR WHAT IT IS
(No one can tell it to you!)
IF YOU LISTEN, IF YOU LISTEN, IF YOU LISTEN
YOU'LL HEAR WHAT IT IS
(And no one can sell it to you!)
IF YOU LISTEN, IF YOU LISTEN, IF YOU LISTEN,
YOU'LL HEAR WHAT IT IS
(The song ends. End of scene.)

On Lincoln's Head
by Julie Jensen

A young woman, Babe, an adolescent, tough, irreverent, is standing on the top of Lincoln's head, throwing firecrackers off. It is night.

(Boom!)

(Boom!)

BABE: All's I gotta say is—I HATE YOU!

(Boom!)

BABE: AND I'M GONNA HATE YOU FOR AS LONG AS I LIVE!

(Boom!)

(Annette appears above her. They can't see one another, really. Annette is a park ranger in her mid-twenties, precise, officious.)

ANNETTE: Excuse me.

BABE: *(She freezes.)* Yeah.

ANNETTE: We do not allow that kind of activity off the top of Lincoln's head.

BABE: What kinda "activity"?

ANNETTE: Standing. Or blowing fire crackers.

BABE: They're cherry bombs.

ANNETTE: Do not allow either one.

BABE: Why not?

ANNETTE: Deface the face.

BABE: I won't do it no more.

ANNETTE: Appreciate it.

BABE: I ain't got no more.

ANNETTE: That's good.

(Pause. Boom!)

ANNETTE: Listen, I can have you arrested. Is that what you want?

BABE: What I want is you to shut up. Just shut the hell up!

ANNETTE: Quiet. Good idea. You first.

(Long, eerie pause.)

BABE: We come up here one Fourth of July. Me and my old man. He was drunk on his ass. He swore to god he was gonna sit on Lincoln's head. And he did. I watched him do it.

ANNETTE: Then you laughed your foolish head off.

BABE: Yeah, I did.

ANNETTE: I thought it was you.

BABE: I mean, that was like him. He got something in his head, he did it.

ANNETTE: A real go-getter, you might say?

BABE: No. A real drunk.

(Pause.)

BABE: He had a thing for Abraham Lincoln. The reading-by-the-fire thing. The low-down-log-cabin thing.

ANNETTE: The penny-in-the-shoe thing?

BABE: Yeah. All that kinda thing. But I am very pissed at him now.

ANNETTE: You still need to get off Lincoln's head.

BABE: I don't know how to do stuff without him.

ANNETTE: You'll figure it out.

BABE: Horse shit!

ANNETTE: Pardon….

BABE: He is the only one that knows what he knows. Like how tall a mile is straight up. Who knows stuff like that? No one!

(She starts to cry, in spite of herself.)

ANNETTE: It's all right. You'll be all right.

BABE: No I won't. And don't talk like that. You do NOT know!

ANNETTE: I do know. And you'll be all right. You will.

BABE: He wrecked his hog. Threw him all across a wash a thousand feet down. They brought him out in shopping bags.

ANNETTE: I see.

BABE: No you don't. You don't see. Quit talking like "you see."

ANNETTE: Young lady was up here last week. She'd hit somebody. Hit and run. Didn't know if anyone was dead. But either way, she was in trouble.

BABE: Shut the hell up!

ANNETTE: She was tucked in there, down from you, under his chin. Telling him, talking away.

BABE: I do NOT care!

ANNETTE: He must have said something to her. Because she came out of there a changed person. But then, that's like him. He's a real talker. Real comfort sometime.

BABE: You're a flipping crazy, you know that? Listen, I want you out of here. I just want to be alone.

ANNETTE: Well, you are not alone up here. They're watching you. Down there at the Visitors' Center.

BABE: Damn tourists. Cameras on their guts.

ANNETTE: Damn security. Scopes on their rifles.

BABE: But they can't see me. I'm in the shadows up here. Shadows of his hair.

ANNETTE: They can see you. They can see things the size of a lizard up here.

BABE: Good. I'm gonna blow another one of these.

ANNETTE: Don't! Please don't. He just can't take it.

BABE: Who can't?

ANNETTE: There was the war. Way too much artillery, if you remember.

BABE: Who you talking about? Your boss?

ANNETTE: And then there was his own death…. He likes to laugh, and he likes to whistle. But the firecrackers, they frighten him.

BABE: You talking about Lincoln?

ANNETTE: Sit down right where you are.

BABE: You are a nut case, ain't ya?

ANNETTE: I know what I'm talking about.

BABE: Crazies always do.

(Babe sits, almost in spite of herself.)

ANNETTE: Now just hum.

BABE: Hum what?

ANNETTE: "Let It Be." He likes the Beatles.

(Pause. Babe begins to hum. After a bar, a whistler joins in.)

ANNETTE: Hear that? It's him. Keep humming.

(Annette's hand comes down from above.)

Now give me your hand.

(Babe grabs hold of Annette's hand as the music swells and the lights fade.)

END OF PLAY

The Technology Project

The Technology Project

From live concerts to live news updates and live webcasts—all available through a dizzying array of media—the definition of "liveness" is no longer limited to the simple act of communication between a live actor and an audience. At the start of the new millennium, it seems particularly important that the theatre, a medium founded on presence, should investigate the question, "What is live performance?"

In order to explore this increasingly complex territory, Actors Theatre—in partnership with the EST/Sloan Foundation Science and Technology Project and Carnegie Mellon University's Entertainment Technology Center—asked three playwrights to interface with technologies that ranged from the mundane to the mind-boggling. The results were exciting and unexpected, and from John Belluso's moving exploration of the limitations of language and technology, to Alice Tuan's wild ride through the endless possibilities of virtual hypertext theatre, to Sarah Ruhl's stunning virtual reality romance, the writers opened up a whole new series of questions about the nature of live performance. Performed in Actors Theatre's public spaces (and some not so public spaces, like the theatre's cavernous basement), these short experiments in form offered our audiences yet another opportunity to celebrate the spirit of innovation and inventiveness that is alive and well in the American theatre.

—Tanya Palmer

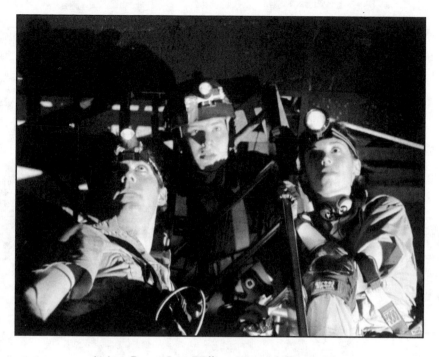

Atticus Rowe, Joey Williamson, and Maesie Speer
in *F.E.T.C.H.*

26th Annual Humana Festival of New American Plays
Actors Theatre of Louisville, 2002
photo by Larry Hunt

Voice Properties
(On a First Date after a Full Year of Februarys)
by John Belluso

BIOGRAPHY

John Belluso's plays include *The Body of Bourne, Henry Flamethrowa, The Rules of Charity, Traveling Skin* and *Body Songs*, a collaboratively-written theatre piece created by legendary director Joseph Chaikin and featuring text by Mr. Belluso with music and lyrics by Elizabeth Swados. His work has been produced at the Mark Taper Forum, Trinity Repertory and Victory Gardens Theater, amongst others, and has been developed by A.S.K. Theater Projects, the National Playwrights Conference and the Public Theater. Mr. Belluso received his Bachelor's and Master's degrees from NYU's Tisch School of the Arts Dramatic Writing Program where he studied with Tony Kushner, Tina Howe and Eduardo Machado, among others. Originally from Warwick, Rhode Island, he is currently living in Los Angeles.

HUMANA FESTIVAL PRODUCTION

Voice Properties premiered at the Humana Festival of New American Plays in March 2002. It was directed by Eric Johnson with the following cast:

Barney . . . . Bryan Buckler
Yolanda . . . . Emera Felice Krauss/Jen Taher
and the following production staff:
Host/Operator . . . . Emera Felice Krauss/Jen Taher
Costume Designer . . . . Mike Floyd
Lighting Designer . . . . Paul Werner
Sound Designer . . . . Vincent Olivieri
Properties Designer . . . . Doc Manning/Mark Walston

CHARACTERS

BARNEY: Male, late 30s, handsome, in an electric wheelchair-scooter, the scooter is a little beat-up, it has a basket and a bell on the front of it like one would find on a bicycle.

YO ("YOLANDA"): Female, late 30s, pretty, self-assured, quick-tempered, just a little reserved.

PLACE
A bar.

TIME
Present.

Voice Properties
(On a First Date After a Full Year of Februarys)

As the audience enters, they put on headphones and the beginning of the song "Bike" by Pink Floyd plays from a speaker system. We see Barney and Yo sitting at the table. They drink red wine; Barney sips his through a straw. He moves slowly but decisively due to his cerebral palsy. He types words into his VOCA; as he presses "enter" we hear the synthesized voice through the speaker system. When Yo responds to him we hear her voice through the speaker system as well; onstage she gesticulates as if she is talking, but her lips do not move.

BARNEY: Flowers.

YO: Excuse me, what? I didn't understand the word you were saying…

BARNEY: "Flowers." I was going to bring you a bouquet of flowers.

YO: Oh, oh my gosh that's very sweet of you! You were going to bring me flowers; a lovely gesture, a very gentlemanly thing to do on a first date! Bring flowers.

BARNEY: Yes. I think they were posies. I left them on my kitchen table.

YO: Oh, I like posies. Yes, sir, those are pretty things; posies; lots of colors, all swirled up together! Posies. Very delicate. Y'know Barney, I should say, right up front, it's been a while since I've been on a first date.

BARNEY: Me too.

YO: I'm going to be honest, I'm a little nervous, not only because I've never been on a date with a guy in a wheelchair, a guy in a wheelchair who uses one of those Stephen Hawking-type things to speak…

BARNEY: Oh. I am…

YO: *(Interrupting, speaking over.)* But you see also, I'm *also* nervous because this is my first date since my divorce, so it's not *only* the fact that you're in a wheelchair that's making me nervous. But I just couldn't help but respond to the personal ad you posted on the internet…

BARNEY: I am glad you responded to my ad.

YO: Yes, it was a very nice ad, the title of it struck me: "Seeking a Warm Evening After a Full Year of Februarys," very poetic.

BARNEY: Thank you.

YO: Can you talk at all? The robot voice is kind of freaking me out.

(Beat.)

BARNEY: I have difficulty speaking because of my cerebral palsy. I mentioned this to you in our last exchange of e-mails. If you were not comfortable with this fact then you shouldn't have agreed to meet me here.

YO: Okay, no need to be nasty.

BARNEY: I wasn't being nasty.

YO: See, it's just, the problem with the, what's it called…?

BARNEY: A Stephen Hawking-type thing.

YO: No I mean, what's it *really* called?

BARNEY: A Voice Output Communication Aid.

YO: Yes, it's just, I can't tell if you're being sarcastic or not, the property of your voice, the character, is that what it's called? The tone, or emotion is removed. But, my ex-husband didn't have much emotion in his voice either and I, well, kind of got used to that. He wasn't *completely* a robot, but, well, close… But anyway; you could, couldn't you just say a few words out loud…?

(Barney interrupts using his VOCA.)

BARNEY: Why do you sign your e-mails with the name Yo?

YO: It's my nickname. Short for "Yolanda." My friends call me that. I don't have any friends.

BARNEY: Oh.

YO: I used to have friends, but not in a long time. I haven't had any friends, *real friends*, not in a long time. My husband left me. He used to call me "Yo," "Yo, get over here!" he'd say. Sounds like he was being rude, but I knew he only meant it as short for my full name, Yolanda.

BARNEY: How long were you together?

YO: Twelve years. He said I was boring. I'm a librarian.

BARNEY: That's a shame.

YO: I take great pride in being a librarian.

BARNEY: I meant it's a shame that he left you. You don't seem boring to me. Not at all.

YO: (Smiling.) Thank you. "A Full Year of Februarys"; like in your ad, that's what my marriage felt like towards the end; long and cold, no choice but to stay inside. Is that what you meant when you said, "A Full Year of Februarys"…

BARNEY: Yeah. The feeling that you're forced to spend every moment looking out the window, watching other people live their lives, while you are snowed in, every day of the year, of your life; snowed in. A ghost in a house, watching the living, as they move through the World.

YO: Yeah. *Yeah*, that feeling. I feel it I… Which isn't to say, I mean, I'm sure it's worse for you. It must be really hard, you have to drag all that stuff around with you; the chair and the "Voice Operated Communicator-thing." I just mean, it sounds, depressing.

BARNEY: But I'm not depressed. Not anymore. Not always. Only sometimes. But I posted the personal ad on the internet because I was tired of feeling alone. *(Indicating the VOCA and the wheelchair.)* And these things, they're not what depresses me. These things, they let be more human. MORE human. They let me move out into the World so I don't have to stay in the house. They let me speak words that people understand.

YO: I just, I wish I could hear the actual sound of your voice.

BARNEY: Why?

YO: Because, I just, I want to.

(Barney pauses, looks as if he is about to speak, pulls back, sips wine, then continues to speak through his VOCA.)

BARNEY: A man walks into a bar with a monkey sitting on his shoulder. He sits down at the bar and orders a beer.

YO: Excuse me. Are you telling me a dirty joke?

BARNEY: Yes. I have dirty jokes programmed into my VOCA, the full-text of a dirty joke is loaded in. I have about seventeen of them programmed in there now; I download them off the internet.

YO: And you just, press a button and the whole joke is spoken through the machine.

BARNEY: *(Presses the buttons.)* I use them as ice-breakers during awkward moments. Are you offended by dirty jokes?

YO: No, I, I like a good dirty joke now and then.

BARNEY: A man walks into a bar with a monkey. He sits down at the bar and orders a beer. The monkey jumps down off the guy's shoulder and runs over to the pool table and eats the cue-ball right off the pool table. Swallows it right down. The bartender says, "Your monkey just ate my cue-ball!!! GET THE HELL OUT OF HERE!!" So the man picks up the monkey and leaves. Two months later the same man comes back with the monkey on a leash. The monkey jumps off his shoulder and grabs a peanut from the bar, shoves the peanut up his ass, pulls it out and then eats it. The bartender says, "Did your monkey just shove a peanut up his ass and then eat it?" The man says, "Yeah ever since the cue-ball incident he checks everything for size."

(Pause, she laughs a little.)

YO: Well, it wasn't so much "dirty" as it was "tasteless." "Dirty jokes" usually have sex in them.

BARNEY: You didn't think it was funny?

YO: It was okay. I think this wine is going to my head.

BARNEY: Me too.

YO: You're handsome.

BARNEY: Thank you.

YO: I've never been attracted to a guy in a wheelchair before.

BARNEY: I don't like the word wheelchair.

YO: You "don't like the word '*wheelchair*'"?

BARNEY: No, I don't. The word wheelchair. It's part of my whole plan to banish anything depressing from my life. People associate the word wheelchair with depression. They use terms like "wheelchair-*bound*", the word *bound*, like it's a ball and chain. Or the term *confined* to a wheelchair. *Confined*. It's a depressing word, and I'm tired of being depressed.

YO: So, then, what do you call that big metal thing you're riding around in?

BARNEY: I call it a bicycle. It's a much less depressing word.

YO: A "bicycle"? Yeah, interesting, it looks a little like a bicycle. I guess that's not really a depressing word, is it? "Bicycle." *(Beat.)* Well, okay, here's the thing; I think that's actually rather, silly. I don't mean to offend you, but I'm not going to placate you just because you're in a wheelchair, you simply cannot change the meaning of a word, just because you want to. That thing you are sitting in; it is a wheelchair...

BARNEY: Well, language is a complicated web of relations which...

YO: *(Interrupting.)* Yeah, well I didn't really come here for an exchange of philosophy, Barney.

BARNEY: ...then why did you come here...?

YO: I wanted to meet you face-to-face, and, I guess what I'm trying to say is, I've never been attracted to a guy in a, in a *bicycle* before or whatever you want to call it. And please, let me finish my sentence here, okay? I'm lonely. I think you're nice. And handsome. So. Do you, would you come home with me tonight?

(Pause.)

BARNEY: Your house. Are there stairs, to get in the front door?

YO: Well, yeah, but we could figure out a way, there's a side door, maybe we could, or we could go to your place?

BARNEY: My apartment is a mess. It won't work out.

(Pause.)

YO: Oh, so, you really, don't want to be with me.

BARNEY: No. That's not it. I'm sorry. I want to make big leaps in my life, I want to change things in my life. I truly do.

YO: I do too.

BARNEY: But, I'm not, ready for that. Not yet. I want to. That kind of vulnerability, it's not easy. I want to be close to you. I really do. But not now. Is that okay?

YO: Of course. Yes, of course.

BARNEY: Can we go out for another drink sometime?

YO: Yeah. Of course. *(She sips down the last of the wine in her glass, looks away.)* Some other time. It's getting late.

(She begins to gather her things, preparing to leave. She pauses, then sits back down.)

YO: Okay, listen very closely: three Boy Scouts, a lawyer, a priest, and a pilot are in a plane that is about to crash.

BARNEY: Three Boy Scouts, a lawyer, a priest, and a pilot.

YO: Three Boy Scouts, a lawyer, a priest, and a pilot are in a plane that is about to crash. The pilot says, "Well, we only have three parachutes, let's give them to the three Boy Scouts. They're young and have their whole lives in front of them." The lawyer says, "Fuck the Boy Scouts!" The priest says, "Good idea, but do we have time for that?"

(Barney laughs out loud; it is the first live sound we hear in the play. A quiet moment between them. Yo speaks in her live voice.)

YO: You have a great laugh.

BARNEY: *(Speaking, smiling.)* Thaa-nk... Yoou...

END OF PLAY

Virtual Meditation #1
by Sarah Ruhl
in collaboration with Students and
Faculty at Carnegie Mellon University's
Entertainment Technology Center

BIOGRAPHY

Sarah Ruhl's plays include: *Passion Play, Melancholy Play, Eurydice, Late, Orlando,* and *Chekhov: Shorts.* Her plays have been heard at the Sundance Theatre Lab, New York Theatre Workshop, New Dramatists, McCarter Theatre, The Flea, Ohio Theater, New Georges, Children's Theatre Company, Trinity Repertory Company, Annex Theare, Chicago Dramatists and Victory Gardens. Her plays have been supported by commissions from McCarter Theatre, Actors Theatre of Louisville, and the Piven Theatre Workshop, as well as by residencies at the Millay Colony, Ragdale Foundation, and Ucross Foundation. She received her M.F.A. from Brown University.

HUMANA FESTIVAL PRODUCTION

Virtual Meditation #1 premiered at the Humana Festival of New American Plays in March 2002 with the following cast:

Voices	Amy Kalson/John Tuft
Host/Operator	Peter Stone
Director/Faculty Lead	Brenda Harger
ETC Co-Director	Donald Marinelli/Randy Pausch

and the following production staff:

Production Manager	Timothy Price
Costume Designer	Sarah Ruhl/Brenda Harger
Lighting Designer	Paul Werner
Sound Designer	Darron L. West
Properties Designer	Doc Manning/Mark Walston
Interaction Design	Brenda Harger/Bryan Jacobs/ Nate Jones/Timothy Price/ Dan Schoedel/Ken Strickland
Programmers/Facial Mapping/ System Architecture	Bryan Jacobs/Nate Jones/ Ken Strickland
Sensory Input Design	Nate Jones
3d Modeler/Facial Animation	Dan Schoedel/Nate Jones
Dramaturg	Tony Sciullo
Web Design/Visual Research	Dan Schoedel
Mannequin and Display Fabrication	Billy Mitas
Sound Engineer	Timothy Price

Virtual Meditation #1

A theater lobby.

Two audience members, A and B, are randomly selected.
They need not be any particular age or gender or ethnicity.
They need not be in love with one another.
They need not be actors.
They will, however, be asked to hold hands during the performance.

Before the performance begins, the two participants are asked to put their heads into a vaudevillian contraption in which only their heads show through a cut-out hole.
Their pictures are taken.

They state their names.
Their names are recorded.

They are shown to a park bench.
They are asked to hold hands.
A device records the pressure of their hand-holding.
A monitor records the beating of their hearts.

Scene One

As soon as the volunteers hold hands, we hear the sound of rain.

The digital images of A and B's faces are projected onto the faces of mannequins.

The projections on the mannequins' faces are pre-animated to represent the following emotions: happy, scared, sad, mad and embarrassed. The pre-animated faces can blush and cry.

The body of mannequin A is wearing a plain man's suit. "A" holds a white helium balloon.

The body of mannequin B is wearing a plain women's suit. "B" holds a black umbrella.

The faces of A and B may be either male or female, depending on the random selection of volunteers.

A and B watch images of their faces become the actors in the play.

The audience watches A and B as well as the images of A and B projected on the mannequins.

There is a projection screen behind the mannequins.

Projection: A sky. Rain. Tulips.

Interaction: Behind the mannequins, rain is falling on the projection screen. The rain falls faster or slower depending on the hand pressure of A and B. The color of the sky on the projection screen is gray and overcast. The sky shifts from black and white to color, depending on the hand pressure of A and B.

A's and B's hearts are monitored and we can hear their hearts thumping softly. Tulips appear on the projection screen with the same constancy as A's and B's heart rates.

A's and B's virtual voices are pre-recorded by actors. The virtual images of A's and B's faces appear to speak the text of the play.

A SUBTITLE FLASHES: Scene 1: In a Park.

B: Do you need an umbrella?
A: I don't know you.
    (A looks scared.)
B: I only want to shield you from the rain.
    (A blushes.)
B: You're blushing.
A: No, I'm not.
B: What are you doing then?
A: I'm—
    (A looks embarrassed.)

B: Don't be embarrassed.

A: I don't enjoy having my emotions discussed in public.

    (A looks mad.)

B: This is hardly public.

A: Thank you for the umbrella.

    (A looks happy.)

B: You really are very feminine, in spite of your best efforts.

    (A looks sad.)

A: You are too. Feminine, I mean.

    (B looks mad.)

A: What's your name?

B: My name is *(Insert pre-recorded name.)*

A: That's a beautiful name. My grandmother also has that name.

B: Your grandmother has that name?

    (A pause.)

B: That's a weird name for a grandmother.

A: Yes. I really loved my grandmother.

    (A looks sad.)

B: I did too. She made me eggs.

    (B looks happy.)

A: Those tulips are so beautiful, they look almost fake.

B: I hate fake flowers.

    (B looks mad.)

A: I hate fake flowers too.

    (They are happy, hating the fake flowers together.)

B: We feel the same way.

A: Yes.

    (They look happy.)

B: What's your name?

A: *(Insert pre-recorded name.)*

    (A pause.)

B: No.

    (B looks surprised.)

A: Yes.

B: *(With more intensity.)* No.

A: *(With more intensity.)* Yes.

    (A looks mad.)

B: Really?

A: Why?

B: Your name doesn't match your face. Who named you?

A: My mother.

B: Does your mother know you well?

A: That's a personal question.

B: Yes. It is. I'm sorry.

(The projection screen goes to black.)

Scene Two

Sound: The silence of a museum.

Projection: A Rothko painting.

Interaction: The saturation of the Rothko painting alters depending on A's and B's combined heart rates.

The two halves of the painting (top and bottom) move towards each other, blurring slightly, depending on the hand pressure of A and B. The two halves of the painting never completely overlap.

A SUBTITLE FLASHES: Scene 2: In a Museum.

B: I love paintings.

A: That's a stupid thing to say.

(B blushes.)

A: You're blushing.

B: That was mean.

(B looks sad.)

A: I've known you for a long time now.

B: Yes.

(A long pause while they look at the painting; the saturation of the painting wobbles, according to their heart rates.)

A: Do you feel better now?

B: I'm happy.

(B looks happy.)

B: Are you happy?

(B looks happy.
A does not look happy.)

The painting changes color.
The projection screen moves to black.)

Scene Three

Sound: The sea.

Projection: The surface of a lake.
The reflection of a full moon in the lake.

Interaction: Slow ripples in the water are produced by the combined pattern
of A's and B's heart rates.

The brightness of the image is affected by the pressure of their hands.

A SUBTITLE FLASHES: Scene 3: By the Sea.

A: I'd rather not take my clothes off.
B: Then we won't go swimming.
    (B looks mad.)
B: I want to go swimming.
A: You can go swimming without me.
    (Pause.)
B: I don't want to go swimming alone.
    (A and B look sad.)
A: That's difficult. I want to be dry and you don't want to be alone.
B: We've known each other for a long time now.
A: Yes.
B: I know how it is when you don't want to do something.
A: I know how it is when you do want to do something.
    (Pause.)
B: It's getting dark.
A: I'm scared of drowning in the dark in the moonlight when the undertow is
    strong.
    (A looks scared.)
B: You're feminine when you're scared. Take off your clothes. I'll dance a
    waltz with you in high-tide.
A: I'd rather not.

B: I'll hold your hand.

A: I don't like holding hands. It's embarrassing to hold hands in public.

(*A looks embarrassed.*)

B: That's true.

(*Pause.*)

B: I love you.

(*A blushes.*)

B: You're blushing. Why are you blushing?

A: There are people around.

B: That's silly. One day we'll be happy and I'll put your soul on my mantelpiece and you'll put my soul on your mantelpiece and we'll call it a kind of marriage.

A: Okay. But I want to be an actor.

B: That's fine. I want to be an actor too.

(*Pause.*
They look happy.
Suddenly, A looks sad.
B looks angry.
A starts to cry.
A tear rolls down the face of the mannequin.)

B: Don't cry.

A: Why not?

B: The moon is turning into a balloon. That's why. I'll give you a moon balloon.

A: Thanks.

(*They look happy.*
The moon turns into a balloon.
The projection screen fills up with moons until the image is completely white.
Music.
The projection of A's and B's faces suddenly disappear from the faces of the mannequins.
The muted sounds of balloons popping in water: pish, pish.
We see, for a moment, the image of blank mannequins against a blank screen.

A SUBTITLE FLASHES: The End.

Lights up on the volunteers.
Lights down.
The end.)

F.E.T.C.H.
(a small installment of Virtual Hypertext Theater)
by Alice Tuan

BIOGRAPHY

Alice Tuan is the recipient of both the Richard E. Sherwood Award through Los Angeles' Mark Taper Forum, and the Colbert Award for Excellence through New York's Downtown Arts Project. Productions include *Last of the Suns* (Berkeley Repertory Theatre), *Ikebana* (East West Players), and *Some Asians* (Perishable Theater). Performances include *New Culture for a New Country* (En Garde Arts) and *Sprawl* (with Rachel Hauck at the Actor's Gang). Ms. Tuan recently finished a residency at East West Players through the NEA/TCG Playwright Residency Program where she assembled the "Turn Asian America Inside Out" Conference/Performance to find new spaces to think about Asian America. She was also the Resident Playwright at the Los Angeles Theater Center through the Los Angeles Cultural Affairs Department. Recent projects include *Hit* (a Public Theater commission), the adaptation of Middleton's *The Roaring Girle* (through the Foundry Theater) and *The 2050 Project* (with New World Theater). Recent productions include *mALL* (Cypress College, Ma-yi Theater); a new version of *Last of the Suns*, directed by Chay Yew; *Ajax (por nobody)* at The Flea and *Coastline* (virtual hypertext theater) at A.S.K.'s Common Ground Festival.

HUMANA FESTIVAL PRODUCTION

F.E.T.C.H. premiered at the Humana Festival of New American Plays in March 2002. It was directed by Eric Johnson with the following cast:

#3	Atticus Rowe
#2	Maesie Speer
#1	Joey Williamson
Mouse/Host	Nehal Joshi

and the following production staff:

Scenic Designer	Paul Owen
Costume Designer	Mike Floyd
Lighting Designer	Paul Werner
Sound Designer	Vincent Olivieri
Properties Designer	Doc Manning/Mark Walston

5 ONE PAGE 'SCRENES'
3 CHARACTERS, 1 MOUSE
1 POLE

F.E.T.C.H.

(a small installment of Virtual Hypertext Theater)

1, 2 and 3 are strapped onto the vertical. Here on this pole, they are sonic icons. Boots hang near them.

PROLOGUE

A spirited Mouse rolls in, holding a flashlight.

I
am
the
mouse

I am
the mouse
the mouse
I am

The clicking mouse
Inside your house
On your pad, man
Like a madman

Scurrying and scurrying
Hurrying and hurrying
Where is it, man
Where is it?
The cursor, man
Where is it?

There it is

Click
There right there
Click click
Then there
Click

There
Click
Clickity click click, o my
Clickity click click, uh huh
Clickity kick kick, uh o
Clickity lick lick, o ho

I am the mouse
Not *a* mouse
But *the* mouse
The mouse of your house
(yeah, we talk of Mickey like y'all talk about Napoleon)

Get to choose with me
lose with me
pray with me
pay with me
vex with me
text with me
cash with me
crash with me
make with me
fake with me
ebb with me
web with me
write with me
incite with me
obsess with me
confess with me
search with me
lurch with me
hex with me

sex with me
hear with me
beer with me
see with me
be with me
e- with me

Yeah soma you see me as old school
What with fancy finger pads
Or extrasensitive buttons
(that feel like clits)
which require only the touch of your fingertip

     (Flash and flicker the cursor.)
Flagpole
Earth's pole
Telephone pole
Cack (you'll see)
Hologram

Our order, choosers
Who knows what it spells?
The mouse asks
Can a story be told out of order?
And if so,
Is it the same story?

That's the beauty of choice:
You never know if it is going to lead you to what you want.
How can it, when the choosers
Don't know what they're choosing?

1, 2, 3: *(From the pole.)* Naïve mouse!
MOUSE: What?
1, 2, 3: Naïve mouse!
MOUSE: What did you call me?
1, 2, 3: Naïve mouse!
    Why do you think it all goes unmysteriously to advertising?

MOUSE : Yes, Choosers,
Our order is random
Or is it?
Will you make sense of it?
Choose.
> *(Mouse models, shows how to curse the letters with the flashlight or clicker or what it is to be.)*

F. E. T. C. H.
> *(i.e. hands cursor to a choose <who wishes to be chosen?>)*

Who'll it be? Which one to fetch?
To first slot, to start, to possibly stretch? *(Mouse announces letter: ( ))*

F-LAGPOLE

We hear lotsa flapping. It's a windy day.
1, 2, and 3 react. Spinning around, trying to hold the pole in one place.

1: yow
2: jeez
3: gripes
1: YOW
2: JEEZ
3: GRIPES
1: YOOOOOOOOOOWWWWWW
2: JEEEEEEEEEEEEEEEEEZZ
3: Guh Guh Guh Guh RIIIIIIIIIIIPES
> *(Flap flap flap.)*

1: Ow Ow Ow
2: OW OW OW
3: ow ow ow
> *(Pause, repeat.*
> *FLAP FLAP FLAP FLAP FLAP FLAP FLAP.)*

1, 2, 3: OW OW OW
3: was that, was that
2: a star
3: a stripe
2: a star
1: a white stripe

3: a red stripe

2: It was it was

3: a red stripe

1: it blanked. It was white

2: it poked. It was a star

3: it bled, it was red.

    (Flap flap flap. They spin around.)

1, 2, 3: ow ow ow ow ow

1, 2, 3: ow ow ow ow ow

    (Insert second slot couplet here.)

E-ARTH'S POLE

2, 1, and 3 try to pull the pole in one direction.

2: See if we tilt the earth's pole, we can get weather better in the places that haven't had it…would solve a lotta grief

3: You're saying if we change the weather of places, their life will improve

2: Why the cack not?

1: Preposterous

    (Cell phone rings.)

2: Hello?

1: You ever been in deep winter Los Angeles?

2: *(On phone.)* No

1: Preposterous

2: *(On phone.)* Yeah

3: Hey mates! I'm in Australia

2: *(On phone.)* Yeah. Yeah, just trying to tilt the earth's pole. Yeah that way. Yeah, no the other, yeah, that way.

1: 78 degrees in mid-January

3: OW! That's what we get down here.

1: No snow at Christmas

3: OW! a sweatin' santa

2: Right right right. 8.11 degrees ongitude, 2 and a half, attitude. Gotcha. Will do. Righty O. Buh-bye now *(Closes cell phone.)* You shift right a little. You shift left a bit.

1: What are we doing?

2: Sun's a bit close to Australia, gonna pull it away a bit. Give some of the heat to the caps, direct it towards Death Valley, fill it back up for the droughtin'. AND—LEAN.

(Insert third slot couplet here.)

T-ELEPHONE POLE

We hear tapping sounds. 2 is rocking out on headphones.

1: I'm terrified. I'm terrified. *(3 tap tap taps.)* Hey I'm terrified!
2: *(Unplugs a headphone muff from left ear.)* What?
1: I'm terrified of heights. The, the crash down
   (3 writes.)
2: Get over it. Just don't look down. *(Remuffs.)*
1: Don't look down? But that, but that…am I supposed to just, just *delete* the bottom quadrant of my sight? But that's, but that's…it limits me! I want to see it all *(Looks down.)* Hah, yah, ah yah. O. *(Looks up.)* What am I on the watch for, again?
3: Sh sh sh sh
1: O great, I can't speak either
3: Gripes! SHHHH!
2: *(Sings real loud to Alicia Keys tune.)* "I keep on fallin'…I keep on fallin'…in and out…"
   (A bird plops one in 1's eye.)
1: O yuck! *(Wipes.)* O yuh *(Looks down.)* Yie yie yie…I'm terrified!
2 AND 3: We're all terrified
   (3 goes back to tappin', almost getting the listened-for info.)
2: If you have to look down, focus on the top of my head. Look
1: I can't
2: Look at the top of my head. Look at it. This crown right here, that's the center of the earth. The rest of it is the cool sand you can dig your toes into, you know when you're on the beach and you can just hug the earth with your toes solid. It's your ground for now, until you reorient. Then go from there. Don't do it all at once
3: Got it. We got it. The code word is—CACK.
1, 2, 3: Cack cack cack cack cack. Cack cack cack cack cack.

(Insert fourth slot couplet here.)

C-ACK

1: What's goin' on with the stack market?

3: Looks like it's lacked up what with the time runnin' out on the clack like that

2: Least they still let us listen to rack and roll. It'd be too shacking to just be strapped here in silence

1: See that cute little frack Judy was wearin' the other day

3: The one with the flack o' geese flying all in that v-shape…look there they are now

   (They all watch the geese fly by.)

2: *(Joyous.)* YOW! V—for victory!

1: Must be approachin' winter, if they flying down to Mexico like that.

3: *Hola Paco, que tal, como estas?*

2: *Bien y tu?*

3: *Bien, gracias*

2: *Bueno, tengo que irme*

3: *Entonces, hasta luego!*

1: Are you two macking me?

2: Just doin' geese talk, ya know, cuz they gotta practice up, have to squack with southerners down there.

3: Yeah, they talk funny. Their ducks go qwuk qwuk. They pay income tux

2: Yeah

1: Yeah

   (Pause.)

3: Hey you two ever wonder how big God's cack is?

   (They start rubbing themselves on the pole.)

   (Insert last couplet here.)

H-OLOGRAM

A drone. Maybe some glowy light on (or off) the pole.

1: Is it real?

2: What we're clinging onto?

1: Is it real?

3: It's just as good as real. Real is overrated. What, you need to touch it for it to be real?

2: It is our support…up here.

1: We're gonna crash down, all of us
   (Louder drone, as 2's and 3's hands pass through, then back to low-grade drone.)

2: How can it support?

3: Stop questioning or we'll fall

1: Why we gotta why we gotta, why we gotta wonder how everything is done?
   Like dissecting magic—we, we gotta allow suspicion. Just, just, you know
   let things be
   (They look up and down the hologrammic pole. The drone gets louder.)

2: Faith got us here. Faith'll keep us here.

1: I thought we got here on God's cack.

3: Are you obsessed with cack?

2: Just up here in all the verticals. Have we so fucked with gravity, that we just
   float? That we are merry astronauts on our own turf?

1: I'm lighter than a molecule

2 AND 3: That's right.

1: Like my essence is my identity

2 AND 3: That's right

1: Better than real, because I have no fear

1: But how much farther in order to fetch?

These texts are installed in the choosing of the 2nd, 3rd, 4th , and 5th letters.

SECOND SLOT COUPLET

MOUSE: Second slot, need another letter
Applaud for your choice, the one you think is "better"
(for the second slot or whatever whatever whatever whatever whatever)

Clap out your choice as we flash it and curse 'em
They'll play it out second, and then we'll reimburse 'em
   *(Mouse shines cursor, determines audience's choice, announces the letter and
   title of screne.)*

THIRD SLOT COUPLET

MOUSE : A third…

less calories

tightenin' up the salaries
goin' to the charities

fattening hilarities
hazin' with their clarities
and whut about disparities?

choose.
a third…
Whaddaya gonna choose?

(Mouse snaps fingers.)

snap it.
snap snap
snap it.

Snap for the one you choose.

(Mouse determines audience choice, announces letter and title of screne.)

FOURTH SLOT COUPLET

Mouse tongue clicks 4 times.

MOUSE: Cluh cluh cluh cluh
Cluh cluh cluh cluh
Cluh cluh cluh cluh

Click it

(Gets audience to cluh.)

cluh cluh cluh cluh

click it

cluh cluh cluh cluh
that's it, click it

go crazy
cluh cluh cluh cluh cluh cluh cluh cluh cluh cluh cluh cluh cluh cluh

OK. Whicha the two?

This or this?

Click the one you want

(Mouse determines audience choice, announces letter and title of screne.)

LAST SLOT COUPLET

MOUSE : *(Announces last letter and title of screne.)*

EPILOGUE

MOUSE : Folks we got a new order now...let's spell it!
( )—( )—( )—( )—( )
We have found the new order of the pole.
( )—( )—( )—( )—( )
The verticals we verse in here.
( )( )( )( )( )
Say it!
( )( )( )( )( )
Again!
( )( )( )( )( )
Last time!
( )( )( )( )( )

What does it mean *now?*

Buh Bye!

(Mouse rolls to stillness. The sonic icons repeat the new word again and again as program has finished and choosers leave, until the next boot up.)

END OF PLAY